The Civil War as a Crisis in Gender

THE

Augusta, Georgia,

CIVIL WAR

1860–1890

AS A CRISIS

Lee Ann Whites

IN GENDER

The University of Georgia Press   Athens & London

The paper in this book meets the guidelines for permanence and durability of the Committee on Production Guidelines for Book Longevity of the Council on Library Resources.

© 1995 by the
University of Georgia Press
Athens, Georgia 30602
All rights reserved
Set in Bodoni
by Tseng Information Systems, Inc.
Printed and bound by Thomson-Shore, Inc.
Printed in the United States of America

99 98 97 96 95 C 5 4 3 2 1

Library of Congress Cataloging in Publication Data
Whites, LeeAnn.
The Civil War as a crisis in gender :
Augusta, Georgia, 1860–1890 / LeeAnn Whites.
p.   cm.
Includes bibliographical references and index.
ISBN 0-8203-1714-4 (alk. paper)
1. Women—Georgia—Augusta—History—19th
century.   2. Elite (Social sciences)—Georgia—
Augusta—History—19th century.   3. Sex role—
Georgia—Augusta—History—19th century.   4. Man-
woman relationships—Georgia—Augusta—History—
19th century.   5. United States—History—Civil War,
1861–1865—Women.   6. Augusta (Ga.)—History—
Civil War, 1861–1865—Social aspects.   I. Title.
HQ1439.A94W5   1995
305.3′09758′64—dc20   94-36540
British Library Cataloging in Publication Data available
Title page illustration: Confederate Monument, Augusta,
Georgia

For My Father,

Roy C. Whites

And in Memory of My Mother,

Verda Mae Bolte Whites

Contents

Acknowledgments

I am deeply indebted to the support, advice, and encouragement that many individuals and institutions have generously given me in the course of researching and writing this book. It is a pleasure to be able to acknowledge their contributions here.

Library staffs at the Southern Historical Collection at the University of North Carolina, the Perkins Library at Duke University, the Georgia State Archives, the South Caroliniana Library at the University of South Carolina, the Howard-Tilton Memorial Library at Tulane University, and the South Carolina Historical Society have been generous with their time and resources. I am particularly indebted to the contributions of the staff of the Augusta College Library and Historic Augusta.

I have also been so fortunate as to receive two residential fellowships in support of this manuscript, a Rockefeller Humanist-in-Residence at the Duke-UNC Center for Research on Women and a Fellowship at the Virginia Foundation for the Humanities and Public Policy Fellowship at Charlottesville, Virginia. Not only did these fellowships give me the time to write, they also offered me new and challenging colleagues, who influenced my work for the better. The History Department at the University of Missouri-Columbia has also been generous in its support, providing me with a Summer Research Fellowship, a semester research leave, and an excellent clerical staff.

Malcolm Call of the University of Georgia Press has been enthusiastic and reassuring throughout the process of publication. Kim Cretors, my project editor, and Mark Pentecost, my copy editor, have kept me close to schedule and have improved the order and clarity of the manuscript. Shelda Eggers has my deepest gratitude for not only rescuing this manuscript from the clutches of a hopelessly antiquated computer program, but proofreading it as well.

Many individual scholars have read all or part of this manuscript, and their suggestions have made it stronger than it otherwise would have been. I wish to thank Tom Alexander, Bill Billingsley, Virginia Ingraham Burr, Lee Ann Caldwell, Catherine Clinton, Jean Friedman, Jacquelyn Hall, John Inscoe, Maurice Manring, Nell Painter, Dave Roediger, and Kimberly Schreck. I owe a special debt to Mike Johnson, who not only read this manuscript in its entirety but, in the more than twenty years that I have known him, has read all my work and has always been a source of support and inspiration to me.

My dearest friends have made the dearest contributions to my work. Carol Montgomery, Susan Bordo, and Ted Koditschek have each in their own way given unstintingly of their considerable knowledge, wit, and compassion. My daughter, Sarah Whites-Koditschek, has given me the faith and the reason to finish.

Introduction: Masculinity in Crisis

CIVIL WAR HISTORY
AS A "VIEW FROM SOMEWHERE"

Since the very first shot was fired at Fort Sumter in the spring of 1861, Americans have discussed and disagreed over the causes, the meaning, and the eventual outcome of the Civil War. Was it the result, as Abraham Lincoln believed, of the inevitability that a nation "permanently half slave and half free" could not endure? Or was it, as the illustrious Progressive-Era historians Charles and Mary Beard later argued, a second bourgeois revolution, finishing the work that the American Revolution began in assuring the final triumph of an urban, industrial North over a rural, agrarian South? Others have argued that the conflict was not as irrepressible as Lincoln or the Beards thought. Perhaps the war was actually the responsibility of inept or corrupt politicians, who valued their own personal or regional interests over the interests of the nation as a whole.[1]

However heated this debate has been, however divergent the positions of its participants, there has been one underlying assumption that has united them all: the conviction that the Civil War constituted a critical watershed in the development of the nation and of the American social order. It is precisely this underlying assumption that the American Civil War was pivotal in the making of America that has made it such a light-ning rod for heated debate and argument, even today. After all, this was the war through which four million enslaved African Americans gained their freedom and, however hedged about, their rights as citizens. This was also the war that cost more American lives than virtually all our other wars combined, more than half a million military casualties and at least fifty thousand civilian deaths. No wonder historians seem to argue end-lessly over the Civil War's significance and underlying causes. Was it a constitutional crisis? A crisis in nation formation? A crisis over slavery? A crisis over states' rights? Perhaps it was really a crisis over the extent of class privilege? Regional dominance? Cultural difference?[2]

More books have been written on the Civil War than any other subject in our past. Is it possible that any stone has been left unturned in what is quite possibly the longest and most intensely contested debate in U.S. history? This work is based on the premise that one critical vantage point has indeed been almost entirely absent from this discussion: *gender*. This absence is, on one level, remarkable. It is hard to imagine any activity that has been more gendered than the conduct of war. Perhaps only child-birth and infant rearing have historically been more exclusively identified with one sex alone than has the fighting of war. It may be only now, as we approach the end of the twentieth century, that a book based on the premise that the Civil War constituted a crisis in gender relations could be written at all. It is only now that the rigid division of these gender roles has begun to fall away, as women enter the military in growing numbers, even filling combat positions, and as men take up expanded childrearing roles, even to the "nursing" of infants. Perhaps only now is it possible to see the gender conventions of the past as just that, gender *conventions*, particular, historically rooted ways of organizing the gender order rather than as timeless, essential characteristics, belonging "naturally" to the male or female sex.[3]

Once the "natural" status of gender is questioned, what in the past ap-peared as natural male or female qualities, such as the "fact" that men fight wars or the "fact" that women nurture, becomes the starting point for historical inquiry. In the case of the Civil War, it suggests that gender roles as well as gender relations played a critical role in the initial outbreak of the war, as well as in its course, its conduct, and its eventual outcome in the "reconstruction" of the South. For individual men and women, this moment of gender transformation in the social order at large created a crisis in the very way that they perceived their appropriate gender roles.

For men, both black and white, the gender stakes in the war were especially high, and tightly intertwined with racial upheaval. Black men stood to win their "manhood," and for that very reason white men felt the ground of *their* masculinity become unstable, uncertain. Consider, for example, the issue of black participation in the military. For black men, military service offered them the opportunity to prove that, as one black soldier put it, "I'se a man now," to actually lay claim to the dominant social construction of manhood itself. For white men, on the other hand, the inclusion of black men in the Union threatened their understanding of manhood as precisely *predicated* on the exclusion of black men from white "manly" responsibilities like military service. If black men could acquire manhood through military service, then white men could lose it, or at least stood to lose their racialized understanding of it.[4]

Even in the North, white men militantly resisted the initial efforts of African-American men to form militia units and to volunteer to serve in the Union war effort. It was, some insisted, a "white man's war." Indeed, by the time of the outbreak of the Civil War black men had been legally excluded from military service throughout the North. The Civil War presented northern white men with a difficult choice. Would they choose, or at least acquiesce in, the "abolition of whiteness," to use David Roediger's phrase, and take black men into the Union military? Or would they choose instead to lose their position as "free men" to an arguably worse threat, the southern "slave power"? Either way, the war presented white men with a crisis for their masculinity, a threat to their manhood as it was socially constructed. Whatever the outcome, they could not simply remain as they were.[5]

The foregoing example underscores that gender roles are historically and socially constructed, along regional, racial, and class lines, and not only for women but also for men. The point that men as well as women are gendered may seem obvious, but in fact our cultural tendency, both among scholars and in more popular understandings, has been to view only *women* as having gender (just as we have tended to view only blacks as having "race"). So, while women are seen as participating in a "women's history" of changing gender expectations and female roles, men simply make "History." This construction of the history of men's activities (e.g., the waging of war) as history *tout court* is a prime example of what feminist theorist Susan Bordo has identified as the "view from nowhere," the understanding of oneself and one's perspective on things as *locationless*. Others (women and blacks, for example) may have "special interests" reflecting their specialized vantage points, but men, identified with "general" interests and events, occupy the "view from nowhere."[6]

One consequence of the failure to acknowledge one's own location is that the world and others in it become mere extensions of that location. Invisible to itself, that location operates as the (concealed) measure of all things. This has been overwhelmingly the case with Civil War history. For example, much of historical writing about women's roles in the war has been to praise their undying "loyalty" to their men. Especially in the case of Confederate women, historians have focused on the intensity with which they supported their men's efforts to secede and to form a new nation. Indeed, according to one history of Confederate women, they formed "the very soul of the war," while another concludes that Confederate women were true "partners in rebellion." Here secession and the war effort are presented without question as the appropriate activity of "real" men, while women appear to fall into their own "natural" role of "standing by their men": sacrificing their homes, their children, even their lives for the defense of their male relations' prerogatives as "free men." Indeed, even in the wake of the postwar military, political, and economic defeat of the Confederacy, Confederate women are generally presented as remaining overwhelmingly loyal to their men. Thus, instead of an exploration of gender roles and ideology, what we get is a history told from the point of view of white men, but unable to recognize that it is, indeed, a point of view.[7]

Only recently have historians begun to question this much vaunted "loyalty" on the part of Confederate women. Drew Faust has suggested that the actual demands of fighting the war in the South went right to the core of the antebellum gender quid pro quo between white men and women, in which men had promised to "protect" and women had agreed to "obey." The war, Faust has argued, ripped apart this antebellum basis for gender relations, much as it undercut the racial basis for the northern white male construction of manhood. Just as northern white men discovered that they could not "protect" their own manhood as they understood it without the assistance of black men, in the context of the war southern white men also discovered that they could not sustain their gender roles as warriors without the active assistance of their women on the home front. Many historians of Confederate women have noted the myriad ways in which Confederate women were not only cut loose from the immediate necessity of obedience by the absence of their men but were actually more or less forced to take up the directive roles on the home front that had hitherto been the province of their men.[8]

Nonetheless, while traditional bases for gender hierarchy clearly eroded during the course of the war, it cannot be denied that most Confederate women stood by their men and supported the Confederate war effort. Indeed, as Victoria Bynum has made clear in her study of North Carolina during the Civil War, women who became disloyal to the Confederate cause did not necessarily do so out of any disloyalty to the men of their own households. Indeed, in the "deserter country" of western North Carolina, loyalty to a husband or brother might well require disloyalty to the Confederacy. There appears then to be more to this quality of "loyalty" than first meets the eye. It perhaps depends on the eye of the beholder. Disloyalty to the Confederate cause could be loyalty to the men of one's family. Breaking with the antebellum gender order under the altered conditions of war could actually constitute a last desperate effort to preserve it.[9]

Once again, the African-American experience is instructive for understanding this process. Historians have discussed at some length the various ways in which the "loyalty" of slaves to their owners was actually motivated by a desire on the part of slaves to preserve or to advance the interests of their own families and of the slave community as a whole. Moments of social crisis in the dominant power structure may have opened the way for revolt on the part of the nondominant but simultaneously intensified the material difficulties of their very survival. This was as true for Confederate women as it was for the slave population. It was no less a salient factor in the persistence of patriarchal southern gender relations than it was a factor in the persistence of exploitative race relations. The quid pro quo of the gender relation between Confederate men and women may have been ruptured by the demands of fighting the war, but the question of how white women and their children were to survive was also never more seriously threatening than amid the exigences of total war and eventual defeat. Confederate women may have stood by their men during the war, and perhaps they did so even more intensely afterward, but what alternative course of action was open to them? Particularly in the economically devastated postwar South, the operative principle may have been that half a "man," some kind of adult male provider, was better than none at all.[10]

In his autobiography, *Up From Slavery*, Booker T. Washington discusses the apparent "loyalty" of some slaves to their owners during the war, even as the old social order of the slave system stood on the verge of collapse. With many slaveowning men absent from the plantations and farms in the service of the Confederate military, much of the coercive force that had held the slaves in bondage was removed. The increasingly difficult economic circumstances of many plantations and the concrete opportunities that the approaching Yankee troops offered for escape also contributed to the collapse of slavery as an institution. Why then did many slaves remain on the plantations? According to Washington, the explanation for the apparent "loyalty" of many slaves was not their lack of initiative or desire for freedom (as some postwar southern whites claimed) but rather the depth of their commitment to their *own* community's integrity and values. As Washington put it, "there are few instances, either in slavery or freedom, in which a member of my race has been known to betray a specific trust." When Confederate men left for military service, Washington pointed out, they left the "protection" of their women and children in the hands of their slaves. According to Washington, the slave community chose not to violate this trust.[11]

While dominant groups are frequently ignorant of the manner in which their identities are defined and sustained by their relations with the non-dominant, those without such obfuscating privilege are more fully cognizant of the ways in which they actually construct others, and this very knowledge demands a kind of responsibility, what might be described as a "loyalty" even to those who dominate and exploit them. Opportunities to abandon this loyalty may well be eschewed when they would entail an abdication of one's own self-respect and sense of humanity. If we look at loyalty from the location of the ex-slave or from that of the white woman, rather than from the view of the white owner or the white male, what has been been glibly dismissed as blind acquiescence assumes a more active, historically significant form. By shifting our angle of vision, by viewing white men not as independent and autonomous, as essentially "free men," by viewing them instead as *socially constructed* by and dependent upon their relationships to others—which is the way they appeared to those they dominated—"passive" qualities like "loyalty" are suddenly rendered active, the very stuff from which the social order itself is built.

Of course, the core assumption here, that the manhood of white men was actually made through their relations to those whom they subordinated, flies in the face of their own articulated reasons for going to war in the first place. White men on both sides of the conflict asserted that they were fighting in defense of their liberties as "free men." We may find it difficult today to enter into the white southern worldview and to believe that Confederate secessionists were actually sincere in their contention that they fought in order to preserve the rights of "free men," when the cornerstone of that "freedom" now appears to us to be the "freedom" to enslave African Americans. But this is exactly a consequence of the "view from nowhere," grounded as it is in the assumption that "free" white men were indeed disembodied, autonomous, independent entities, "self-made" men. The slave social order was a system that perfectly embodied the white slaveholder's "view from nowhere," as owners had the power to define the world so totally as an extension of their own experience that they could even define a war fought in defense of slaveownership as a struggle for greater freedom and liberty for their society as a whole.[12]

At its most basic level, this work is dedicated to deconstructing this white southern "view from nowhere" by insisting that it was in fact a "view from somewhere." Until we recognize that whites have race and that men have gender and that both have a *social* history, then gender studies will remain incomplete. Marginalized as discussions of the experience of the "victims" of race or gender exploitation, gender studies will be unable to generate alternative systemic analyses of general historical processes. In order to generate those analyses, we must recognize that there is indeed a "white man's history." We find ourselves in a curious position in this regard, for while we now have women's history and African-American history, white man's history apparently still does not exist. We have gender studies, but they are overwhelmingly dedicated to the experience of women's gender role construction. Any quick survey of university press advertisements for their publications in U.S. history will confirm this observation. White men's history, if it can even be considered to exist, is routinely identified simply as "American History," much as the "free men" of the mid-nineteenth century routinely identified the defense of their own individual liberties as white men with the defense of liberty as a universal social good.

If, however, the white man's "view from nowhere" appears still enshrined in our very categorization of the latest work in American history, the emergence of so many other histories alongside it that self-consciously speak from "somewhere" else gives hope that we have arrived at the point where we can seriously entertain the proposition that white men also constituted a similarly located, socially constructed group. Indeed, the continued expansion of these very histories will ultimately "locate" the history of white men as well. This, after all, was the effect produced by those black men who asserted their right to serve in the Union military at the beginning of the Civil War. By thus drawing attention to their own different location, they both forced and enabled white men to see themselves and their war for what it really was, a "white man's war." Before the whiteness of the Union war effort could be abolished, insofar as it ever was, it first had to be perceived.

In jettisoning the possibility of a "view from nowhere," a view that has already lost much of its paradigmatic power with the emergence into autonomy of various nondominant historical fields, we are empowered to recognize that *all* history is indeed socially located. The introduction of new angles of vision will only enrich our power of sight and contribute to a fuller understanding of dominant forms of manhood or race identification, as they are today and have been in the past. The Civil War era offers us especially critical opportunities in this regard, for just as the Civil War constituted a critical test for racial and gender identities in general, it ultimately marked a decisive watershed in the apparently seamless universalization of white men's history, the unquestioning equation of American history with the experience of white men. This was particularly the case for southern white men, who in losing the war to the North lost the right to construct their sense of manhood exactly as they pleased.

Military defeat at the hands of the North, regional and political disempowerment, the loss of their slave property, as well as the general economic devastation that the war produced—all cut to the root of the material underpinnings that had hitherto sustained southern white men's understanding of themselves as free men. As a result, they were confronted with a crisis in their understanding of their manhood. This crisis required a fundamental "reconstruction" before southern white men could reattain their "view from nowhere," even in modified, attenuated form. Indeed, some might argue that these men never really managed to recover from their loss. The point is readily illustrated by a quick tour through any local bookstore. All the great southern slaveholding planters from before the war, like George Washington, Thomas Jefferson, or James Madison, have managed to retain their places in the "American History" section of the shop. Beginning with the antebellum sectional crisis, however, all white southern men, no matter how notable, are relegated to the "Southern History" section. To truly occupy a "view from nowhere," one not only needs to be raceless and genderless, one also needs to be above region.

As Nina Silber has argued in *The Romance of Reunion*, defeated white southern men were forced to acknowledge the northern vision of what it meant to be a "free man." This meant that they were damned if they did and damned if they didn't. The very act of living under a vision of manhood that was not their own made it difficult for them to ever participate fully in the prevailing northern "view from nowhere." Henceforth they would forever be unmanned in this dominant vision of manhood. Of course, this was not the outcome of the sectional conflict that Republican Party strategists had envisioned with the formation of the party in the 1850s. Northern Republican strategists confidently assumed that nonslaveowning southern white men would come to see that the northern Republican vision of what it meant to be a "free man" was the vision that best reflected their own circumstances. According to this northern Republican vision, the greatest threat to the economic and political independence of the southern white male majority was not the black Republicans of the North, but rather the illegitimate power that slaveowning conferred upon their own southern political leadership.[13]

It was this "slave power," to use the Republican terminology, that threatened the liberties of all nonslaveholding white men, in both the North and the South. As Eric Foner has so astutely argued in *Free Soil*,

Free Labor, Free Men, the Republican Party counted on the appeal of its own particular understanding of what it meant to be a free man. On this antislavery basis they expected to divide nonslaveowning southern white men from any residual identification with the southern slaveowning planter class. Given the opportunity that the formation of the Republican Party clearly offered the southern white yeomanry, it was assumed that such men would readily recognize the superiority of a more market-oriented, nonslaveholding definition of white manhood.[14]

At root, then, the sectional crisis was not only a debate over the proper vision of "free manhood," it was also a struggle about the proper foundation upon which that construction should be based. According to the northern vision of manhood, slaveholding not only failed to create the basis for a legitimate white manhood, it actually threatened to undermine the very white freedom on which this manhood was to be based. Yet, while northern Republicans looked to the South and saw the ways in which the "slave power" threatened their own interests, they failed to see that nonslaveholding southern white men's manhood was constructed differently than their own. They failed to understand that for white southern men, slaveowners were simply the tip of an iceberg of economically autonomous male household heads, in which the nonslaveholding household heads constituted the submerged bulk.[15]

Of course it was not surprising that northerners failed to understand how white male identity was constructed out of the particular form of domination and dependency characteristic of the South, since these northern men also failed to recognize the construction of their own freedom out of the particular, highly gendered form of household dependency peculiar to their own burgeoning system of separate spheres. Indeed, as Eric Foner has suggested, northern men focused on the "illegitimate" empowering of southern white men through slaveownership in part as a way to *avoid* seeing the major transformation that industrialization and proletarianization was having on their own identity as "free men." And while the most radical fringes of the northern abolitionist movement may have entertained the idea that the northern subordination of women was no more legitimate than the subordination of the southern slaves, many more of the abolitionists were taken by the domestic rhetoric of abolitionist spokeswomen like Harriet Beecher Stowe, who presented the newly formed northern separate spheres system as a veritable "antidote" to the southern slave system, as an apparently "natural" basis for the making of truly free men.[16]

Not surprisingly, white southerners resisted this invitation to become second-class white men through what they perceived as an attenuated form of white male autonomy. While the Republican Party found some support among nonslaveholding white men, many more of them lined up behind their state's secessionist movements and the Confederate war effort. As Michael Johnson has argued in his analysis of the secessionist movement in Georgia, secession constituted a veritable "revolution against revolution." In passing legislation to make the slave and landowning basis of southern white manhood open to a wider sector of white men, the secessionist legislature attempted to empower all white men in relation to their dependents. The aim was to make them even more "free" in the southern construction of that term, while at the same time intensifying the formal political power of the planter elite on the level of state government. Johnson aptly describes this overall strategy as a move toward the creation of a more "patriarchal republic."[17]

This work takes up the story of this move toward a more "patriarchal republic" in Georgia at the point of the actual outbreak of the war. It does this through a consideration of the ways in which white manhood and womanhood, particularly elite white manhood and womanhood, were transformed in the context of the war and its aftermath in Georgia's second largest city, Augusta. This work is therefore doubly a "view from somewhere," located as it is in a particular place as well as in the experience of particular residents of that place. The first chapter begins in the spring of 1861, as hundreds of Confederate men marched out of Augusta to join the war. Here I examine the worldview that could envision secession, the formation of a slaveholding Confederacy, and the war in defense of it, as an articulation of the universal principles of liberty and freedom that all Americans presumably held dear. While the war effort is thus considered as an expression of Confederate men's commitment to this vision of "free manhood," this chapter also examines the ways in which the war came to constitute a test of the "loyalty" of their dependents, particularly of Confederate women, and the willingness of these dependents to sacrifice in the name of this vision.

At first blush, the outbreak of the war seems only to have strengthened Confederate women's identification with their men. Indeed, the initial outbreak of war served to intensify gender role difference, as Confederate men set forth to fight and to aggressively defend their "manhood," while Confederate women redoubled their commitment to the support and succor of their men. Nevertheless, it was not long before the war drove home the probable cost of this support for Confederate women. However enthusiastically they may have supported secession and their men's enlistment in the war effort, the actual departure of their men to the front was a sobering development. These women were called upon to sacrifice their sons, fathers, and husbands to a cause that they hoped would empower them as individual free white men. At the moment of departure, however, they were forced to contemplate the very real possibility that rather than being empowered, these men might well end up disabled or dead. In the first chapter, we will see the ways in which Confederate women confronted this situation by falling back on their female kin networks and the personal strengths they had developed in the female gendered experiences of childbirth and infant loss.

The second chapter considers not only the ways in which the domestic loss of their men actually served to strengthen same-sex female kin networks, but the ways in which it empowered the domestic labor of Confederate women as well. As the demands of fighting the war mounted, wartime exigencies shifted the center of economic power from the production and marketing of cotton to the production and supply of the troops. As a result, it shifted the center of social power from the rural, male slaveholding household head to the urban, industrial producers of textiles and armaments, as well as to the domestic and subsistence labors of the household dependents. Men's primary significance now became as conscripted bodies that must fight and die for the cause. In this they now came increasingly to resemble their women, whose worthiness had always been vested in their bodies and their potential to produce offspring, or even their slaves, whose bodies were expected to produce staple crops and more bodies to work those crops in the future.

At the same time that Confederate men found themselves positioned more like their dependents, Confederate women found themselves positioned more like their men. The same war effort that embodied their men caused their previously "hidden" domestic labor to gain new public stature in its own right, outside the structure of the household and outside the domination of the male household head. If only to "stand by their men," Confederate women were now called upon to breach this subordinate position and participate in a massive formation of women's voluntary organizations, whose purpose was to organize sufficient domestic labor to "mother" the troops on a collective basis. By the end of the second year of the war, this reorganization of Confederate women's labor had proceeded to the point that the stage appeared to be set for a fundamental breach of traditional gender relations. As Confederate women's public status expanded, their newfound autonomy threatened to undermine the very basis for the social construction of white manhood that they were supposed to be propping up.

The third and fourth chapters analyze the ways in which class and race divisions among women in Augusta served to blunt this transformation of gender relations that began in the public organizational activities of elite white women. As less privileged white women in the city began to assert publicly the legitimacy of their own domestic position, more elite Confederate women began to realize that public empowerment for all white women could also entail a loss for their own class. While chapter 3 examines how these class divisions among white women served to remind elite white women of the class base of their men's ability to keep them secure and "protected," chapter 4 considers the ways in which the mounting threat of Sherman's troops from the outside and the rising autonomy of the African-American population from within translated such fears of class loss into reality. In Sherman, Confederate women encountered a white male dominator who made the gravest shortcomings of their own men look friendly by comparison. At the same time the rapid erosion of the antebellum racial order in the last year of the war confirmed just how high economic and social loss would go in the Confederate social order.

Chapter 5 considers how these class and race dynamics set in motion by the war actually created the parameters within which the domestic reconstruction of southern white manhood would take place in the war's aftermath. While Confederate men discovered that the continued loyalty of their own women and children was frequently all that remained to them of their antebellum social construction as "free men," Confederate women discovered that they could achieve a kind of persistence of their wartime domestic empowerment by virtue of the expanded significance that was now attached to their roles as the "makers" of their men.

Chapter 6 considers the public face of this domestic reconstruction in the continuation and even the expansion of associational activity among ex-Confederate women in postwar Augusta. In this chapter, I discuss how the Ladies' Memorial Association not only rehabilitated the tattered honor of defeated Confederate men but in doing so made a vital contribution to the redefinition of the Civil War itself. Rather than taking their men's participation in the war as a militant assertion of "free manhood" or as the defense of slavery, the ladies redefined it as dedicated in the first instance to their own domestic defense. Here Confederate men, rather than having fought the war in defense of their right to dominate those household dependents—the slaves—who were now lost to them, were reenvisioned as having loyally stood for the defense of those household dependents—their women and children—who in the postwar era continued to stand loyally by them. White women, especially elite white women, acquired a new kind of public voice and a public cultural power by virtue of their special role and status in articulating and celebrating this reconstruction of white southern manhood, while at the same time the very form of their empowerment was set squarely against the self-realization of the new freedpeople, who were rendered mute in this remembering of the war effort.

In chapter 7 the transformation of Confederate gender relations that was initially set in motion by the war is closed off in the emergence of two structural developments: the formation of the Confederate Survivors Association and the takeoff in industrial development that would, by the 1890s, transform Augusta into the "Lowell of the South." The massive expansion of industrial employment for white women and children allowed white men to continue to "protect" them, although not exactly as the men might have wished. The formation of the Confederate Survivors Association indicated that "reconstructed" white men were now able to take up the task of memorializing their own fallen comrades and to tell their own, albeit domesticated, story of the war and its consequences. This last chapter discusses the way that, despite the war, white southern defeat, economic loss, and the emancipation of the slaves, this Confederate history provided many white southern men with a vehicle through which they could cling to what they understood to be their timeless, essential manliness, their "view from nowhere." Their women, having experienced white southern men's sojourn from the heated antebellum sectional politics of "free men" to the cold pedestals of their own memorial association's construction, continued to cling to what remained of their men in the "somewhere" of their daily lives.

I cannot express to you in any words, my regret at leaving you and my dear little Stanhope, but you know it is the duty of every man to stand by his country in this hour of her greatest trial. If our separations are painful, we must remember that they are the price of liberty and justice, without which life is not worthy of a moment's consideration. If we expect to hand down to our children the glorious inheritance of true freedom and honorable peace, we must cheerfully endure the sacrifices necessary to secure them.
—Joseph Jones to Caroline Davis Jones, October 8, 1861

1

Independent Men and Dependent Women

AUGUSTA AND THE OUTBREAK OF WAR

For the citizens of Augusta, the Civil War constituted a test. It tested their commitment to the slaveholding, cotton plantation economy and the values that it generated—an economy that by the outbreak of the war had made Augusta one of the largest and fastest-growing urban centers in the South. As a major southern cotton factoring center, Augusta depended on the prosperity of the surrounding countryside. Not only was the commercial welfare of the town dependent upon the profitability of the larger slave-based plantation economy, but Augusta's own cotton factors, among the wealthiest commercial men of the town, were also frequently large landowners or closely allied to the local planter class through inter-marriage.[1] Even Augusta's industries, which absorbed the largest concentration of manufacturing capital in the state by 1860, were offshoots of the plantation economy. The prosperity of Augusta's textile industries rose and fell with the fortunes of cotton.[2]

Despite these ties to the larger regional cotton economy, the secession of Georgia from the Union in February of 1861 was met with mixed emotions by the city's citizens. Some of the most prominent among them were origi nally native to the North, having migrated to take advantage of economic opportunities.[3] Men of this class had familial relations or long-standing business connections north of the Mason-Dixon Line. Severing such relationships was not to be done precipitously and certainly not without considerable debate and even more anxiety.[4]

The outbreak of hostilities at Fort Sumter in April of that year swept away much of this controversy surrounding divided loyalties. Local society suddenly became much more united in its support for the Confederate cause. Joseph Jones, a professor at the Georgia Medical College and a member of a prominent planter family, described with enthusiasm local troops departing for the front in June of 1861:

> We are constantly enlivened by the arrival and departure of troops for Virginia. Augusta has contributed more than 1,000 of her own citizens for the war. Yesterday evening the Augusta Companies which had been stationed near Fort Pickens left for Virginia and the crowd of citizens assembled was immense, it could not have been less than several thousands. . . . It is difficult to resist the temptation to join them.[5]

In that fateful summer of 1861, the total population of Augusta numbered close to twelve thousand, and roughly one-third were slaves. The fact that as many as one thousand adult white male volunteers could be mustered out of a total white male population of some four thousand indicates that the citizenry had united behind the formation of a new nation.[6] Indeed, this newfound enthusiasm for the war was based on the specter of an even more immediate and fundamental danger than the prospect of loosening ties of nativity, friendship, business, or kinship. Whatever individual Augustans thought of the wisdom or folly of the decision to secede, the North, in forcibly denying them the right to do so at Fort Sumter, called into question their status as free men, male householders who were masters of their own political fate, empowered to maintain whatever economic and familial connections they might wish. The North's forcible denial of the South's right to secede and to form a new nation was, therefore, not just a denial of their right to autonomy as a region. More critically, it appeared as an attack on their independence as individuals, an attack, in fact, on the very essence of their free manhood. As one writer to the local newspaper concluded upon the outbreak of hostilities, in actually firing on Fort Sumter, the North threatened to "subjugate the South" to a "yoke more intolerable than the bondage of the African . . . to rob you of your birthright and place upon you, your children and your children's children the brand of slavery." [7]

This writer slid easily from the threat that the northern invasion posed for the independence of the South as a region to the even more fundamental threat that it represented to the liberties of individual white citizens. According to this writer, the forcible denial of the South's right to regional autonomy would lead directly to reducing the free southern man to a position lower than the lowest member of the southern social order, the black slave. Much has been made of the fact that only a minority of white southern households actually owned slaves. Why would white southerners who did not themselves own slaves fight a war to defend the slave property of the privileged few who did? This writer gives us an answer. The language of slavery as he employed it signified something more than the actual ownership of slaves. The extreme form of "liberty" that the slaveowner obtained by virtue of control over his "property" served to exemplify the values to which all white southern men could aspire in a system that grounded white liberty in black slavery. Conversely it suggested the potential or actual position of "enslavement" into which white men might fall if black slavery were indeed abolished. If we understand slavery as a constituent part of the southern household structure, we can see how the northern abolitionist attack on the slaveholder—the ruler of the most extensive household dominion and therefore the most powerful of all male household heads—could thus be construed as a challenge to the independence of all male householders, whether or not they actually held slaves.[8]

While from other perspectives the Civil War may have constituted a test of competing economic systems (agrarian versus industrial), or a test of competing labor systems (slave versus free), or even a test of diverging regional cultures, from this vantage point it was a test of the individual privilege and prerogative of southerners as "free men." While some might also envision the war as a battle for economic, regional, or racial hegemony, the one principle that could and did unite them all, slaveholders and non-slaveholders alike, in their defense of the Confederacy was their defense of a common social construction of manhood as largely autonomous and self-directing household heads.[9]

Both the North and the South can be understood through this lens. Both fought in defense of their version of what it meant to be a free man. If to many southern white men this entailed the persistence of black slavery, to many "free men" of the North, it meant not having to compete with what they perceived to be the unfair advantage that slaveowning conferred upon white southerners, what the Republican Party termed the "slave power." What was at stake, then, was the basic structure of the household itself and the scope of "liberties" that it created for its white head.

In an article urging militant support for the Confederate cause in the spring of 1861, the editor of the *Augusta Chronicle and Sentinel* argued that support for the war effort was now the "plain duty of every citizen." "Perish forever all dissensions among us," he wrote. "Let denunciations on the one hand, and murmurings and revilings on the other, cease, till we have redeemed our fair land, conquered our independence from a ruthless, and insolent, and despicable foe." Whatever differences had previously divided them, this writer concluded that the citizens of Augusta should now stand together "as brothers" and resist to the bitter end the "domination of a fanatic, puritan horde of agrarians, abolitionists and free lovers, while there is a dollar or a man among us."[10]

The three groups identified by this editor, the agrarians, the abolitionists, and the free lovers, reflect the way in which the northern threat was understood as a threat to the position of the southern white household head. The agrarians threatened the sanctity of rural property holding, the fundamental economic basis for the independence of most southern "free men." The abolitionists and the free lovers threatened to emancipate not only the slaves from the household, but white women as well. The reference to "free lovers" was thus a derisive comment alluding to the close relationship between the abolitionists and the feminists in the North and indicates that, in questioning the proper authority of the white male household head, the North threatened to transform the status of all household dependents.[11]

The "plain duty" of every white male citizen was clear. But what was the "plain duty" of their household dependents? If it was indeed their subordination to the white men of the South that created the basis for the very form of free white southern manhood that was under attack from the North, then the war itself constituted a test not only of white southern men's willingness to fight and die for their manhood but also and perhaps more critically of their household dependents' willingness to support the cause of white men. Although there were some cases of active support for the Confederacy among slaves, they generally appear to have bided their time or, when the opportunity presented itself, to have worked actively to subvert this "slave power." By contrast, white women appear, at least initially, to have stood firmly by their men, identifying with the Confederate cause and at the same time with their own properly subordinate and supportive place within the white southern household structure.[12]

Southern men, at the time and for years afterward, have written in understandably self-congratulatory tones about the loyalty that their women demonstrated during the conflict.[13] Histories of the war tell us that Confederate women throughout the South sacrificed those nearest and dearest to them for something they could never hope to obtain, the liberties of free men. Some historians have gone so far as to argue that Confederate women were even more intensely committed to the war than were their men, packing the galleries of secessionist congresses, hissing at the delegates who opposed secession and cheering its advocates. There is the perhaps apocryphal story of the young woman who sent her underwear to her fiancé with the note, "enlist, or wear these." In the heightened gender rhetoric that accompanied secession and war, few women seemed to have wanted anything less than a manly man, as their culture defined it.[14]

The larger discussion that took place between Joseph Jones and his wife Caroline Davis Jones around the issue of his enlistment indicates that white women's support for the cause was nonetheless not without its tensions. For while Joseph Jones stood by in June as the first massive departure of local troops took place, he was not able to resist the mounting temptation to enlist, and by October he too had left for the front. He wrote a letter to his wife in that month, explaining why his enlistment was necessary to defend "liberty and justice" and "true freedom." He concluded that, "I know my Dearest that you feel & appreciate all this, as a noble and true woman." Joseph Jones relied here upon his wife's understanding and internalization of her appropriately supportive gender role. Because she was a "noble and true woman," an honorable individual in her own gendered way, Joseph Jones expected that his wife would support his need to defend his prerogatives as a free man, even if it cost both of them his life. In the short run it would surely cost her his presence and his support of their household.[15]

Indeed, Caroline Davis Jones had made peace with her proper place within the southern social order when she entered into marriage with her husband. Not without some internal conflict, however, as the course of their courtship in the spring of 1859 reveals. In that year, Davis made it clear to Jones that she recognized that their marriage would cost her her individual freedom, her independence, with which she was loathe to part. He replied by pointing to the benefits that her position as a dependent in his household could confer upon her. "Will the possession of a friend who will be your protector and defender when all friends and relatives fail, involve the loss of freedom?" he queried. In exchange for her subordination to his will, to the construction of his identity, he promised to use his position to promote her interests. Their domestic interests would, he promised, be as one. "Will the possession of a heart which will beat responsive always to yours; share your joys, bear your sorrows, encourage the right and forgive the wrong, involve a loss of freedom?"[16]

Caroline Davis accepted Joseph Jones's suit shortly after this exchange, and they were married a few months later. Having given up her own autonomy, she informed her fiancé that she would, "be always ambitious for [his] success in life because *we poor women* have no name or existence of *our own*, we pass *silently* down the stream of time without leaving a single trace behind—we die unknown." She would look to him to maintain and enlarge his power to "protect and defend" her through his achievements in life. She would now live as an individual through him. He replied in turn that women's acts of "humble piety and devoted love," their self-sacrifice in abandoning their own individual autonomy in favor of contributing to their male relation's self-realization, were in fact of "greater consequence than all of men's monuments, wars, etc." The extent to which he would in the course of their married life turn his dominant position to their mutual domestic interests would therefore prove that he recognized and duly honored her sacrifice.[17]

As part of this quid pro quo, "true and noble" women like Caroline Davis would support the drive for southern independence and their husbands' efforts to defend their own independence as southern men. Joseph Jones was not to be disappointed in his wife's response to his enlistment. In reply to his letter defending his participation in the war, she wrote that while he was "more to me than everything on earth," she understood that "life would be valueless under such rule as these miscreants would force upon us & that honor & feeling & everything else compels you to take part in this struggle."[18]

Insofar as white southern men in their position as heads of household really did turn their individual economic and political position to the interests of their families, their prerogatives as free men and the interests of their women and children were as one. The letter of one young woman, identified only as "GEF," to the local Augusta paper upon the outbreak of war certainly reflected her intense identification with the cause and the role in it of the men in her family.

> You will pardon the liberty I have taken to address you, when I tell you that my great inclination to do so assails me so constantly that I can only find relief in writing to you. . . . My father and family have ever been the strongest of Whigs, and of course not in favor of immediate secession; but as that has been the irrevocable act of the South I submit to it, and say "as goes Georgia, so go I." But at the same time I am conscious that that very act has increased our responsibilities tenfold. We have outwardly assumed the garb of independence and now let us walk in the path our state has chosen. And shall man tread it alone? . . . No, no, a thousand times no.[19]

This young woman went on to paint a picture of a hardworking father, now doubly burdened with the added role of creating a new nation, "going forth until his strength is almost spent" to support his "three blooming daughters" in the "excess of idleness." Although she granted that this picture was "somewhat on the extreme," she contended that it was "applicable to a great many Southern families." Urging other Confederate women to join her in the cause, she suggested that they "hurl the destructive novel in the fire and turn our poodles out of doors, and convert our pianos into spinning wheels." Not only would such a return to home manufacturing make a critical contribution to their male relations' pursuit of political autonomy, she argued, the drive for political independence would make women more independent as well. As she concluded, "I feel a new life within me, and my ambition aims at nothing higher than to become an ingenious, economical, industrious housekeeper, and an independent Southern woman."[20]

Clearly GEF identified intensely with the ideals of independence that her father's role in the war effort was meant to defend. Yet she also assumed that independence for women, although clearly possible and desirable as southern men took their stand, would have to take a very different form. Rather than aspiring to liberty as her male relations conceived of it, a liberty grounded in individualized public interaction among men, GEF envisioned independence for women in a more intense commitment to women's domestic labor *within* the private realm of the household. Confederate women could support the Confederate cause through their labor, but only if that labor remained dependent, as it must if it would actually promote the continued independence of their men at home as well as at war. As GEF concluded, "Now I, for one, intend to lead a more useful life; if I can't make money by my work, I can save what little I have."[21]

Under the constraints of their place within the household, Confederate women could identify with their men's pursuit of war. The expansion of home manufacturing by white women was, from this perspective, a way to save money for redirection into the support of their men's war effort. As with their men, Confederate women could look with renewed pride upon their particular gendered role in the social order. As their men expanded their efforts to defend what they understood to be their manly prerogatives as free men, their women responded with an expansion of their role as laborers within the households of such men. Whatever increased status might accrue to Confederate women as a result of this intensified wartime demand for their labor, the underlying assumption, at least on the part of GEF, was that Confederate women would remain subordinate to and dependent upon the household head and the other men of their households in whose interests their own wartime efforts were undertaken.

When GEF wrote this letter to the local press in April of 1861, she clearly foresaw the ways in which the Confederate war effort would increase the significance of women's domestic role. What she could not clearly envision was the way in which the demands placed on the civilian population would also transform the privatized and subordinated character of this role as well. Here GEF simply reflected the social order she knew as a white, middle-class woman. In her experience, white women's lives were ordered by the patriarchal boundaries of the particular households to which they belonged. Indeed, according to the manuscript census, not one identifiably middle-class white woman residing in Augusta claimed to be gainfully employed in 1860. White women who labored in the textile mills did not, of course, share this experience, but even here the pattern of employment points to the dominance of privatized domestic labor for white women across class lines, for only four married women were listed as working in the mills out of a total of 192 workers. Out of all the married white women listed in the 1860 census for the town, only twenty-nine were marked as having gainful employment and of these twenty-four were seamstresses, who apparently worked out of their homes.[22]

The same experience of privatized domestic labor for their own households certainly was not the case for most African-American women, whether married or single, slave or free. The overwhelming majority of free black women were employed as domestics in white households. Indeed, in the mid-nineteenth-century United States, the most common form of gainful employment for women as a whole was domestic labor. In Augusta, however, and under the southern slave system more generally, domestic labor for other than a woman's immediate kin was connected to slave status. The limited employment of white women outside their own households, regardless of class, stands as perhaps the starkest contrast to the distribution of black women's labor, whether slave or free.[23]

Thus, while the particular form that white women's labor took within their households undoubtedly varied by class, the larger racial division of labor served to underwrite a common structural experience for white women as economic dependents of largely male-headed, slaveholding or potentially slaveholding households. The impact of this racial division of labor was to render all white women more economically dependent upon the patriarchal white household structure than they would have been in comparably sized towns in the North. The formation of the Confederacy and the outbreak of war appears only to have increased the basis for this commonality among white women. As their men became "brothers" in defense of the Confederate cause, they, however momentarily, found themselves rendered "sisters" through the common sacrifice of their husbands, brothers, and sons. And when GEF advocated that more privileged white women not only support their men in spirit but actually throw away their novels and take up home manufacturing, the course she suggested would not only declare their allegiance to their men but would also lead elite women to take up domestic labor that their less privileged white sisters already carried out as a matter of course.

While common commitment to the Confederacy, common sacrifice of their men, and increasingly common labor in the household served to unite white women, the same attachment to the Confederate cause had the effect of widening the gulf between white women and black men and women. Historians of antebellum southern women have debated the extent to which white women in slaveholding households identified with the men of their race and their class or with other subordinate members of the household, the slaves. In the particular instance of secession and the outbreak of war, white women revealed little inclination to align themselves with other subordinated members of the social order. Instead many appear to have identified militantly with the cause of their men in forming a new nation, a new nation that was now overtly committed to the defense of slavery as an institution.[24]

The diary of one planter-class woman, Susan Cornwall, whose husband owned a plantation in Burke County in Augusta's hinterland, illustrates the way in which secession and war served, if anything, to intensify her commitment to her husband, the master of her household, and to the subordinate status of their slaves, with no apparent recognition of any ambiguity in her own position. As in the case of GEF, Susan Cornwall identified intensely with the cause of her male relations, as she recorded in her diary. "*We* of the South see nothing in Union but danger to *our* sacred rights" [my emphasis]. Her immediate concern, however, was with the threat that she perceived to the survival of the slave system. As she asserted, "the Black Republicans rejoice that they are to be the instruments of final emancipation for that is undoubtedly their aim in spite of their declarations that they will not interfere with slavery in the states where it now exists." This threat to the racial hierarchy of the southern plantation household elicited from Cornwall a militant defense of both the autonomous position that it afforded the household head *and* the subordinate position that it imposed on the slave. This was a relationship that she considered appropriate to the nature of master and slave and therefore "a condition highly honorable to both parties."[25]

In the North's determination to undermine this "natural" hierarchy within the southern household, she foresaw only disaster. As she concluded, "What does the thinking mind see in freedom for the black race? Freedom which is to the white man the 'Open Sesame' to a career of honor and everything desirable or conducive to happiness is with the African merely a synonym for idleness." And upon the actual outbreak of war, she went so far in her identification with the position of the master as to write, "Do they think then that *we* are as degenerate as *our* slaves, to be whipped into obedience at the command of our self-styled masters?"[26]

While secession and war brought forth a torrent of racist diatribe on the part of Susan Cornwall, not all planter-class women had so internalized their subordinate status or identified so entirely with the position of the household head. Gertrude Clanton Thomas, who was daughter and wife of two of the wealthiest planters in the Augusta region and who herself inherited a large number of slaves from her father's estate (ninety at the time of emancipation), expressed herself on the slavery question in very different terms. She was not entirely in sympathy with slaveownership and recognized in the subordinate status of their slaves some reflection, however dim, of her own subordination. As she concluded upon the division of her father's estate in 1858, "Southern women are I believe at heart abolitionists, but then I expect that I have made a very broad assertion but I will stand to the opinion that the institution of slavery degrades the white man more than the negro and so exerts a more deleterious effect upon our own children."[27]

Clearly, Thomas's identification with the slaves, insofar as she did identify with them, was always couched in relation to the hegemonic position of the household head. In other words, she called herself an abolitionist, not because slavery demeaned dependents—the slaves or even herself—but rather for the way in which it empowered or degraded the household head and his offspring—presumably his sons. Here Thomas was primarily concerned with sexual relations between men of the master class and their slaves. The result, she asserted, was that "the happiness of homes are destroyed, but what is to be done?"[28]

As an example of this sad state of domestic affairs under the domination of the slaveholding household head, she gave the example of a nearby neighbor, George Eve, who lived openly with one of his slave women, "and although it was known to all that he lived constantly with her violating one of God's ten commandments, yet nothing was thought of it. There was no one without sin, 'to cast the first stone at him.'" When, however, reports circulated in the town that he had taken this woman to the North and married her, "public opinion was outraged." His father was so "mortified" that he tried to prove that his son was a lunatic. "He preferred having him live in a constant state of sin to having him cross the bounds of caste."[29]

Thomas thus recognized the way in which the class relationship between master and slave allowed some planter men to violate their domestic commitments to planter women in the very exercise of their class prerogatives over the women they held as slaves, and this recognition caused her not only to label herself an abolitionist, but also to rail against the extremity of the sexual double standard that slavery created among the slaveholding elite. "While no man was without sin," she wrote, "he was still empowered to cast the first stone at his wife or sister, for a woman of the planter class who had fallen was cast aside beyond recall." Even more distressing to Thomas than the behavior of slaveowning white men was the manner in which many white women allied with them. Arguing that women should "at least pity" other white women accused of adulterous behavior, she asserted that instead most white women treated them only with "a glance of cold scorn or indifference, expressive of, 'stand aside, I am better than thou.'"[30]

For men of the master class to have sexual relations with their slaves was to act within the scope of male prerogative. For their wives or sisters to do the same was to violate their subordinate position, to act autonomously in disposing of something that did not properly belong to them any more than it did to the slaves: the use of their bodies. While Thomas could bring herself to advocate that other women should "at least pity" such women, in the case of slave women, she could not even envision the possibility that they might be so empowered as to protect themselves against sexual exploitation by their white owners. She did, nonetheless, at times claim in her journals to identify with the situation of slave women. "A woman myself, I can sympathize with my sex, whether white or black." Her sympathies, however, were engaged not by the slave woman's loss of freedom, but rather by the distortion of domestic life that slavery caused.

She concluded, "I know that if I had the sole management of a plantation, pregnant women should be highly favored."[31]

Ultimately, however, in a world where women like herself generally did not have the sole management of plantations, she could only conclude that "a servant educated" was done a "disservice," as they were "sometimes sold for debt and bought by men only one degree removed from brute creation." Slave women were best left entirely within their place and not encouraged to expect any of the privileges accorded white women. Women of her own class were expected to avoid the entire question of sexual exploitation and the double sexual standard it created. As she concluded, "I know that this is a . . . subject thought best for [white] women to ignore."[32]

Although in the privacy of her journal Thomas was critical of slavery for the sexual double standard it fostered within the white elite, her criticism of the sexual exploitation of black women was limited by her commitment to the interests of white domesticity as well. While planter-class men may have violated their domestic obligations to the women of their class by using their position as slaveowners, or even just as white men, to command sexual favors of slave women, it was this same power of the planter-class male, a position grounded in his status as head of household and as slaveholder, that made the domestic world of elite white women possible at all. As Thomas could not envision a fundamental transformation of the position of the household head—the kind of domestic reform she desired would have required a change, most likely a decline, in her own class position—she could not conceive a solution to the violation of black women's sexuality by white men. Her criticism of slavery, therefore, was as much limited by her commitment to the interests of white domesticity as it was radicalized by these interests.

If Thomas, a self-avowed "abolitionist" and advocate of women's domestic rights, could only envision the good will of the master as the basis for a sexual single standard, it should not be surprising that Susan Cornwall, an avowed supporter of the racial hierarchy, should do the same. Not only was Cornwall among those women who, according to Thomas, would shun a "fallen woman" and leave her "cast aside, beyond recall," for violating the rights of white men in their women, she went further and damned such women for all eternity. As she asserted in the very first entry of her journal, in March of 1857, "How fearful for such beings [adulterous women] to contemplate the future. Death is to them the beginning of an eternity of anguish, while to the Christian O blessed contrast it is the beginning of eternal happiness." And as if an "eternity of anguish" were not sufficient, she went on to conclude in the case of one woman who had committed adultery, "This now wretched woman has been the favorite of man, now, who will call her friend?" Certainly not Susan Cornwall, who even doubted that "her innocent babe will ever be taught to reverence her who bore her." [33]

After thirteen years of marriage and five children, Cornwall had little in the way of illusions regarding what frequently appeared to her as the thankless tedium of a planter's wife's lot. "In a life like mine there is so little to write about, so much monotony that I would have to stop writing for want of something to write about." She struggled daily to resign herself to the "petty trials" that made up her daily domestic existence and the occasional "sarcastic remark" from her husband. "Well, well, patience and hope, little woman and you'll learn to do right yet even if you don't get praised for it." Having disciplined herself to the self-sacrifice required by her place in the social order, she reserved her resentment not for the sarcastic remarks or the neglect by her particular Lord of Creation, but for women in her own position who dared to violate it, adulterous women who appeared by their behavior to treat with contempt her own struggles to adhere to her place. [34]

For all that Susan Cornwall and Gertrude Thomas stood at opposite ends of the political spectrum, they both stood within the confines of the same male-dominated household structure. Their differences were therefore more apparent than real. Whatever Thomas's criticisms of slaveholding, she was not about to violate the authority of the household head—in fact she explicitly exempted her own husband from any such criticism. For all that Cornwall damned women who violated their place, she was herself frustrated in her domestic life and, like Thomas, could only find voice for her frustration in her journal.

In fact both Thomas and Cornwall harbored the ambition to be writers. They both expected, however, that their only real audience for their journals would be their own children. As Cornwall wrote, "It may be that some stray thoughts will meet the eyes of my little ones after I am gone home, which will interest them as coming from one who loves them as only a mother can love." In a similar vein, Thomas expected only her daughters to find interest in her journals, and "for no intrinsic merit . . . but because . . . they were written by your mother." Of course, such disclaimers were, in one sense, ritual gestures, to expiate what both women recognized as an inappropriate ambition, literary aspirations that could not be acknowledged forthrightly but which could be made more acceptable when cast in terms of maternal roles.[35]

When Susan Cornwall received a request to become a contributor to a newspaper, she was at first overjoyed. "Is it possible that the dream of my childhood is to be verified and I am to become an Authoress?" However, she immediately squelched this thought with renewed expressions of deference to the parameters of her place, what she described as "the fear that this to me delightful employment may cause me to neglect my domestic duties." She strove to reconcile her desire for individual public recognition with the proper confines of her subordinate status. She asked herself, "But if I can realize anything from it [her writing] should I not try to succeed in order to aid my dear husband in his labors?"[36]

Both Cornwall and Thomas sought a vehicle for individual expression and self-realization at the same time they were both intensely committed to the domestic arena. Although they differed over what that domestic commitment entailed, they both ultimately embraced the hegemony of the household head. Therefore, although Thomas disagreed violently with Cornwall on matters internal to the structure of the household, when the household was threatened from the outside, and that threat came as an attack on the prerogatives of the household head, Thomas, in language strikingly similar to that of Cornwall, expressed a militant identification with the cause of the men of her class—without any recognition of the way in which it might contradict her identification, however hedged about, with the position of the household dependents.

In her journal Thomas described secession and the outbreak of war as "events transcending in importance anything that has ever happened within the recollection of any living person in *our* country." She was sure that she would never forget "the state of intense excitement which pervaded the city of Augusta when it was announced that the fight was going on down at Sumter." By July 15, 1861, Augusta, according to her, had done "much to be proud of," having already sent ten companies off to the front. Her own husband's elite cavalry corps, the Richmond County Hussars, had received orders to hold themselves in readiness to leave, and she concluded, "I can write this without one wish to have him remain with me. When Duty and Honour call him it would be strange if I would influence him to remain in the lap of inglorious ease when so much is at stake." After all, the North was attempting to "deprive us of that glorious liberty for which our Fathers fought and bled and shall we tamely submit to this? Never."[37]

How could Thomas support her husband in fighting a war that others, like Cornwall, viewed as a defense of an institution that Thomas herself seriously questioned? Like the non-slaveholding men who actually fought and died in battle, Gertrude Thomas understood the war primarily as a threat to the position of the male household head, a position that (rightly or wrongly) included the prerogative of owning slaves. Although she was critical of particular aspects of the power that position conferred upon white southern men under normal circumstances, when these men were threatened from the outside, she perceived her interests to lie with those of her husband, the head of her household, and with the men of the Confederacy more generally. In fact, she perceived the struggle to be a dual one: directly for the liberties of the household head, and by extension for the well-being of the household as a whole that male liberties were expected, at least ideally, to underwrite. The more the North transgressed upon southern soil, the more the latter danger became apparent. So, upon hearing a rumor in the fall of 1861 that the Federals were within ten miles of Savannah and that several carloads of women and children had left fearing the attack, she concluded, "I have never so fully realized that we are engaged in a war which threatens our firesides. . . . We lack arms and ammunition. In that respect they have the advantage over us, but our men are fighting for liberty and homes."[38]

Although clearly outmanned and outgunned, the Confederacy would prevail, according to Thomas, because its soldiers were fighting not only for their own independence but for their dependents, to protect and defend their families and their homes. From this perspective the war was in fact transformed from an expression of male prerogative into a struggle to protect white domesticity.

Here elite white women and children were deflected from any even marginal identification they might have developed during peacetime with the plight of the slaves. As women united with the men of their class and race to protect the interests of their households, the political and economic privilege to which the status quo entitled them, the political spectrum of white women's racial politics narrowed. Secession and the outbreak of war initially worked to intensify white women's loyalty to the men of their race and class, not only because they were reared to a common set of values, but also because a threat to the powers of the male household head constituted a threat to their place within the household more generally.

As in the case of the young men who volunteered for the war thinking that it would be short and glorious, women, like Thomas or Cornwall, found that the actual conduct of war called into question their dedication to the principles that they held dear in the abstract. Despite her brave commitment to those same principles of honor, duty, and liberty that her father and husband venerated, Gertrude Thomas found the actual departure of her husband to be a wrenching experience. After being notified by the captain of her husband's regiment that the unit was leaving, she found herself confronting the "momentous decision" of "should I be willing for him to go," despite having already committed herself to the proposition in principle. Walking into the room where her newborn lay sleeping, she kissed the child, and at that moment named him Jefferson for his father, "and having baptised him with this name under such circumstances I felt that God will cause him to be a solace and comfort to me during Mr. Thomas' absence." Between her child and her God, she then found the resources to "say nothing that should cause him [her husband] to falter."[39]

Katherine Cumming, wife of Joseph Cumming, a prominent lawyer and member of a long-established family in Augusta, described a similar course of action in her recollections. Upon hearing that her husband would be leaving with the Clinch Rifles, "my heart died within me," but she determined "to be brave for his sake." Her husband, in fact, "broke down more than I did at the final good-bye, when I had to call in to play all my courage to keep him up to the sticking point."[40]

Despite the widespread commitment, not only to the cause of independence, but also to the presentation of a brave front to their male relations, even "to the sticking point," not all women were able to carry out this duty. In a letter to his sister, Julia Bryan Cumming, Goode Bryan described the heartrending behavior of his wife at the train station: clinging to him constantly and crying whenever he left her side, despite the fact that they had agreed together that he would enlist. In response to this behavior, he wrote, "I wished that I had never thought of the war and could I have done so without disgracing myself, would have given up commission and everything else, to have remained with her."[41]

Goode Bryan apologized to his sister for this momentary fainthearted-ness, although he obviously expected that she would also understand the intensity of his wife's anxiety. Julia Cumming, herself the mother of seven grown children, saw three of her four sons immediately enlist in the war. She accepted this with a stoic face to the world, but privately she confided to her daughter Emily, "I can say nothing to dissuade them [her sons] from going, but you may well imagine how bereaved and anxious I feel." The sight of her sons' empty rooms, the "silent awful gloom," threw her into despair. She comforted herself with the observation that she was not alone, domestic life in general in the town seemed to be in a depression. "This, I believe, is almost a universal feeling, I never knew so little visiting, so few interchanges of neighborly hospitality, or gatherings of friends."[42]

Julia Cumming clung to her one remaining son, Julian, and wrote to her daughter on his birthday, "Tell him not to think of going to the war just now to have some thought for your father and myself who have given up all but him—tell him to *wait*." At the same time she recognized the pressures upon her son to exhibit, as Gertrude Thomas described it, "a noble, manly spirit" by enlisting. As she concluded in her letter to her daughter, how "immensely more painful is his state, than that of any of them who go to face even all the *horrors* of honourable warfare." Julian Cumming wrote his own sardonic comments on his situation to his sister, noting the "thinning out of our population," leaving only the "patriotic ladies" in the area, who, by giving birth to several infants, were "much to be lauded for their praiseworthy zeal in preventing the entire extinction of the human race." He apparently found the challenge to his manhood overwhelming, however, and despite his parents' protests, also enlisted within the next six months.[43]

The absence of fathers, sons, and husbands had the effect of impressing upon the women left in the family circle the depth of their attachment to them, intensifying domestic ties at the very moment when these became most threatened and most tenuous. Julia Cumming wrote to her daughter that she could "hardly endure the sadness of the change, the diminished family circle." Her daughter wrote to her own husband, Henry Hammond, of the "blank dreariness" that had taken possession of her since parting from him, "you who give color and tone to my life, you who are its chief interest, and delight." Gertrude Thomas wrote frequently of her prayers to "reunite the severed tie." Only in her loss, she wrote, did she fully recognize the intensity of her attachment to her husband. "Oh Darling I never knew before how much I loved you. Absence has taught me the more fully to appreciate your many noble traits of character!"[44]

Not only did the absence of their male relations heighten these women's consciousness of the depth of family ties, it also intensified their feelings about the place in which those ties were imbedded. Catherine Barnes Rowland, wife of a young Augusta merchant, described in her diary her sadness upon attending church without her husband. "Never since I was married have I ever been to that church without Charlie and as I went in, & took my seat in our pew, where we sat the last time we were in church together, & when I saw the *vacant* place where he always sat, my heart was very, *very* sad, and the tears fell thick and fast, I could not keep them back in spite of all my efforts to do so." Catherine Rowland broke up independent housekeeping upon her husband's enlistment and moved back to her parents' plantation, Ivanhoe. She found return visits to their prewar home especially difficult. "It was a bitter trial to me giving up that happy home, & I wish I could have kept it. When I went in & looked around upon everything, recollections of so many joyous days come up before me, & I could not bear to stay in the house." Gertrude Thomas felt a similar ambivalence about her home upon her husband's departure. "I do not wonder that people leave a place which reminds them so much of a loved one. Mine is not the disposition to enjoy the sight of objects which in reminding me of Mr. Thomas make me miss him more."[45]

Many young married women of the Augusta elite, like Catherine Rowland, moved back to their parental households during the war. Both Gertrude Thomas and Emily Cumming Hammond returned to Augusta to live with their parents. To a certain extent, then, families were able to regroup during the war, to compensate for the absence of men through closer and more tightly knit relationships among female kin. Catherine Rowland frequently recorded the particular importance these ties held for her under wartime circumstances. "I am once more at my dear old home [Ivanhoe] and right glad I am to be here for I am happier here than anywhere else when away from Charlie." There she found the welcome company of her mother and her sisters, as well as the unspoiled beauty of Ivanhoe, unspoiled, at least for her, with associations of personal loss.

"The country is to me the sweetest place in the world & the quiet is so in accordance with my feelings that I love to be here."[46]

As important as their female kin and their place of origin were in consoling these women in their men's absence, their children were even more critical in filling the void. After naming her child "Jefferson" after her husband and thereby steeling herself for his imminent departure, Gertrude Thomas reflected upon how she would pass the time in his absence. "If the war continues I shall endeavor in my children to find my principal comfort, teaching my children to be proud of their father's example." Catherine Rowland also found a similar consolation in the companionship of her young son. "I took a delightful walk with my darling little Willie this afternoon, bless his little heart, he is so sweet and is a great deal of company for me during Charlie's absence and I enjoy many hours with him, that would otherwise be lonely!" Joseph Jones sent a message to his young son encouraging him to act as his substitute during his absence. "Tell my noble little son that he must take good care of his dear Mother & be a little man. . . . Tell him that he must love his Mother very much whilst father is away & must put his arms around her neck, & hug her tight & kiss her every morning & night for his dear father."[47]

Although their children helped to fill the void left by the departure of their husbands, the children themselves were threatened by the high infant and child mortality rates that prevailed in the mid-nineteenth-century South. By the outbreak of the Civil War, Gertrude Clanton Thomas had already lost one child, and she would eventually lose two more. During one brief, two-month period during the war, Catherine Rowland saw all three of her sister's children die painful and gruesome deaths by typhoid fever. Of one of the children, Clara, she wrote, "I think she must have had a hundred convulsions; as one would leave her another would come on." Of a second, Lizzie, she recorded, "Dear little thing! How great were her sufferings & her screams were terrific."[48]

As concerned as Catherine Rowland was about wartime threats to her husband's well-being, and in some ways precisely because of those threats, the ever-present war against childhood maladies loomed even larger in her mind. Every childhood fever, every cold that her young son contracted threatened to strip her, as it had her sister before her, of her one great consolation in life, her son. "I have spent a quiet day, though a very anxious one as my little darling has had a fever all day, but Mother and Aunt Maria say it is caused by a heavy cold he has. I pray that he may be spared to me & may soon be well though I cannot help feeling anxious, as dear little Lizzie & Clara's sudden deaths come up before me."[49]

The ability that these women possessed to put up a brave front, to see their husbands off to war, "saying nothing that would stay him," while their hearts "died within them," was a hard-bought but critically necessary quality that they had already acquired in their struggles with child and infant loss. Catherine described her sister's outwardly calm acceptance of the death of her third and last child. "Truly Sister has been sorely chastened, but she bears her afflictions with beautiful Christian resignation." This surface calm reflected a deep striving for the quality of resignation, for acceptance of that which they had no power to change. As Gertrude Clanton Thomas recorded upon the death of her first infant, "The Lord giveth and the Lord taketh away. Blessed be the name of the Lord." In her next sentence, however, she burst forth, "But oh it is hard. Nature rebels and turns shudderingly away from the thought that tonight my poor little darling will sleep its first sleep in its grave." To be resigned, even to God's will, was never a question of a simple, passive acceptance. It required a constant struggle and real courage to face that severed tie and turn it into the ground.[50]

Gertrude Thomas was grateful for her husband's support and sympathy during this trying experience. She wrote, "He has shown the greatest possible kindness and sympathy and done everything in his power to alleviate my grief." Their mutual loss brought them together, according to Thomas, and made them "nearer and dearer" to each other than they had ever been before. "Tis in grief true affection appears." This grief, however, was always expressed by Gertrude Thomas as her grief, not her husband's. Her husband's role was to participate in *her* grief, to alleviate *her* suffering, to have sympathy for *her* affliction. Jefferson Thomas could offer his wife a "manly and strong heart to lean on for sympathy and support," precisely because he was *not* prostrate with grief. Being free from "the trials of life," as Gertrude Thomas put it, that is, the trials of a childbearing woman's life, Jefferson Thomas was also freed from the necessity of acquiring the quality of resignation. He did not need to learn how to accept the unacceptable or how to recognize his own essential dependence upon forces outside his control. In fact, in order to act in a "manly way," he could not do so.[51]

As much as the loss of their infant drew them together as a couple, it created a fissure between them as individuals; it gendered them. As Gertrude Thomas wrote, "Now I do indeed begin to know what are the trials of life," trials that would force her to recognize her own dependence upon forces outside her own control and eventually teach her the hard lessons of acceptance and resignation. Gertrude felt blessed by having a companionate marriage, in having a husband who would turn his freedom from such trials into the ability to offer shelter and support to her during such difficult periods of her life. But however much she may have appreciated her husband and turned to him for sympathy, it was her mother who "remained with me the night my little babe was buried." Her husband could sympathize with her grief, but he could not identify with it, and in that sense he could not lead her as her mother or other female relations, who had walked the path before her, were able to do.[52]

Ultimately, however, each woman faced her loss alone and in the process acquired character as an individual. What a woman in her loss could not bear, she gave away to her God, giving up a part of herself and her own will; she gained in return a growing capacity for resignation. Catherine Rowland's sister could bear the loss of her children because "God has made His grace sufficient for her." Contemplating the imminent possibility of a similar fate in the wartime loss of her husband, Catherine Rowland wrote, "I pray that God will strengthen me to bear whatever He has in store for me."[53]

Nevertheless, the departure of men to the front, combined with the continuing threat of child and infant mortality at home, presented these women with the possibility of such a totality of domestic loss that it strained the limits of even this hard-bought fortitude and religious faith. Julia Cumming, who saw all four of her sons enlist in the war despite her efforts to keep at least Julian by her side, confessed to her daughter her fear that her depressed state reflected insufficient faith, insufficient, at least, for the crisis at hand. "I resist it [an intense anxiety] in every way I can but not successfully. . . . I still feel as if this was something more than it should be and that a true Christian faith should give me more confidence and serenity than I now feel."[54]

From the outset, then, the war reinforced gender among Confederate men and women. When the men like Joseph Cumming or Charles Rowland rode off to defend their independence, they acted not only as citizens in a democracy that affirmed their right to do so, but as men in a society that defined the essence of masculinity in the freedom from ties of dependency that it permitted. If they had any say in the matter, neither they, nor their children, would be "reduced to a bondage lower than that of the African." For their female relations, however, the departure of these men, although promising to insure the autonomy of the male members of the family, had the immediate impact of intensifying their own sense of domestic dependency. These women, like Catherine Rowland or Gertrude Thomas, were left to contemplate the temporary if not the permanent loss of their men. They resigned themselves to this loss, as they resigned themselves to the ever-present possibility of child and infant mortality, by recognizing and accepting their dependence upon forces outside their own control and by intensifying their religious faith. As Caroline Davis Jones wrote to her husband during his enlistment, "In these awful times I wish to take my Beloved ones to Jesus feet & there continue until this calamity be overpast. . . . What can we do now but humble ourselves before Our Father and pray for mercy."[55]

In the case of child mortality, the force outside women's control was beyond all human agency, that of men as well as women. Men, like Jefferson Thomas, could only stand by and offer what comfort and shelter they could provide their wives on the long and rocky road of largely uncontrolled childbearing and child loss. The war, by contrast, was brought on by human agency, that is to say, *male* human agency. These men proposed not only to defend their rights as free men but to establish a new and independent nation to represent them. They proposed to do this not only for themselves, but for their "children and their children's children." Domestic loss, in this context, was not attached to the female world of necessity and resignation, but rather to the male world of individual autonomy and self-assertion. Husbands, fathers, and sons might be lost in the war, but greater independence might be won as a result.

Whereas in the everyday order of things gender relations were inward-looking, with each couple bound together in a symbiotic relationship directed toward the process of reproducing familial life, the war had the effect of turning that relationship outward, of shearing apart male and female gender roles, as men dedicated their energies not to the immediate support of their families but rather to the pursuit of their own individual and collective political rights. Of course they argued, and with some reason, that to defend their rights as free men was to expand their ability to give shelter to their families in the long run. But in the short run it deprived their families of their immediate ability to do so.

Secession and the onset of the war therefore placed Confederate women in a highly contradictory situation. As much as it intensified their vulnerability to domestic loss and thereby intensified their privatized and dependent domestic position, it simultaneously attached that possibility of loss to a new assertive, independent, and outward-looking basis. Rather than being given the task of struggling to resign themselves to the loss of yet another child, Confederate women found themselves called upon to sacrifice their men to a cause that ultimately promised to enable them to *gain* control, if not over their own life's course, at least over the future of their households and their region more generally. Rather than constituting the basis for the private, inward-looking nature of gender relations, critical events in the course of women's lives, in particular the loss of their children, became in the context of the outbreak of war of central, public, and political concern.

Women in their role as mothers found themselves in a particularly critical political position. As much as their ties to their children created the cords that bound them to their dependency in peacetime, these same ties now drew them into the center of the struggle for the establishment of the Confederacy in a time of war. As much as women were uniquely tied to their children, their children were also tied to them. If men, especially young men, were to participate in the war effort, their women, especially their mothers, would at least have to acquiesce in their departure. Women thus became as capable of political and patriotic behavior as their male children became critical to the war effort. Gertrude Thomas proudly recorded the way that Confederate women rose to the occasion, contributing not only their wealth and their labor to the Confederate cause but, most importantly, their sons. She gave as evidence of such ultimate patriotism a perhaps apocryphal conversation between one mother and her son. On his way to the front, the young man said to his mother, "Mother, if one word of yours could keep me at home what would you say?" The mother, according to Thomas, "with a tear in her eye but a smile on her lip . . . replied, 'my son I would bid you go.' Such is the patriotic spirit with which we bid our hearts idol go and do deeds of glory." [56]

Women exercised authority over their sons as they did over no other men in their culture. As the *Augusta Chronicle and Sentinel* noted, "The man who does not love his mother and yield to her influence is not of the right stuff to make a patriot of, and has no business in a patriot army." With such influence came responsibility, especially as the extreme youth of many of the enlistees made them literally little more than children. They went off to the front as a gay lark, leaving their mothers to contemplate the darker possibilities of their enlistment. Take for example the plight of Philoclea Edgeworth Eve, wife of a prominent planter in Richmond County. She saw two of her sons enlist, the elder, Francis Edgeworth, only sixteen and the younger, according to his sister, Eva Berrien Eve, only fourteen. Of the fourteen-year-old his sister commented, "The child is daft, and his uniform is irreproachable. He smiles blandly and tries to affect dignity." [57]

While such young men reveled in the excitement of the moment, their mothers were left to confront the danger that lurked behind the dashing uniform. Letters to the local paper therefore urged women to consider the future impact the war might have on their sons. "Let them not, in future years . . . be forced in sadness of heart and reproaches of conscience, to say that in all this they took no part." Mothers should, according to this writer, consider with what "humiliation" sons would be forced to recognize that they were "unworthy of the liberty and home secured for them by the valor of others." Mothers should exercise their influence to secure the long-range interests of their children. Ignoring the probable immediate cost, they should focus their sights upon the principles involved and the larger goals to be achieved. They should raise their eyes from the immediate details of domestic life and focus them instead upon public concerns and potential benefits to future generations.[58]

Wives as well as mothers found their roles turned outward with the departure of their men. While they did not have the same kind of authority over their husbands that mothers had over their sons, wives' support for their husband's participation in the war was critical. Some wives went so far in their identification with their husband's struggle as to actually enlist in the war themselves. The *Chronicle and Sentinel* described one such woman who arrived in town with her husband, the captain of the Light Guards, "determined to share with her husband . . . all the dangers and privations of the War." She was described by the press as being "armed to the teeth, carrying a belt around her waist, a very formidable bowie knife and pistol." She was called upon by local citizens when in town, who were "highly delighted with her agreeable manners and her heroic purpose." Other women who actually enlisted with their husbands also elicited favorable comments. There was Mrs. Amy Clarke, for example, who was described as "heroic and self-sacrificing," having enlisted with her husband as a private and, after he was killed in an early battle, having fought on alone in the ranks as a common soldier until she was twice wounded and taken prisoner, where "her sex finally discovered, she was taken as a regular prisoner of war, but required to don female garb."[59]

Here we find an apparent breakdown of gendered conventions altogether, as women warriors are held up for public admiration, even to the point of commending women who arm themselves and dress up like men in order to accompany their husbands to the front. Of course, no one was suggesting that women should enlist and fight for the cause themselves. The message here was rather to stress the extent to which women should be willing to go in support of their men's cause. In that sense, these examples of the fluidity of gender roles during wartime, the falling away of appropriate dress, sphere, and activity for these particular women, reflect the *underlying* principle of gender division that under normal circumstances conventional behavior reflected. Whether it meant giving up their children to the war effort, actually accompanying their male relations to the front, or contributing through their expanded domestic labor, patriotic Confederate women should even be willing to violate their domestic place itself if this became necessary to defend the underlying basis of that place—to support the position of the male household head. So although the immediate impact of secession and war was to intensify white gender roles, the ultimate recognition of the patriarchy actually lay in the willingness of Confederate women to go one step beyond these very domestic roles, to transcend their own privatized domestic place in the name of the basic patriarchal principle that animated it.

Do impress upon the soldiers, that they are constantly in our
thoughts, that we are *working* for them, while they are *fighting*
for us—and that their wants shall be supplied, as long as there
is a *woman* or a dollar in the "Southern Confederacy."

—Anonymous letter, *Augusta Daily Constitutionalist,*
August 13, 1861

2

Fighting Men and Loving Women

THE MOBILIZATION OF THE HOMEFRONT

Southerners who gave their support to secession and war in
order to defend what they understood to be the rights of free white men
found themselves confronted with a perplexing contradiction. The demands of national independence, not to mention the demands of fighting
a war to defend it, increasingly appeared to run counter to the defense
of those individual liberties that secession and national independence
were supposed to insure. In the antebellum South, the domination of
the southern market economy by the slaveowning, staple-crop producing
plantation system had not only made the region as a whole wealthy and
powerful in relation to the North, but had also produced an extreme form
of white and male domination within the household. In the altered context

of national independence however, the extreme economic dependence of the South upon a few staple crops was transformed into a serious weakness, threatening to render the newly formed Confederacy as dependent upon exchange with the industrial nations as it had previously rendered white male heads of household independent of those they dominated.[1]

In Augusta, mounting support for political independence was accompanied by a discussion in the local press of how regional economic independence could also be achieved. One writer to the local Augusta paper argued that a wholesale shift away from staple-crop production and the rapid development of domestic manufacturing and subsistence crops were critical. "To secure our complete independence," he wrote, "we must determine to be so." Southern manufacturing in every area should be encouraged and patronized. "Southern clothes, southern shoes, southern hats must be worn. . . . All our food must be produced at home, both for man and beast."[2] Augusta's industrial interests had made the city one of the largest manufacturing centers in the South prior to the outbreak of war and stood to benefit immensely from this newfound regional commitment to economic self-sufficiency. As the editor of the local paper concluded, "Anything which looks to the advancement of our manufacturing interests we go in for most heartily. There is enough energy and 'go aheadativeness' among our own people to insure all kinds of manufactures, for which we have heretofore depended on the North."[3]

This "go aheadativeness" of the Augusta citizenry had already promoted a plethora of small manufacturing concerns by the mid-nineteenth century, including an ice company, a machine works, a brick factory, and flour and lumber mills. By far the most significant industrial undertaking, however, was the Augusta Factory, a textile mill that employed some six hundred hands by the year 1860. The construction of the mill in 1847 had resulted from the efforts of several of the town's leading citizens, most notably Henry Cumming, Amory Sibley, and William Schley. Before it was possible to actually found the mill, it was first necessary for these men to promote the construction of a canal with town funds in order to create the necessary water power for such a mill and eventually for the other industries that would come to line the banks of the Savannah. Public opinion ran high in some quarters against the construction of this canal precisely because of fears of the factories it would bring. Such enterprises were derided because they portended the emergence of factory wage labor, a social condition that was deemed to be an affront to the dignity of free white men. Within the context of a land of small, independent producers, such a condition was anomalous. It was even more alien from the perspective of the slaveowning planter, for whom a "hand" meant not a free laborer, but a slave.[4]

However, the men most responsible for the construction of the canal and the mill did not view this experiment in industrial social relations as a challenge to those principles of white male independence that they themselves held dear. In fact, they saw the construction as a way to reinforce these underlying values. The mill promised to offer employment to the growing numbers of poor people, especially white widows and their children, who had migrated to Augusta from the surrounding rural areas looking for employment. As the price of cotton declined, so too did the power of the male-headed household structure to provide for all women and children. The most vulnerable rural households in economic hard times were those that lacked adult male heads, as the influx into the city of predominantly female-headed households indicated. The mill promised to reinforce the basic cotton economy that undergirded the town's prosperity by making cotton profitable even in unpromising times. Simultaneously, the mill promised to provide an alternative means of support for women and children who had been deprived of male "protection" by the death or economic failure of the household head.[5]

While industrial development may have represented a potential threat to the free and autonomous status of some white men—namely factory hands—for local notables like Henry Cumming or Amory Sibley, manufacturing served to secure their independence on a larger plane. Factories provided a hedge against fluctuations in the price of cotton, which had periodically undermined the viability of the patriarchal household structure as a shelter upon which all women and children could rely. From this vantage point, industrial development actually promised to enhance elite white men's ability to protect *all* white women. Even those men most committed to the wisdom of industrial development, however, were loath to identify themselves primarily as industrialists. Of the three men most responsible for the canal and the factory, only William Schley eventually became a full-time industrialist in the 1850s, after a lifetime as a prominent lawyer. Henry Cumming never did so. Despite heavy investments in the mills, he remained one of the town's leading lawyers until his death in 1866. Amory Sibley continued to build up his cotton factoring business in partnership with his brothers. By the outbreak of the war it had become Sibley and Sons, one of the largest businesses of its kind in town and, as the name would indicate, a path to wealth and honor for the younger generation of Sibleys as well as for Amory himself.[6]

The boast of the Augusta newspaper editor about the "go aheadativeness" of the town's population was therefore not entirely justified. More accurate, perhaps, was a letter to the newspaper claiming that although planters "have a finger in every [manufacturing] concern," they "hide behind joint stock companies." Although planters and merchants were at times willing to invest their surplus capital in manufacturing, even the most stalwart supporters of industrialism among them, men like Cumming or Sibley, were not willing to completely identify with it or to exercise the aggressive entrepreneurship necessary to make it work. As the major employer of women and children in the town, the mill was viewed as much as a quasi-charitable institution for those "deserving" poor who lacked male protection as it was envisioned as a path for autonomous economic development in its own right.[7]

However, in 1861, from the vantage point of the new situation created by the demands of *national* independence, attitudes about industrial development began to change. Now the reluctance of men of wealth to be clearly identified and actively involved in manufacturing appeared to be detrimental to the well-being of the society as a whole. In the radically altered context of secession and independence, one writer to the local paper concluded, "the problem with our capitalists is that they are not enough individualists."[8]

If secession and the creation of the Confederacy served to change the basis for independence and autonomy, the outbreak of war intensified this transformation. The key to success as an independent nation was not grounded in successful cotton production but in the ability to produce the materials necessary to support a war: soldiers and the food, clothing, and arms necessary to sustain them. Especially after the North cut off trade with Europe through its naval blockade, the South's success in the war depended upon the mobilization of internal resources. From a basis in cotton and what cotton could purchase on the world market, the southern economy needed to make a radical shift to subsistence crops and home manufactures. As the planting season approached toward the end of the first year of the war, planters recognized this changed state of affairs. "It must be apparent to all, except those who habitually take the most gloomy view of things, that we can be subjugated only by starvation, and equally apparent that we can, if we will, avoid this, and that it can be done only by planting no cotton, or at least very little." A letter to the editor put the point more succinctly in April in 1862 when it concluded, "In the next few days our planting friends must decide whether they choose, on the one hand, cotton and subjugation, or corn and triumph."[9]

When the planters and farmers were forced to choose between their farms and plantations and their nation, that is, between planting cotton or corn, or between their individual liberties and the interests of national independence, they tended to choose that which preserved their status as free men. Fortunately for the health of the Confederate war effort, the choice for the Confederate citizens of Augusta, especially those who had already invested in manufacturing concerns, was a more straightforward one, because their economic interests had become more diversified. Having promoted the development of an economic form, the factory and wage-labor system, that potentially threatened the independent producer economy that the Confederacy was dedicated to defend, Augustans were, ironically, in a better position to make the transition that the exigencies of wartime had thrust upon them. Nevertheless, the coming of the war inevitably magnified the importance of manufacturing in the economy of the town. As long as the ideal of the autonomous, independent producer remained hegemonic, manufacturing stayed marginal in the local economy, limited largely to those members of the population, white women and children, who were already dependent, being so unfortunate as to have no place in a male-headed household.[10]

Now, in the wartime context, manufacturing became positively associated with the pursuit of white male independence, albeit collectively, on a national scale. Corn to feed the troops and the animals would be of little avail in the struggle for southern independence without the proper clothing, equipment, food, medicines, and arms. If the conduct of war required that the planter's production be turned to the immediate needs of subsistence, it also required that urban centers such as Augusta shift from mercantile activity toward manufacturing so as to fabricate local substitutes for lost imports and to provide industrial material for the conduct of the war. In the first year of the war, therefore, Augusta became the site of many of the strategic manufactories of the Confederacy, including the largest powder mills in the country, machine shops, gun factories, the state's center for the manufacture of uniforms, and a confederate bakery.[11] The Augusta Factory enlarged its workforce to 750 hands, and in recognition of the critical contribution of textile production to the war effort, skilled male workers in the mill were exempted from the draft until the last year of the fighting.[12]

Although the Augusta Factory ran at full production throughout the war, the mill could never begin to produce sufficient quantities of cloth even for the soldiers, much less for the population at large.[13] Given the largely preindustrial nature of the southern economy, an economy where production was still organized within the framework of households, the main source of domestic goods could not, at least initially, come from the expansion of preexisting manufactories like the Augusta Factory or even through the desperate efforts of the Confederacy to establish a whole new industrial infrastructure. Of necessity such production rested, particularly in the early years of the war, upon the redirection, rationalization, and expansion of the previously privatized and subordinate domestic labor of women within their households. The demands of the war effort, therefore, not only undercut the primacy of staple crop production, the economic basis for the preeminent position of white men as household heads, but it also moved to the center of the economy that labor associated with reproduction and domestic manufacturing.[14]

This intensification and rendering public of women's domestic labor in the context of wartime had already occured on a smaller scale during the American Revolution. Then, spinning bees and the weaving of homespun had become political and patriotic activities of central importance to the success of the war effort as a whole. In later wars, especially the two world wars, the phenomenon reasserted itself, as in the massive public organization of women's labor, in factories, the Red Cross, and the nursing corps. In this long-term trend the Civil War represents an intermediate stage. This was particularly true in the South, which occupied a midpoint between the overwhelmingly rural, subsistence context of the American Revolution and the largely urban and industrial context of twentieth-century wars. Southern society was still largely of the old preindustrial order, but in a handful of urban, industrial centers such as Augusta, embryonic elements of the new order were ready to emerge.

Cities like Augusta had the economic surplus, contained largely within the structure of the male-headed household economy, that made it possible to engage in a massive shift toward what was in many ways the antithesis of the southern socioeconomic order as a whole. Nevertheless, in the context of wartime, these antithetical arrangements had become necessary to counter an enemy whose overall industrial capacity and economic self-sufficiency were considerably more advanced. This shift was experienced in human terms as a radical tearing of household dependents from their traditional place in the household. This process has occured to some extent in all our wars. In the case of the Civil War South, particularly in places like Augusta, the experience was particularly wrenching and dramatic, as well as pivotal for the ultimate outcome of events.[15]

Thus, while Confederate women of Augusta turned to their religious faith at the outset of the war to resign themselves to the temporary and perhaps permanent loss of their men, a loss that reconfirmed them in their subordinate domestic status, where "God's will be done," structural shifts in the economy created by the war simultaneously placed them in a position to make a critical contribution to the shelter and protection of those who, under normal circumstances, were supposed to protect them. Mothers who gave up their sons to the war faced not only a bitter test of their ability to resign themselves to domestic loss, but also a new, public political power as the producers of warriors. Women in their everyday domestic labor of sewing, cooking, and nursing found not only the service to their offspring that bound them in peacetime to their subordinate position, but also a newfound power to contribute to public life, previously the province of their men.

In the course of the war, Richmond County, of which Augusta was the largest town, sent more than two thousand men to the front.[16] The immediate practical demands of outfitting these troops was immense, and the remorse and pain that many women felt at the departure of their fathers, husbands, and sons was both reflected in and relieved through the intensity of their domestic labors to outfit them properly for the conflict. Catherine Rowland recorded in her diary her feelings upon the departure of her husband to the front. "It is a great comfort to know that God overrules all things and that he is doing what is best for us, it is with this feeling, I look upon my separation from Charlie and trust I have had strength given me to bear it." Having steeled herself to accept the worst, she then went on to record with some pride her own efforts to care for her husband. "I packed Charlie's valise with a heavy heart and had many cries over it. I put in many little comforts which I hope he will find useful. He had a very nice outfit and I made nearly all of his clothing with my own fingers which was a pleasure and a satisfaction to me."[17]

While GEF had envisioned the increased contribution domestic labor could make to southern independence within the context of individual households, she could not imagine the radical restructuring of the entire economy that would occur as a result of the war. In an economy now abandoning its total dependence upon a single crop and depending for its very life upon the success of its soldiery, not only was there a shift to manufacturing and subsistence crops, but the entire realm of hitherto secondary reproductive labor was suddenly pushed to the forefront. The most immediate and pressing demand was for the fabrication of uniforms. Although women initially attempted to do this within their own homes, it became almost immediately apparent that the individualized and privatized nature of women's domestic labor was not sufficient to the task at hand. It was effective enough in the case of the elite, whose households contained sufficient resources to meet the needs of their own menfolk. Gertrude Thomas was more than able to provide her husband with his officer's uniform, and to outfit him for the cavalry as well. However, for the general population, the demands of outfitting the men exceeded the domestic resources that their households could muster. This was true not only because women could not spare enough of their labor, but also because they lacked the requisite materials. Although the common-to-middling families provided the majority of the soldiers to fight the war, their households did not contain sufficient resources to provision them for the manifold requirements of a military campaign.[18]

In order to supply a war on such a large scale, women's domestic labor needed to be organized in a more rational and comprehensive fashion than the isolated household structure allowed, yet any reorganization along such lines would entail a fundamental breach of women's privatized position and, from the perspective of gender relations, a breach in their subordination to the authority of particular men. Here Confederate men faced a choice between their understanding of the proper "place" of their female dependents and their newfound need to empower their women in the larger struggle for independence, between the previously subordinate status of their household dependents, which had created the basis for their individual position as free men, and the new goal of Confederate nationhood.[19]

When the larger political interests of individual men as well as those of the new nation required that all men receive the fruits of women's labor, it was necessary to go beyond the system of household manufacture. A collective pooling of domestic labor was called for to address the needs of all the enlisted men. As a result, the daughters of the elite, who, according to GEF, had previously been "languishing in the very excess of idleness," were now encouraged not only to sustain the men of their own families but to make a direct contribution to the success of the Confederacy as well. In response to the overwhelming demand for their domestic labor, 225 ladies of the town and hinterland met on May 28, 1861, at the Masonic Hall in Augusta to form the Ladies' Volunteer Association.[20]

The Ladies' Volunteer Association was defined from the outset as a working society, where no dues were required for membership but all members were called on to contribute their labor. The initial leadership included some of the most prominent women of the town. The wife of the mayor, Mrs. Robert H. May, was the first president; the first vice president was Mrs. William Schley, wife of the textile manufacturer. The twenty directoresses who were to give out the work and keep records of supplies on hand and garments made also included many members of the merchant and planter elite, such as Gertrude Thomas and Mrs. William Sibley, wife of one of the sons in the factoring firm of Sibley and Sons. Although this initial membership reflected a clear grounding in the local elite, the ladies expected to garner much more widespread support throughout the community, projecting at their initial meeting that membership would swell to over one thousand women—about half the number of local men who ever served in uniform.[21]

To a certain extent, the Ladies' Volunteer Association continued to reflect conventional gender hierarchies. Its organizational meeting was opened by one of the local ministers rather than by any of the women present. The ladies also recognized the exceptional nature of the circumstances under which their organization was formed when they wrote in their charter, "The existence of this society and its duties, will terminate with the war." They also acknowledged the preeminence of male autonomy and independence when they stated that it was only because "Northern fanaticism and cupidity [had] rendered it necessary for the men of Georgia to resort to arms" that the ladies of Richmond County, "desirous of contributing to the comfort of our defenders," had joined together to organize the society.[22]

As much as these ladies may have been aware of the ways in which public organization challenged their properly privatized domestic place and were therefore careful to recognize the exceptional and limited nature of the association, they were equally convinced of the ways in which the association actually served to further their domestic interests. Like Catherine Rowland, these women sewed as a way of concretely manifesting their attachment to the family. This attachment, in the first instance, was to their own sons, fathers, and husbands. In the context of war, their familial attachments were extended to the soldiery at large. As the Ladies' Voluntary Association concluded, for the "citizen soldiery" who had "gallantly volunteered for the defense of our southern country," we "deem it a laudable undertaking, as well as a pleasure, to sew while in the service of their country; and to do all in our power to alleviate the hardships and privations of a soldier's life."[23]

In a rudimentary and fragmented form, this extension of women's domestic labor outside the framework of their immediate households predated the outbreak of the war. No doubt this was why the ladies were able to muster such an effective and formidable organization on such short order after hostilities began. The most common and widespread form of public domesticity during the antebellum period had been individualized charitable work among the poor, especially among poor women and children. Carried out on a sporadic and ad hoc basis, as their own household resources permitted and as the needs of the poor required, this donation of women's domestic labors to the needy reinforced the male-headed household structure of the society as a whole by helping those women who lacked effective support from men. Most of Augusta's poor during the antebellum period were poor precisely because a male breadwinner was absent. A society that empowered men to such an extent and offered women such circumscribed roles necessarily left widows and their children impoverished unless they had inherited substantial assets.[24]

Women who gave to the poor out of the bounty of their own households were thus serving the function of redistributing the economic resources generated by the men of their own class to the households of those who had been deprived of male support. Such charitable giving by women reinforced the stability of the patriarchal system as a whole, while it was accepted as appropriate and desirable activity for more prosperous women to undertake. Catherine Rowland reflected the value placed on this form of domestic charity when she described the death of a close neighbor, Mrs. Plumb, who "will be much missed and is a loss to the community, for she was an excellent, good woman and always doing good to the poor."[25]

While such individualized giving was encouraged, indeed made necessary by the very needs of a patriarchal society based on individual households, the formation of organizations, especially autonomous organizations run by women, was generally disparaged because this appeared to pose a challenge to the predominance of the household and opened the possibility that women might gain autonomous control over their own lives. Nevertheless, there had been a few women's voluntary organizations in the town prior to the war. Most notable were the Ladies' Sewing Circle and the Ladies' Foreign Missionary Society of the Presbyterian Church, first organized in 1828. Both these organizations took women's domestic labor, in particular sewing, as the basis for forming working organizations to support causes they deemed worthy, the education of ministers and the support of foreign missionaries.[26]

During the war, women within households containing a surplus of domestic resources were able and willing to donate some of that surplus to care for the needs of soldiers, in part because many of them already had experience with antebellum organizations to which they had donated their domestic labor to support the needs of young men called to the army of the Lord. Women who had "mothered" these young aspiring ministers before the war now "mothered" the soldiers in the same way, extending their maternal role into the public arena.

During the antebellum period these organizations had operated within the confines of the church, which sanctioned them while limiting their possibilities for independent development. As the history of the sewing circle explained, "The minister was always present to lead in prayer, and close in benediction."[27] The direction of the minister paralleled that of the household head, and the church provided a substitute structure to replace that of the household. Nevertheless, these prewar organizations formed the prototypes for the wartime organizations that followed. Although the potential for women's autonomous political expression was effectively constrained within the church, these organizations provided opportunities for women to exercise leadership that would stand them in good stead when they faced the challenge of war. This connection can be seen clearly in the case of one Augusta family in which the leadership of these organizations was handed down from one generation to the next. Anne McKinne was one of the organizers of the first Presbyterian Sewing Circle in 1828. Her daughter, Elizabeth McKinne Whitehead, as well as her daughter-in-law, Maria Whitehead McKinne, were officers in women's wartime organizations. Elizabeth's daughter, Catherine Whitehead Rowland, assisted her mother during the war.[28]

Although the structural shifts brought on by the wartime economy created the possibility for a reordering of women's domestic labor, this was actually accomplished by women who had long experience in antebellum domestic organizations. This experience took one of two forms: in the case of the McKinne-Whitehead Rowlands it was a tradition of participation in church organizations; or, as in the case of Mrs. Plumb, it occurred on a less organized, more private and individualized level.

The charitable connections between elite women and the poor, or women's voluntary church organizations and aspiring young ministers, served as rudimentary forms of women's domestic politics, creating the basis for elite women to develop as self-conscious political agents—a development that would remain largely invisible until the traumas of wartime breached the walls of the male-headed household structure. So while the initial meeting of the Ladies' Volunteer Association took an obligatory bow in the direction of patriarchal authority when the minister opened their meeting, this was the beginning and the end of male oversight. Women were now able to organize and act collectively on their own. The universality of the call for aid to the enlisted men drew them into an experience of social mothering unbounded by constraints of family or church for the first time.

As early as June of 1861, the ladies of Augusta were calling for similar organizations of women throughout the entire Confederacy. "Believing, that through out our Confederate States, there is not a lady who would not cheerfully give her mite to thus aid their protectors," the organization called upon the "cheerful patriotism of our sisters throughout the South" to come forth and create their own working societies in each "city, town, village and neighborhood." Not only did the war place all soldiers in a position akin to that of their own sons, husbands, or brothers, it made the ladies of the Confederacy akin to their own sisters. Thus Confederate women as a group were urged to apply their domestic labor collectively and publicly in support of the national Confederate cause. According to the ladies of the Augusta organization, such a national organization of women's labor could make four vital contributions to the war effort. It could promptly supply the soldiers' wants; it could assure the best goods and workmanship; it could economize costs for the Confederacy; and lastly, "we will in this small offering of service secure to ourselves the heartfelt satisfaction that patriotism always inspires, and this will serve as solace to each of us, for the absence of those whose lives are so dear to us." [29]

From the perspective of these women, patriotism took on a peculiarly domestic cast. While their men may have enlisted to defend their position as "free men," their women entered the war to protect their position as dependents, as mothers, wives, and daughters. After taking their children, patriotism constituted a continued, and in fact an intensified, commitment to the domestic labors they normally carried out. In the largely preindustrial southern household, no clear-cut distinction existed between labors of reproduction and labors of domestic manufacturing. It all fell, as the ladies of the Voluntary Association put it, within manufacturing, which was itself seen as an "offering of service." They could therefore find great solace in sewing the sleeve of a garment, since the act itself was freighted with significance as a labor of love for their husbands and children. They were also capable of incredible dedication to the cause, as patriotic acts of service to the nation came to mean for them the externalization not only of their domestic labor, but of the domestic attachments that this implied. Given the direct connection between domestic manufacturing and reproductive labor within the structure of the household, they could view their contributions to the war as an extension of their attachment to the men of their families, and could thus believe that no sacrifice was too great. [30]

Upon receipt of uniforms from the Augusta association in June 1861, the Confederate Light Guards indicated that such sentiments were understood and reciprocated. "Nothing can be more cheering to the soldier's heart," wrote the unit's Sergeant Ellis, "than news from 'the loved ones at home,' but when the news comes accompanied by such substantial tokens of regard for him and his welfare . . . as have so recently reached the members of this corps from the ladies of Augusta, our duties are indeed lightened and our hearts made brave to battle for the firesides of our noble countrywomen."[31] These men may have gone to war initially in defense of what they perceived to be their prerogatives as free men, but the actual demands of fighting the war made them conscious of their own dependence upon women's love and labor in ways that had hitherto been obscured by the latter's subordination within the household. As one young soldier wrote home in the summer of 1862, "I will close by saying—all honor to the ladies of *Georgia.* I wish I had the language to tell you how they treated us in Augusta. If I say like their own brothers I will not have said too much. I will remember the ladies of Augusta to the last. I feel proud that I am allowed the privilege of fighting for the women of old Georgia."[32]

The more the war called forth women's domestic labors into the public arena, making public those "small gifts of service," the more the war itself was transformed from a struggle of men in defense of their prerogatives as "free men" into a battle for the "firesides of our noble countrywomen." Women seized this opportunity to lay claim to a more *reciprocal* basis for gender relations. As one woman wrote to the local newspaper, "Do impress upon the soldiers, that they are constantly in our thoughts, that we are *working* for them, while they are *fighting* for us—and that their wants shall be supplied, as long as there is a *woman* or a dollar in the 'Southern Confederacy.'"[33]

The demands of conducting the war made public women's previously privatized domestic labor and therefore opened up the possibility of shifting their relationships to their men in a more equitable direction. Historically, this process of externalizing domestic manufacturing from the household was more typically the result of industrial development. Industrialization severed domestic attachments, as manufacturing labor ceased to be a voluntary offering of "service" and was incorporated into market relations by profit-seeking capitalists. In the Confederate South, however, this externalization and rationalization of manufacturing, at least initially, occured within a domestic rather than a market framework. Women themselves organized this new public form of their labor. The entrance of their labor into the public arena constituted an intensification of domestic values of love and service rather than their atrophy, which would be expected if this change had taken place in capitalist terms.

Nevertheless, as their charter indicated, the ladies realized that the demands of collectivized wartime production would require a wholesale reorganization of domestic labor to make it more rational, efficient, and standardized. Public organization guaranteed that the troops would be clothed at a minimal cost to the country and also insured that the job would be done quickly and with the "best goods and workmanship." The individualized nature of women's labor within the household could not serve the needs of equitable wartime distribution, nor could it sustain the most efficient organization of women's labor or insure proper standards of quality control.

The massive wartime demand for uniforms on short order revealed the inefficient and wasteful nature of individual piecemeal domestic labor within the household structure. With a limited supply of sewing machines, the ladies centralized their equipment in the Masonic Hall. They hired cutters for the garments and gave out the cut and partially machine-sewn garments to women to take home and finish off by hand. The town was divided into wards, each with a directress to distribute partially finished garments to the women of her ward, collect these garments in a week, and inspect them for quality work. This wholesale rationalization of women's labor was viewed with considerable interest by "a friend" who suggested in a letter to the paper that mechanization might be carried even one step further.

> In order to facilitate the hard work which the ladies have been under going, and still continue to undergo, in making up clothing for the sol-diers, a friend begs leave to suggest the application of sewing machines, to be propelled by water power. Such fixtures can be easily arranged, and applied so as to operate in the Masonic Hall, or any other building in the city, at but very little expense; affording, at the same time, the advantage of performing double the work with half the labor.[34]

This suggestion for water-propelled sewing machines elicited a re-sponse the following week, signed "Steam Engine," indicating that "A Friend" was undoubtedly intending to "poke fun" at "somebody" (presum-ably the Ladies in their efforts to rationalize their labor) when he suggested the use of water power at the Masonic Hall. For, as "Steam Engine" con-cluded, "The canal, which is the water power of Augusta, could not be conveniently extended to the Hall, and I presume the Masons would not like to have the Hall moved to the canal." Notwithstanding such occasional outbursts of sarcasm, the reorganization that the ladies orchestrated demonstrated how much more productive women's labor could be when it was organized efficiently beyond the household. As a result, the women of the Augusta Ladies' Volunteer Association were able to produce 4,185 garments in the summer of 1861.[35]

By mid-June the ladies had also come to realize that they not only needed to rationalize domestic labor, they also needed to establish control over the sources of funds and raw materials necessary to support their work. They urged the community to recognize their association as the sole public source of supply for the troops. This recognition was critical, according to the association, if an "impartial distribution" of donations was to be realized. It was, according to the ladies, the "duty" of all patriotic citizens to acknowledge the critical role of the ladies' organizational structure. Just as they recognized their duty to support their "brothers in arms," so men must recognize their duty to contribute to an association which had become central to the supply of war materiel.[36]

True commitment to the cause, patriotism itself, required not only that men accept public organization on the part of women, but that they turn over control of the necessary economic resources to enable the women to do their job. Not only did the demands of war require the reorganization of women's domestic labor beyond the household, it also required directing previously privatized economic resources of the household as well. As women gained organizational control over their own labor, so they gained control over the allocation and distribution of finances that had previously rested with the male household head.

Not content, however, to rely entirely upon the beneficence of individual donors, women in the town organized fairs and bazaars to pry loose additional donations. These fairs were the particular province of the young ladies, who made their own contribution to the cause by staging frequent "Tableux Vivants." Young ladies were especially active in the summer of 1862. The local newspaper printed up one announcement after another of local entertainments. The mayor regularly wrote letters of thanks to these young ladies for their generous contributions to the cause. The fair held in August of 1862 by the Misses Mary Sibley, Mary Barber, and Anna Guieu at the residence of Mr. Josiah Sibley garnered a total donation of $150. The mayor wrote to thank these young women for their "marked evidence of patriotic feeling," and to note that the "proud consciousness" they would carry "in time to come of having been the agents of good to many who have suffered and toiled for the independence of their country" would be their true reward.[37]

These fairs offered young women a vehicle for their own contribution to the war effort and allowed them to receive public acclaim and status as patriotic citizens in return. Perhaps more critically, however, these young women were acting in support of their mothers' organizational efforts. Just as young women were apprenticed to their mothers within the household, they now took up the role as their mothers' assistants in the public arena. The fairs and bazaars put on by the young ladies in the summer of 1862 were dedicated not only to supporting the Confederate cause but also to supporting the development of the Augusta ladies' second major organizational effort, the creation of a soldiers' wayside home.

Much as in the case of the externalization of sewing from the household, the labor of feeding and nursing emerged from the household structure. Demand for nursing outstripped the existing supply from within the household, even when supplemented by individual charity. With the initial calling-up of the troops, women went as individuals to the nearby rail connection to the passing troops. The efforts, for instance, of Mrs. Anderson W. Walton, who "provided fatigued soldiers with a bountiful supply of coffee and other refreshments" in the summer of 1861, were held up for general emulation by the local press. By the end of that first summer, however, the ladies had banded together in the Ladies' Lunch Association for the purpose of feeding the increasing numbers of troops passing through on the railroad line. Their arrival in ever-growing numbers posed a challenge that ad hoc personalized charity could no longer meet. The establishment of the Lunch Association, according to the local paper, "makes it a duty of all charitably disposed citizens to look after the Refreshment Fund—lest, as we have before intimated, the tax fall too heavily on a few individuals."[38]

More than the feeding of soldiers on the way to the front, however, it was the growing number of returning wounded and diseased soldiers that necessitated a further reorganization of the hitherto privatized domestic labors of nursing and cooking. By the spring of 1862, the ladies were calling for the creation of a wayside home, a house to be located at the Millen rail stop outside Augusta, that would be used by the ladies to nurse and feed the soldiers coming through the area. Here the ladies were calling for a new kind of public household, a household dedicated entirely to domestic labors, in particular the nursing and feeding of soldiers in need. Shorn of its male "productive" aspect, not to mention its male "head," the wayside home would be entirely under the control and direction of the women. By July, the local paper had taken up the cause. "It has been suggested, and we heartily endorse the suggestion, that in view of the number of sick and wounded soldiers daily passing through the city, a way side hospital should be established here for their benefit. The ladies, who are ever foremost in good works, have already had this benevolent object under consideration, and it is to be hoped that they will succeed, with the aid of the 'lords of creation,' in accomplishing it."[39]

The ladies, however, were not willing simply to rely upon the generosity of the male citizenry to finance their proposed civic household. They turned as well to their own domestic lines of authority, and in particular to their daughters to meet the wayside home's staffing needs. While the departure of fathers and husbands and sons had intensified the privatized domestic attachments among the women who remained at home, the externalization of women's domestic labor served to give the mother-daughter relationship an increased status, both at home and in public. Catherine Rowland gave up independent housekeeping during the war to return to her family of origin and particularly to the solace that her mother and sister could offer her during the absence of her husband. But with the emergence of women's voluntary organizations, Catherine discovered that her mother was also frequently called away to her duties as an officer in the Millen wayside home. Her mother's increasing involvement in public life both increased Catherine's recognition of the crucial role that she played within the family and drew Catherine herself into the public arena as her mother's assistant.

Rowland recorded several occasions when her mother was off nursing the soldiers at the wayside home and members of her own household became ill. "We have been anxious all day about Lizzie, she is worse than she was yesterday and our anxiety is increased by mother's absence." Rowland's mother was the nurse, both in the wayside home and on the plantation, Ivanhoe. Her domestic skills served as the basis for her new public authority, but they also enhanced her role at home. The possibility of death was an ever-present one, and not only for the soldiers. "Home was not home," according to Catherine Rowland, when her mother was gone, because it was her mother who possessed the skills necessary to secure that environment. When Catherine's sister contracted typhoid fever, Catherine again called on her mother to return. She nervously awaited her arrival at the railroad station and recorded that "Mother came up this afternoon and it is a great relief to have her with us, she is such an experienced nurse that I always like to have her with me in sickness."[40]

While the emergence of Catherine's mother as a critical public figure enhanced her domestic value in the family's eyes, it opened the way for Catherine, at her mother's insistence, to participate in the work of the way-side home. Other young women helped their mothers by staging charity bazaars and fairs. Rather than being apprenticed to an overwhelmingly privatized domestic role, young women now found themselves acquiring the rudiments of a training in public organization. As Rowland recorded, "I have been assisting mother lately in her society matters. I have been doing some writing for her and I am very glad to relieve her as she has a great deal of work to do."[41]

Mothers and daughters of the town's elite and surrounding hinterland were thus empowered by the primacy that the war gave to questions of domestic and subsistence production. On this basis they formed public organizations, took direction of their own labor, and created a new public domestic space. There were limits, however, to how far these women's public activities could extend without actually threatening to deconstruct their men's understanding of their manhood more than it promised to reconstruct it under the altered conditions of war and national independence. When in the spring of 1862 the ladies organized a campaign to raise funds for a gunboat, they reached this limit. The ladies approached the problem of providing gunboats for the Confederacy as they had previously dealt with the problem of clothing the troops. After all, was not a gunboat a kind of good warm coat, simply a solid metal protection for their sons and husbands? Though the ladies may have viewed this activity as an extension of their maternal responsibility, it was not a case of simply making public labors that had hitherto been private, as was the case with the wayside home and the Ladies' Aid Society. The financing of defense industries moved women into an activity regarded as the proper province of men. This distinction was duly noted by a protest written to the paper and signed "Gray Beard."

I see by the newspapers that a call is made upon the women of Augusta to contribute towards the construction of gun boats. If this is allowed, the next call, of course, will be for women to man them. Have we no men left, that this thing should be tolerated? It is well enough to ask the aid of women in their proper sphere of usefulness . . . but the idea that great whiskered men should ask them for help to build a few gun boats too, is, to say the least, shameful. Why not call upon the men? Have they done too much, or is their patriotism already exhausted? [42]

Gray Beard concluded by submitting an offering of five dollars for the construction of a gunboat, with the proviso that if the other men of the town failed to follow his example and instead "chose to let the women undertake the defense of the country," his own contribution could go into the ladies' fund. The editor's response to this critique was to conclude that in a competition over patriotism, "we will bet on the ladies." Despite further queries to the paper about the lack of overt male participation, men seem to have been content to allow the women to run the show. In April the city council contributed twenty thousand dollars to the Georgia Ladies' Gunboat Fund and by May the ladies were holding fairs, tableux, and concerts to raise more funds. [43]

The "Gray Beard" strictures underscore the extent to which Confederate women's public activities and the sanction they received from the press and local authorities were beginning to undermine the very basis of white male gender-role construction. The position of white men as heads of their households was legitimized in part by their ability to protect and defend their dependents. When men would not or could not do this and their women were instead taking up the role, the whole gender order appeared to be verging on disarray. As Gray Beard concluded, in taking up the financing of gunboat construction, the ladies had gone beyond empowering the men who were protecting them; they were coming dangerously close to manning the ship themselves.

A second incident that also occurred in the spring of 1862 made the increasingly open-ended nature of elite women's domestic politics even more apparent. The issue arose, appropriately enough, around the question of the disposition of cotton. Hand in hand with the decline of the authority of the male household head, the value of cotton had descended to a new low. The commodity that had once been "king" had become useless and ultimately, in the spring of 1862, dangerous. As the possibility of enemy invasion grew, the problem of what to do with the unmarketed cotton that had accumulated in the town as a result of the blockade became pressing. The plan put forward by the town fathers was to burn the cotton in the streets to avoid having it fall into enemy hands. The burning of such large quantities of cotton, however, would have had a devastating effect on the city itself. As the ladies noted in a letter of protest:

To the Gentlemen of Augusta:

Gentlemen: We learn that in the *Superior* wisdom that characterizes your government of the affairs of the world, you have determined to burn all the cotton in the city upon approach of the enemy. Now *we* in our *inferior* wisdom suggest that as the cotton, if burnt where it now is, would inevitably burn the whole city, you should take immediate measures to *remove* it. All that some of us possess are our houses and our homes, and though we don't object to you burning *your* own property, we have a very serious objection to your burning *ours* and thus leaving us and our children houseless and homeless, especially as we by our sacrifices will gain no credit, it will all be ascribed to your patriotism.

—signed, Ladies of Augusta [44]

This protest reflected a basic severing in the logic of Confederate women's domestic subordination to their men. Not only had the war shifted the relationship between activities associated with production; not only was women's domestic labor now public, protecting those who were supposed to protect them; but the traditional symbol of power and source of riches, cotton, had descended from its position as king. Now cotton not only did not empower men to protect women, it constituted a positive menace to women in their homes. As a consequence of this severing of male productivity from women's domestic pursuits, male patriotism was being cast into doubt. No longer was it possible for these men to assume that simply by promoting their own interests, they would promote the interests of their women and children as well. According to the ladies of Augusta, the men who proposed to burn down the homes of women and children in order to protect that which remained of their own honor and autonomy were acting not as responsible heads of households but rather as irresponsibly foolish. [45]

Men's vision of patriotism as the pursuit of independence both for the nation and for themselves was increasingly being severed from the vision of patriotism that centered on the defense of home and domestic life. As dedicated as these ladies were to the interests of their men when those interests appeared to sustain domesticity, women were capable of forming their own independent and even critical judgments when the course of war caused men to violate their domestic trust. No question of male authority and leadership was more fraught with contradictions in this regard than the conduct of the war. Although the burning of the cotton threatened the homes of women and their children, the decisions of the generals threatened their lives, most immediately the lives of their sons. By the summer of 1862, the commander of one company was so inundated with letters from local women anxious about their sons, husbands, and brothers that he resorted to the town newspaper to respond to their expressions of concern. Taking a defensive tone, he wrote, "In the time of battle, I have no control over the dead and the wounded, nor have I when one is taken very sick. . . . As far as it is in my power, I shall preserve the lives and advance the health and comfort of my men. I am sensible of the great responsibility resting upon me and am determined to discharge my duty faithfully and will endeavor not to be charged with negligence on my part."[46]

As the casualty lists lengthened, however, rather than simply pressing officers to remember their domestic duty, some women began to question the authority of the generals themselves. One woman, signing herself "Mother," wrote to the newspaper after one particularly costly battle in the spring of 1862. "I know I am a poor, silly woman and a cowardly one too; at most, not so brave as some of our country women seem to be." Not so brave, that is, as those women who continued to uphold the direct relationship between their men's pursuit of war and a general vision of patriotism. However "cowardly" from the male vision of honor, she had the courage of her domestic convictions. She went on to say, "I know Generals have no right uselessly to throw away precious lives, merely because the generous fellows will go where they are bid. If, however, the claims of humanity are to be ignored and the tears of mothers treated as only so much brine, then let me appeal against the policy of so brutal a course." She stepped then upon the general's own terrain and proceeded to analyze the likely result of gallant encounters that resulted in large casualties. Although swept up in the "excitement and enthusiasm" of the battle, seeing in the aftermath the "dead and wounded bodies of their comrades covering the plain," this mother predicted that the loyalty of the common soldier to the cause might be transformed into demoralization and defeatism when the men saw that the generals sacrificed the general good to their own self-interest. "Our leaders know that not only their fortunes, but their very lives, are in danger, if captured, and are determined to sacrifice the army to save themselves. Ten thousand lives may go for one, ten thousand hearts wring rather than one neck."[47]

She closed her letter, as she began it, with a ritualized recognition of her own "unworthiness." "It may be but a mother's weak fears, but I have them, and having, must speak them out." It was undoubtedly the case that this woman felt the press of her own insubordination heavily, but that the drive of her domestic commitments both impelled her to self-assertion and legitimized her speech. Having spoken, however hedged about by allusions to her own weakness and cowardliness, she had at the same time drawn her own sword and cut to the heart of the pretenses of military leaders when she accused them of a cowardice much more damning than her own. For as the newspaper pointed out, "A Mother," "having three gallant sons in the army," had a right to be heard. She had more than fulfilled her duty to the cause in offering up her sons. The generals, however, who failed to recognize the reciprocal commitment to protect her domestic sacrifice and who considered only their individual advancement and honor over their social duty, created the ground for this woman to stand on and the necessity of her doing so.[48]

The bread of dependence is too bitter to be swallowed by the proud poor, of which there are more than the proud rich.

—*Augusta Chronicle and Sentinel*, June 12, 1862

3

Benevolent Men and Destitute Women

THE DOMESTICATION OF THE MARKET

The demands of fighting the war created a fissure in Confederate men's gender roles. As the months of fighting turned into years, it became increasingly difficult for them to maintain both their public position as citizens and their private responsibilities as fathers and husbands. While their duty as citizens now called upon them to take up arms in defense of the Confederacy, they were still expected to provide for the members of their own households on the home front. The increasing difficulty they confronted in holding together both their public and private roles as "free men" under wartime conditions was manifested most immediately

by the rising levels of destitution among soldiers' wives and children. Indeed, as soon as the first troops from the county departed in April of 1861,
the city council was called upon to address the needs of some of the soldiers' families who were already in "destitute circumstances." The council
recommended the establishment of a town committee to cooperate with
a committee established by the citizens in order to "solicit and receive
subscriptions for providing for such families."[1]

Although this committee was able to collect over a thousand dollars
for needy soldiers' families within the next month, rapid price increases
quickly undercut the ability of this fund to meet their needs.[2] The situation was made more difficult by the continued departure of troops from
the county during the spring and early summer of that year. The more
men who left, the more women and children there were who were thrown
into poverty. By October, the mayor, R. H. May, was so inundated by
requests for aid from soldiers' families and so frustrated by steadily rising
prices that he lashed out at the town's merchants. In a letter in the local
press, he charged them with "speculating in the prime necessities of life,"
of holding back their goods and waiting for higher prices. He pointed
out that the situation of poor women and children was already difficult
enough without the added burden of artificially high prices.[3] "Common
patriotism," he concluded in his letter to the local paper, "demands that
all our citizens should make sacrifices for the common good, and not that
advantage should be taken of those least able to suffer. I sincerely trust
that while these troublesome times shall exist, our merchants and traders
will be satisfied (as they were before) with *living profits*."[4]

Although by the second year of the war the "Ladies of Augusta" were
criticizing the town authorities for threatening to burn their homes to the
ground in defense of their cotton, many of the wives, daughters, and
mothers of the common soldier had faced the immediate threat to the survival of their households from the war's outset. In contrast to the county's
planter and mercantile elite, the labor of the common soldier frequently
constituted a critical portion of the basic sustenance of his household.
Without slave ownership or the resources to replace the labor of absent
menfolk, these women experienced their men's departure to the front as a
critical and largely irreplaceable loss from the outset. While all Confederate women were called upon to part with their husbands, fathers, and sons
and to entertain the possibility that they might never see them again, for

the women of the common folk, the pain of this parting was compounded by the immediate economic problems it created for their households. How would they live and how would they provide for their children without the critical labor of their men?

Relatively free from economic constraints by virtue of their class position, the "Ladies of Augusta" experienced the benefits of the increased significance of their domestic labors in the context of war without suffering the same economic hardships. At least initially, the contribution, first of their men and secondly of their domestic labor to clothe and feed the soldiers created the basis for the first independent organizations among women in the town. Based on these critical contributions to the war effort, they began openly to demand that men in positions of power, whether they be the city fathers or Confederate generals, should become more responsible to *their* domestic needs. In contrast, white women of the common folk discovered that the same basic contribution to the war effort on their own part, the sacrifice of their brothers, husbands, and sons, not only did not have the effect of empowering their public position, but instead left them ever more deeply enmired in the struggle simply to survive. At worst, it threw them upon the limited mercy of the town's charities.

Indeed, the economic distress of soldiers' wives revealed much more dramatically and immediately the way that fighting the war stressed the basic gender quid pro quo, where women and children would subordinate themselves to the empowerment of the household head in exchange for protection and economic well-being. For while the "Ladies of Augusta" might worry over the damage their households stood to experience from the policies of men in power, at least some of the wives and daughters of the common soldier knew from the outset of the war the domestic suffering that war could create. The responsibility for this suffering was not, however, attributed to the domestic dereliction of the common soldier, much less to any basic problem in the way that white male gender roles were constructed. Instead, the town's merchants, and the workings of the market economy more generally, received the brunt of the criticism in the local press. As one Augusta citizen wrote in an open letter, "The patriot's heart is saddened when he sees the almost universal wish to get rich at the expense of all that makes and constitutes a good citizen." It was the local merchant class who, in the face of opportunities for profit making, had lost sight of all other values. "Friendship, honor, country all are absorbed in the all-engrossing rush after the panacea [wealth] which alone can make the man tolerated who has sacrificed everything to attain it."[5]

As increasing numbers of male citizens in Augusta turned their energies to supporting the common cause of national independence by actually taking up arms, stay-at-home merchants were criticized for not following suit. As in the case of the choice presented to the planter—corn or cotton, subsistence or profit—merchants were increasingly called upon to choose between their public standing as men of honor and social responsibility and their individual pursuit of prosperity. Their success as competitors in the marketplace, which had previously brought them wealth and social esteem, now threatened exactly the reverse, as in the context of war profit and a good public reputation quickly parted company. The most withering criticism was reserved for those merchants who made a profit by hiking prices on basic foodstuffs, which most directly intensified the difficulties of poor women and children struggling simply to put food on their tables.

Thus just as the departure of men to the front called upon elite women to act as social mothers to the troops, the women and children that those men left behind called upon men, especially men of wealth, to act as social fathers. "Do not," queried one writer to the local paper, "our soldiers and their families deserve all our care? And is there one heart in all this land that answers not to such a call, that is cut off from that grand sympathy that makes us all in this sore trial, one family, one brotherhood?"[6]

From this perspective, the war effort had rendered all Confederate men brothers in their common struggle for the cause of national independence. It was this common cause that had taken them away from their individual household responsibilities. The growing number of destitute women and children on the home front called upon Confederate men to expand their commitment to that cause, to act as one brotherhood, at home as well as at the front. As one writer asserted in the local press:

Did you ever conceive the idea that your patriot sons, when they bid adieu to home and friends, and buckling on their armor, went to the ensanguined field, brave and unsuspecting, as the brave alone can be, that they were leaving an enemy in the rear more dangerous than that in the front? Did you, in promising the son, of whom you had a right to be proud, that he need have no fears about his wife and little ones that a father's protective care would be over them, did you expect that perhaps on the very day that your son was confronting the deadly fire of the foe, a more cruel and detested enemy would be waging a war of want and famine upon your family?[7]

Insofar as the war was indeed based on the defense of "one brotherhood," it revealed the ways in which the capitalist market system caused that brotherhood to make war on itself. Particularly galling was the fact that the households of the common soldier, men who arguably sacrificed the most in the collective defense of white men's liberties, were also the most impoverished of households, while those of men who remained at home to carry on business as usual profited from the war.

It was this increasing hegemony of the domestic tie—the familialization of social relations—that brought market behavior previously regarded as equitable into increasing disrepute. In the context of war it became increasingly apparent that the imperatives of private property and profit making that fueled the operation of normal market productive relations might be incompatible with the hitherto subordinate domestic and reproductive relationships which had now suddenly become central to the survival of the Confederacy itself.

Under normal circumstances, the mediatory function of the market rendered poor those who had nothing but their labor to sell, while those who had the resources to purchase labor power became rich. The resultant social hierarchy was equitable in men's eyes, at least in the eyes of the men who benefited. The common labors of the war, or at least the collective cause of the war, revealed the inequities of this situation through a different lens, focusing not on the wealth or earning power of the household head but on the life he had to give for the cause of his country.

Merchants in Augusta did not simply accept this condemnation of their business practices. They responded by arguing that higher wartime prices were not their responsibility but rather the result of "natural" workings of supply and demand. Shortage created high prices. Insofar as they were actually willing to take any responsibility for their prices, they argued that it was only an attempt to protect themselves against the uncertainties of a wartime economy or to cover the increased costs of procuring goods. While one Augusta merchant went so far as to admit that there were indeed a "few landsharks among us," he nonetheless insisted that there was no reason to assume that most merchants "fall into this category of humanity."[8]

While some of the town's merchants undoubtedly did deserve this new-found reputation as "landsharks," most were indeed following the logic of the capitalist market system, as they had in the past. By antebellum standards they were, as the above writer claimed, "fair traders." They were only following the same practices that previously had not only made them wealthy but placed them among the most socially respected citizens of the town. In the altered conditions of war, however, the highest social value was now attributed to behavior that supported the war effort. Even the long established and well regarded house of Sibley and Sons was criticized for contributing to the common soldier's inability to both fight for his country and provide for his household. Josiah Sibley, the head of the establishment, was so plagued by rumors of hoarding that as early as May of 1861 he was forced to defend his reputation in the local press. "It is not pleasant to come before the public," he wrote, "but circumstances not only justify but demand such a course." He vehemently denied the rumor circulating widely through the city and the county that his firm had bought up large quantities of flour, lard, and butter in an effort to reap windfall profits. In defense of his house and his own good name he pointed to his longstanding reputation as a charitable citizen. "I do not profess to boast loudly; but if the feelings of others are as well shown to the wants of the poor as mine have been, those who talk so much would by contrast be silent."[9]

The solution to the growing distress among soldiers' families was not, according to Josiah Sibley, to criticize the behavior of the merchants or the workings of the capitalist market, but rather to expand the previously private role of men as household providers to encompass not only the needs of their own immediate dependants but those of those of the Confederate soldiery at large. Just as the need for uniforms was met voluntarily through the public organization and redistribution of the domestic labor of the more class-privileged Confederate women, Sibley suggested that the resources of the citizenry who remained in the town could be redistributed through the same voluntary means to provide for those women and children who now found themselves struggling with the absence of brothers, husbands, and fathers.[10]

To a certain extent, the problem of destitute women and children could be addressed, as it had been in the past, through the individual charitable activities of more prosperous Confederate women. These women could work, as they did with the soldiers, to redistribute some of the resources contained within their own households to those less well endowed with the world's goods. In her Civil War journal, Catherine Rowland recorded her efforts to bridge the gap between the meager wartime incomes of impoverished women and children in the town and the rapidly inflating prices of life's necessities. Women with men in the military could at least expect the paltry eleven dollars a month that each man in the service received. As was the case before the war, the Confederate women who found themselves in the most difficulty were those who lacked even this reduced remnant of adult male economic support. Catherine Rowland described the situation of one such widowed woman and her daughter, Harriet Tyndall. "I went this afternoon to see Harriet Tyndall, poor girl. What a sad life is hers having to support herself and her mother by her needle." Despite her most diligent efforts, Harriet Tyndall was not able to provide for herself and her mother adequately, and Catherine Rowland recorded that she "carried her some money I had received from several friends to get her a pair of shoes as she was without any and she was very grateful and her eyes filled with tears when she thanked me for it." [11]

While Rowland made efforts to aid the poor women and children of the town through the same type of individualized charitable giving that she had engaged in before the war's outbreak, she found that her efforts were no match for the rapidly inflating prices of wartime. Indeed, not only did these rising prices intensify the suffering of poor women like Harriet Tyndall, they made it increasingly difficult for more prosperous women, like Catherine Rowland herself, to meet their own needs, much less contribute to the needs of others. By the end of the war, Catherine Rowland could only express her outrage and disbelief at the economic dislocations it had brought. "I was startled and amazed," she wrote in the winter of 1865, "to find how greatly the price of everything had advanced, it is awful, and how the poor can *live* I cannot imagine." She was appalled at the "spirit of speculation" that seemed to be "running higher than ever," as "every man tries to get the very highest prices he can for his goods." She did not limit her criticism to the town's merchants, however. She was perhaps even more distressed by the behavior of some of the elite women of the town, who seemed determined to flaunt their own continued economic well-being. "I noticed while on the street this afternoon," she wrote, "that the ladies seemed to be dressed finer than ever and it made me feel dreadfully as it strikes me as being so perfectly heartless." [12]

Catherine Rowland asserted that she, at least, took "pride and pleasure" in dressing as plainly as possible when there was so much "distress and suffering throughout the land" and would do no differently if she were "worth a million." Apparently the impact of the war was to intensify her identification with other women, regardless of their class position. She was therefore repulsed by the sight of other elite women who "dressed finer than ever," flaunting, in effect, their class difference in relation to poorer Confederate women. By literally displaying on their person the economic gains of their men, these ladies were, at least in Rowland's estimation, being as unpatriotic in their sphere as their husbands were in the sphere of market relations. And while she condemned this blind striving for material gain by the men, she clearly was more offended by the behavior of the women, from whom she seemed to expect a more self-sacrificing, socially responsible attitude. "It makes my very heart ache," she wrote, "when I see all this and the Yankees too at our very doors and makes me feel that certainly if this state of things is kept up we cannot gain our independence." [13]

Although Catherine Rowland's own response to rising levels of economic distress among Confederate women was to assert an egalitarian commitment to meeting the domestic needs of all white women regardless of class, in the face of the rising tide of shortages and need, other privileged Confederate women failed follow her example. Rather than considering the needs of women poorer than themselves, they turned instead to the comfort and sense of security that their position as dependents of wealthy men could still offer them. Some were even inclined through gestures of conspicuous consumption to flaunt their continued access to precisely the kind of male protection that ever larger numbers of women in the town lacked. [14]

While Confederate women who behaved in this fashion were responding out of their own need to cope with the pressures of war, their behavior reflected a more long-standing response to a social order deeply rooted in the economic dependence of white women upon the power of the individual men of their households to protect and provide. For self-supporting white women of any class, the options were limited even under the best of circumstances. In the context of wartime privation and inflation, when making ends meet was becoming difficult for all, these women found themselves reduced to a state verging upon absolute destitution.

Historians of the antebellum South have discussed more generally the way the most extreme form of subordination in the social order, slavery, served to reinforce the dependence of all women upon the household head. According to this view, slavery created a situation in which race and class took precedence over gender identity and women were so divided as a result that they were only minimally able to cohere along gender lines. Here I am suggesting that the war, while in some ways bringing white women together across class lines, if only to support the common cause of their men, was at the same time limited from the outset also by class difference. Indeed, while the departure of Confederate men empowered elite women to form their own independent organizations in support of the war effort, the very same departure of the common soldier disempowered women who lacked the economic resources to replace their men's contribution, much less to find themselves "freed" to step into the realm of public organizational activity.

Thus, on the one hand the war initially empowered elite women who both retained economic privilege relative to poor women and children and gained new influence with the increased public status of their previously privatized domestic labor; on the other hand, it stripped the wives of common soldiers of even minimal economic subsistence and thereby revealed to all women their basic, continuing dependence on the ability of their men to protect and provide for them. Whatever tendencies emerged within elite women's individual organizations to criticize the efficacy of male protection, and to use their new experience of social mothering as a basis for claiming an independent status in the world, they were met by the sight of these struggling women whose position seemed to indicate what expanded female independence really involved. Consequently, as much as wartime conditions may have amplified the significance of domestic labor and led Confederate women to an apparently more independent position in the social order, they also served to underscore even more graphically women's unchanging dependence on the economic position of their men.

So although the war drew elite women's domestic concerns out from under the constraints imposed by their subordinate location within individual, male-headed households, these women did not develop a politics grounded in independence for women. Rather than turning their newfound public space and power toward a generalized critique of male dominance, they instead criticized the town fathers and Confederate authorities for failing to provide the level of protection which their dominance ought to have insured. Rather than agitating for a general structural change in the dependent position of all white women, they employed the new public power of domestic concerns to demand that men be more responsible to the needs of the women and children that they at least in theory were committed to protect and provide for. They demanded, in other words, a more paternalistic patriarchy.

The experience of Gertrude Thomas illustrates the manner in which women's dependent economic position created clear-cut limits to the development of a common politics among white women in the context of wartime demands. Gertrude Thomas was moved by the emergence of an organized domestic politics in Augusta, but to a greater extent than Rowland she was limited by the boundaries of her class position as daughter and wife of the planter elite. Like Catherine Rowland, Thomas participated wholeheartedly in the organized and individual activities of the Confederate women of the town, making uniforms for the soldiers, nursing them when they returned ill or wounded, even making cartridges at the Confederate Powder Works. She also engaged in individual charity among the wives and children of the soldiers. She described the desperate situation of some of these women who had taken up living in abandoned railroad cars at the local depot. She wrote of a Mrs. Church, living in the cars with her three children, "having chills nearly every day and no stove in the car."[15] She hired Mrs. Church to sew for her and gave her a cooking stove. While Mrs. Church's difficulties distressed her, she found the story of another woman, a Mrs. Kirksey, whose husband had been taken prisoner, to be even more distressing.

> Alluding to the difference between this Christmas and the last [Mrs. Kirksey] added while the tears coursed down her cheek, "Oh, Mrs. Thomas, my husband was such a good man. Every Christmas he filled the children's stockings with something for Santa Claus presents. . . ." The idea occurred to me that next Christmas I might be unable to provide my children with Christmas gifts and I placed five dollars in Mary Bell's [her daughter's] hand and told her to give it to the lady to buy some apples for her children. I also gave her some potatoes and meat."[16]

While the outbreak of war made the intensity of her attachments to her male kin more apparent to Thomas, the increasing distress of women deprived of their own men drove home the lesson that the loss of men and men's power to provide would wound not only the heart but the stomach as well. Her gift of apples, potatoes, and meat can be seen as an offering to ward off a fate that even she, for all her economic resources, might eventually suffer if conditions continued to deteriorate. Although both she and Rowland extended a helping hand to poor women during the war, they did so out of a recognition that they all shared a common economically dependent state. Hence, she was not at the same time immune to the more blatantly self-aggrandizing attitudes of the ladies who so shamelessly, in Rowland's view, attired themselves with their husband's ill-gotten wartime gains.

Although Thomas gave to poor women, that relationship was clearly mediated by her own economic position, a status that she recognized had made charitable giving possible in the first place. Rowland also recognized this power when she claimed that were she "worth a million," she still would not exercise her class privilege at the expense of her gender identification with other women.

In the case of Gertrude Thomas, however, the relative primacy of her class identification was made clear in an incident that occurred early in the war. Her father, Turner Clanton, one of the largest planters in the county, sent a notice to the local paper declaring his willingness to sell his corn below the market price to the families of soldiers. "You will please mention," he wrote, "that families of all volunteers now in service from Richmond and Columbia counties, can obtain meal at my mill on my Rowell Place for one dollar per bushel." [17] In taking this action, Clanton was acting in a patriotic and honorable fashion. Unlike at least some of his fellow planters or merchants, he was willing to sacrifice his personal gain for the good of the whole. He recognized in this action his social responsibility to protect those women and children whose husbands were offering up their lives in defense of the common cause of independence. Gertrude Thomas took particular pride in her father's generous offer and was shocked when poor women and children did not appear to share her appreciation of his paternalistic largesse. For rather than eliciting an outpouring of gratitude, Clanton's offer generated a spate of sarcasm and recrimination. "As Mr. Turner Clanton has been so kind as to furnish meal at one dollar per bushel to the volunteer's families," queried one woman who signed herself "Soldiers' Wife," "we would like to know who will be so liberal as to furnish bacon to eat with it?" Others asked what good was the meal if one had no wagon with which to fetch it? And who could be expected to live on meal alone? [18]

Gertrude Thomas reacted to what she described as the "impertinence" of these women, who were "clearly not ladies," by writing a response to the local paper. "Perhaps this 'poor' soldier's wife would like Colonel Clanton to send her a load of meal, then a load of wood to cook it with and then (as she appears averse to labor) a servant to prepare it for her." [19] Thomas's response is interesting because it reveals a good deal about her own anxieties and fears. In point of fact, it was Thomas herself who never washed a dish or cooked a meal until after the end of the war, when her "servants" left her without warning.[20] What was "impertinent" about these soldier's wives from her perspective was their apparent expectation that they should receive a level of "protection" from the male elite similar to that which these men provided their own women. The soldier's wife was no lady, according to Thomas, not simply because she was not a member of the local elite, but also because she refused to recognize her proper place in the class hierarchy, as the dependent of a mere common soldier. Mrs. Kirksey, on the other hand, although no more well connected in life, was considerably more cognizant of her *place*, that is, she expressed her *gratitude* for upper-class charity. Thomas therefore actually referred to Mrs. Kirksey as a "lady." She knew her place.

Thomas's very conception of what it meant to be a good woman, "a lady," was determined by a woman's recognition that her "place" was defined by her relationship to the men whose economic position in the world determined her own. Ultimately what was offensive about the soldiers' wife's response to Turner Clanton's offer of meal was precisely that they really did assume an equality of domestic interest. They took seriously the notion that market relations ought to be familialized, something the local press had presented as a nationalistic ideal. In the context of wartime sacrifice of *their* men, they expected, as did elite women, that what were previously private domestic issues would now become matters for common and collective redress. Gertrude Thomas was a militant supporter of the domestic critique of male behavior only as long as that critique was consistent with the domestic interests of the women of her class. It was legitimate, therefore, for elite women to criticize the town fathers for threatening to burn down their homes or to lambast the generals for needlessly sacrificing their sons on the battlefield. A similar articulation of domestic interest by women of the lower classes she viewed quite differently, however. This was no manifestation of the common effort to articulate women's interests as a group but rather an inappropriate attack on her father's class position, and by extension on her own domestic interests.

When soldiers' wives saw Turner Clanton's offer to sell his corn below the market price for what it was, a half-measure, they were expressing their right to an equivalent replacement from society at large for the support that had previously come from their own fathers and husbands. They were therefore only making the same claims for recognition of domestic duties owed to them as were elite women. These women expected no servant, as Thomas sarcastically suggested, no standard of living similar to her own. What they did demand was their equal right to have their domestic needs met, as had been the case before the war. Turner Clanton's offer to sell his cornmeal at half the market price was perhaps generous from the perspective of his class, but from a domestic perspective it was inadequate to enable impoverished women and children to survive the full or partial loss of their men.

When poor women applied the logic of domesticity to their own situation, women of the elite, like Thomas, were forced to recognize that their own class interests might well set limits to the scope of a gender ideology that, in the context of war, they were forging with ever-greater militancy. Lower-class domestic demands, if carried to their logical conclusion, might undercut elite men's ability to maintain them as ladies in their own "place." The servant who really concerned Thomas was not the imaginary one she saw as the desire of the ungrateful recipient of her father's charity. It was rather her own very real one whom she was afraid of losing and whom in the end she eventually did lose.

While the patriarchal household structure was conducive to the development of Ladies' Aid Societies to mother the soldiers, it created serious limits to any comparable response in addressing the needs of their wives and children. The Augusta ladies' organized activities on behalf of the common soldier had served to reinforce their own men's war effort, while simultaneously enhancing their own social position. Beyond a certain point, however, any alliance with lower-class women only threatened their own domestic interests. Indeed, poor women posed a double threat to the position of more prosperous women in the town. As the war progressed and the number of these poor women increased, this threat deepened. In the first place, the demands of poor women on the ever-shrinking resources of the prosperous men of the town threatened elite women directly since it entailed a diversion of resources that they required to maintain their own increasingly fragile and endangered households. Secondly, as the specter of poverty climbed higher and higher up the class structure, economic distress and public destitution threatened to replace voluntary organization and public domesticity as the most characteristic female experience of war. While the Ladies' Volunteer Association betokened the ways in which wartime conditions might empower Confederate women, the experience of female poverty served as a chilling reminder of what independence had more typically meant for white women before the war.

Thus the individualized charitable endeavors that elite women undertook to help poor women and children did not lead to the same massive organizational efforts that had characterized their work for the male soldiers from the war's outset. The hope expressed by merchants like Josiah Sibley that the solution to the problem of the town's poor women and children might be found through voluntary efforts was doomed to remain largely unfulfilled. Elite Confederate women could not provide out of their own labor, as they did for the soldiers, a sustenance to poor women and children, even if they had been inclined to do so. Instead, the crisis of poor women and children in the town required a modification of the very way that support for household dependents was organized. It demanded a reorganization of men's roles as providers.

The solution, insofar as there was one, had to come directly from Confederate male leaders themselves. Indeed, the town fathers, in the institutional form of the Augusta City Council, had attempted from the beginning of the war to respond to the crisis of the soldiers' wives. They repeatedly earmarked more funds for poor relief. As early as the fall of 1861, however, the inadequacy of this form of aid was apparent. A local citizen wrote to the paper suggesting that the gentlemen of the city follow the example set by the citizens of Mobile and New Orleans, who had established an association to distribute provisions to the poor and needy through a "free market." Local merchants and planters donated their products or sold them below the current market rate to these "free" markets, and these goods were then distributed to the poor who had been deemed worthy by a committee of the association. The benefits of this organization were, according to the writer, twofold. On the one hand this "free market" rescued the poor from the "grasp of sharpers, who are heartless enough to speculate upon the wants of the people." On the other hand, it did not give out goods or money indiscriminately as did county relief, which tended to corrupt the respectable poor. Surely, the writer concluded, an "Augusta Relief Association," modeled on the plan of these other cities, would be preferable to the current system of ad hoc individualized charity and/or official relief.[21]

In the fall of 1862, the Augusta City Council did in fact establish such an organization. The Augusta Purveying Association was empowered to regularize and standardize a new relationship between men of wealth and poor women and children that had already been emerging in an improvised and sporadic way, as the example of Turner Clanton and the soldiers' wives indicates. In his annual message of October 1862, the mayor described this innovation in the social structure of the town as "the duty of Council and those who have ample means." He proposed that to procure provisions and a site to distribute them, twenty-five thousand dollars should be raised, half from the city and half from private sources. Merchants and planters were also encouraged to donate their produce or to sell it to the purveying association below the market rate. The association would then either give the goods to the "worthy" poor or sell to them at a price substantially below market.[22]

Much as the formation of the Ladies' Aid Society made possible the redistribution of domestic labor to all men, regardless of the resources of their particular households, the formation of the Augusta Purveying Association made possible the redistribution of the resources of wealthy households to the poor women and children of the town and the county. Where the Ladies' Aid Society required a breach of women's subordinate position in the name of preserving the larger framework of patriarchal gender relations, the creation of a partly publicly subsidized "free market" required a breach of capitalist market principles in order minimally to protect "dependent" women and children and thus preserve credibility for the workings of the market. As the mayor concluded in his annual message, participation in the purveying association was "a noble work in which every man of means can unite with eternal honor to his name."[23]

By December of 1863 the association was already supporting some eight hundred families. It sold goods to these families at its own cost, which was considerably below the going market rate in the town. Meal, for example, which was selling at $6.00 to $7.00 a bushel on the open market was sold for $2.50 in the Purveying Store, and other staples like salt, syrup, and flour were sold at roughly half the going rate. The association also served as a vehicle for the distribution of direct donations to soldiers' families and to the town poor. In a letter to Governor Joseph Brown, Mayor May asserted that it was the "universal sentiment" of the town's citizens that the institution was "indispensible" and of "inestimable advantage" to the cause. "The institution," he wrote, "has grown to be of vast proportions; its influence is felt for good by every class of society; by those indigent who rely upon it for many necessaries it would otherwise be impossible to procure, and by those of our citizens in better circumstances whom it relieves from the incessant appeals for charity and assistance which would be made to them were it not attainable."[24]

This subsidized "free market" created by the purveying association constituted a domesticated shadow market reflecting the new and uneasy balance between Confederate men's familial roles as providers and protectors and their economic, class position—a balance normally maintained by the subordinated and privatized position of women and, therefore, of domestic concerns generally. Now, as the pursuit of war destroyed this equilibrium, as women emerged in the public arena in their own right, the old logic of the male-dominated capitalist marketplace was revealed to be an inadequate mechanism for insuring the provision of the basic needs of the population. A more truly free "free market" was therefore necessary to restore some balance between a free-enterprise economy, which had privileged white, elite men, and the domestic interests and needs of women and children, especially women and children with the least class privilege, whose needs in the context of the war had become public needs and concerns.

Not all elite men were moved, however, to do the honorable thing and contribute to what was essentially a mechanism redistributing rather than consolidating their wealth. Some of the town's merchants appear to have been retrograde. They, after all, more than the planters or the manufacturers, lived by the principle of market competition violated by the "free market." On the face of it, this interference with the market pricing system threatened to undercut their profits, threaten their livelihoods, and undermine their legitimacy as merchants altogether. Different circumstances applied to the town's manufacturers, especially the Augusta Factory, whose business boomed astronomically with wartime demand and whose price rates were regulated by their main customer, the Confederate government. Indeed, requests of the Purveying Association that businessmen give some of the products and profits that wartime opportunities had brought them were eagerly taken up by Augusta's manufacturers, who saw in them an opportunity to improve the image of the factory and the status of industry within the community.

In the fall of 1863, for example, the Augusta Factory contributed forty thousand dollars to the town's poor, the most "munificent donation," according to the mayor, that had been made for the poor and soldiers' families in the course of the war. This "princely gift" was "in keeping with the past reputation of the Augusta Factory for liberality and patriotism."[25] One citizen, signing himself "Canaan," wrote in a similar vein to the local press.

> We cannot refrain from an expression of gratitude and admiration at what you justly style the "munificent donation" of the Augusta Factory. . . . As this corporation very rarely permits any public announcement of their liberality, many persons might suppose it to be the first act of the kind, and a sort of tardy recognition of the claims of the needy . . . but this would be a mistake. The course of this company has been characterized by a princely liberality ever since the war began. . . . All honor to the proprietors of the Augusta Factory and their kindhearted President Jackson and Superintendent Coggins. The prayers of many a household are constantly ascending in their behalf.[26]

Not only did the factory frequently donate funds to purchase goods for the poor, they also furnished large amounts of cloth on a weekly basis, to be sold at low rates to the needy, and other consumer goods such as bacon, when such items were all but impossible to buy on the open market, goods they procured in trade for their textiles. Without these contributions by the factory, the mayor asserted in his annual message of 1863, "the power of the Association to do good would have quickly cramped, and that, too, at times when aid could have been obtained from no other quarter." The mayor singled out the president of the Augusta Factory, William E. Jackson, for a particularly glowing tribute, describing him as a gentleman with a "liberality that does him infinite honor," a liberality which would undoubtedly be "gratefully remembered in pleasanter days to come by all those who have been, and are, the recipients of his kindness."[27]

While the reputation of the manufacturers rose, that of the merchants continued to suffer by comparison. By the spring of 1863, when the price of goods had increased to such an extent that many ordinary Augustans had difficulty putting bread on the table, one writer to the local paper, a William Gibson, noted once again another generous cash donation by the Augusta Manufacturing Company to the Augusta Purveying Association and took the opportunity to castigate the the laggard merchants. "Trust not to them or their tender consciences, or to 'supply and demand,' or any law of trade by which enemy extortion is attempted to be justified." Instead, in the immediate crisis of high bread prices, the city fathers should rely upon the generosity of the town's manufacturers and should appeal "directly to the liberal and patriotic hearts of our noble planters, and my word on it, ample supplies will be obtained, and many will be the grateful hearts of our people, who will call the Augusta Purveying Association 'blessed.'"[28]

In the context of sore destitution, the poor were undoubtedly wont to call the Augusta Purveying Association "blessed" and pray for the "kind-hearted President and Superintendent." By the fall of 1864, it had become "the sole dependence of many within its sphere," according to the mayor, and by the end of the war some five hundred families were dependent upon it for their support.[29] At the same time, however, there is evidence that some of the recipients of this elite largesse, the families of the soldiers, were not as universally grateful as Mr. Gibson assumed. "The bread of dependence," wrote one critic of the Augusta Purveying Association as early as the summer of 1862, "is too bitter to be swallowed by the proud poor, of which there are more than the proud rich." The proper solution to the dilemma of poor women and children was not, according to this writer, to institutionalize their dependent state through a domestication of the market. The answer was not to expand the protective power of elite men to include ever-larger numbers of women whose own husbands and fathers could no longer provide, but rather to allow poor women to occupy the independent status in relation to the market that their husbands had previously held, by giving them employment sufficiently well paid to support them and their households. "Such [women] should be," according to the writer, "placed in a way of earning an independent living. Give those wives, who can and will use their needles, the soldiers' clothes to make, and pay them liberally for the work." Moreover, this critic recommended that "the ladies who have so nobly, but we believe mistakenly, devoted themselves to the work, take the thimble from their own fingers and give the work and compensation to the poor—they can best support the soldier in the field by supporting his family at home and they who are rich enough to live without work, will do most good by giving the work to those who want it, not to be doing it themselves."[30]

While the needs of the common soldier had elicited the voluntary domestic labor from elite women in the Ladies' Aid Society to engage in social mothering, the resultant destitution of soldiers' wives and children had led to the creation of the Augusta Purveying Association and the emergence of social fathering among elite men. However, these redistributions of social resources were highly convoluted. From a lower-class perspective, it made little sense to have elite women clothing the common soldier, while his wife and children suffered for lack of employment and as a result were thrown upon the humiliating and insufficient benevolence of the male elite. How much more reasonable simply to hire soldiers' wives to produce for the soldiers' needs and thereby restore the integrity and viability of the lower-class family.

Where, however, would the resources come from to pay such women a living wage? The writer suggested that elite women should employ poor women to do this labor instead of doing it themselves. Indeed, before the war this had been the most common way that white married or widowed women found remunerative employment. Out of the 554 white women listed as gainfully employed in the 1860 town census, some 43 percent of them were listed as seamstresses. The second largest form of employment, textile mill work, employed 192 women, 34 percent of the total. Of these mill workers, however, the overwhelming majority were single women. Only 3 percent of the women who labored in the mills were married or heads of household. For married or widowed white women, seamstress work provided virtually the only available employment. Only five married white women in the entire town were listed in the census as holding any other job.[31] In describing the domestic situation of several of her antebellum seamstresses, Gertrude Thomas indicated how this form of employment served as a substitute for the earning power of an absent or disabled husband.

I have bought me a very pretty blue silk and had it made by Cousin Mary Ann Cooper. Poor creature. She appears to have a very hard time of it—She is nursing Jim Cooper and sewing for a means of subsistence. He has had rheumatism for a long while and for the last fifteen months has been constantly confined to his bed. . . . I had rather I believe work for a sick husband than an idle trifling one like Mr. Blalock. There is Sarah [another of Thomas's seamstresses] sewing hard all the while and he, although in the enjoyment of health and strength, doing nothing. Standing idle while his wife—a woman—is sewing for the bread she eats.[32]

Although Gertrude Thomas continued to employ white women as seamstresses, the living that they could hope to earn, especially in the context of high wartime prices, was entirely inadequate. Therefore, when Thomas employed Mrs. Kirksey to sew, she also gave her food. Similarly, when Catherine Rowland described her visits to Harriet Tyndall, she consistently mentioned her "busy efforts with the needle," but these efforts were clearly insufficient for self-support, as Rowland's visits to Tyndall were basically charitable. Not only were poor women hard-pressed to make ends meet through sewing, the ability of elites to continue hiring them diminished as the war began to eat into their own resources.

While Gertrude Thomas continued to employ seamstresses to do her sewing throughout the war, she was unusually well off and expressed in her journal a particularly strong aversion to sewing. Other elite women found that they had to take up sewing that they normally would have hired out. Take for instance the case of Caroline Davis Jones, who was the wife of Joseph Jones, a young doctor and professor at the Medical College in Augusta. Despite their class position, however, the Joneses had great difficulty managing during the war. Joseph Jones enlisted in the summer of 1861, and as early as the fall of that year he was already writing to his wife about their straightened financial situation. "I know my dearest," he wrote, "that you do all in your power to economize in these days of embarrassment and hardship." The Joneses were fortunate to have prosperous, planter-class connections. As a result, Caroline Jones was able to acquire foodstuffs that were otherwise unavailable or very expensive in the Augusta markets. In November of 1863 her in-laws sent them a real blessing, a cow. As Caroline Jones wrote gratefully to her mother-in-law,

Mary Jones, "Milk is now selling for 60 cents per quart, and rising almost daily. Our good cow gives us now three quarts per day with the promise of much more when she has recovered from her grief for her lost family and friends and when she is a little better fed. The times are very hard & with the progressive tendency in the hardest direction for poor folks. This day I paid $35 for a cord of inferior wood."[33]

Under the circumstances, both Caroline and Joseph Jones did whatever they could to cut back on their expenditures. Joseph Jones wrote to his wife of his efforts to save all that he could from his pay, and Caroline wrote frequently of her own various efforts to economize. She despaired of being able to buy cloth, finding the price of "factory cloth" so high that she "retired from the struggle [at the market] in deep disgust." She congratulated her mother-in-law on her efforts to produce her own cloth. "I hope the result will equal and surpass the expectation, certainly these are times when one needs all such aids." For herself, one of her main forms of economizing was to do all of her own sewing, an experience so novel for her that she kept a record of her labors. As she wrote to her mother, "I am going to make a catalogue of the items of my summers work, as a curiosity and I think that the fact that my machine is a private one to that I have not had an hours assistance taken into consideration, will swell it to a very respectable length."[34]

With women such as Caroline and Mary Jones making their own cloth and clothing rather than buying it, or hiring seamstresses, the available labor for poor women only shrank. The efforts of elite women, not only to clothe their own men but to sew for the common soldiers, eliminated possible jobs for needy Confederate women. Since they also found themselves increasingly hard-pressed to make ends meet as the war continued, they were no longer able to hire these women themselves. As their own personal economic situation was rapidly deteriorating, it seems unlikely that the more prosperous of Augusta's citizens personally could have paid to employ a veritable army of poor women and children to sew for the troops. The greatest resource of the town's elite in this regard was the willingness of their own women to engage in greater self-exploitation for the cause.

Ultimately what opened up employment opportunities for poor women and children then was not an increase in privatized sewing for particular households, but the intervention of the state and the Confederate governments in the production process. While the garments produced by the ladies' aid societies had the attractive feature of being inexpensive, the system also had certain weaknesses, which became more apparent as the war progressed. In the first place, outfitting troops through the voluntary organization of local groups of women presented problems of consistent and regular supply. Not all localities were equally well organized or sufficiently wealthy to support their own troops. Indeed, this reliance upon the ladies' aid societies increasingly appeared to reveal some of the same deficiencies that had characterized the original reliance on soldiers' individual families, which had led to the creation of the aid societies in the first place. As in the case of individual households, the goods produced by local ladies' aid organizations were not always of standard quality, nor were they always distributed equitably.

Perhaps more critically, the resources of the voluntary organizations themselves were increasingly strained to meet the continued demands of outfitting the troops. As early as November of 1861, the Augusta Ladies' Aid Society had been required to request payment from the troops they supplied.

> We have . . . distribute[d] to the volunteer companies from our county four thousand one hundred and eighty five garments; and in consequence of heavy drafts made upon our treasury it has become exhausted; and as the winter approaches our soldiers will have to be supplied with almost an entire outfit for the winter campaign, which will be more expensive than the summer clothing; and we feel our community cannot supply us with the means to meet their wants, as they have already poured out their liberality until they are well nigh exhausted and we have not the heart to tax them further. We must, therefore, ask the Captains of each company to contribute six dollars and seventy-five cents for each member of his company . . . every six months for clothing.[35]

Recognizing these problems, the Confederacy moved to establish sewing manufactories in major cities. One such establishment was opened in Augusta in the fall of 1862, and in the following spring the state government opened another, similar establishment in the town. Under the direction of a Major L. O. Bridwell, the Confederate manufactory distributed cloth to women who made the material into coats and pants in their homes.

Hundreds of poor needlewomen have been furnished with garments to make up, and the highest price in cash is paid for their labor. The pecuniary benefits received by this large and industrial class are incalculable in these times of scarcity and inflated prices for the necessities of life. Throngs of poor women flock there daily, receive their work, and when finished it is returned, carefully inspected by a competent hand . . . and more given out.[36]

The local paper estimated that some five hundred women were employed in this manufactory, and another five hundred were given jobs after February 1863, when the state government set up its works. "A large number of industrious needle women are given constant employment, a numerous corps of other employees are usefully engaged, and the most durable and comfortable clothing are gotten up for the Georgia troops, so that various classes of the community are benefited thereby."[37]

In providing this employment, the state offered the women and children of the soldiers absent at the front an additional way to support their own households, rather than relying entirely upon the benevolence of the local elites or the town's purveying association. Paid employment thus created the basis for a greater independence for these women and their children, who were otherwise increasingly reduced to a form of dependency that many found to be a poor substitute for the kind of autonomy that a viable integration into the market could provide. As poor women and children gained this basis for a continuation of their households' self-sufficient status, even in the face of the rigors of war, their households simultaneously lost control over the direction of their labor.

After all, they were no longer producing garments directly for the members of their own households, who in turn they could rely upon for a contribution to the support of the household as well. Now they labored for the state bureaucrats who reimbursed them with a wage. They had gained an independence for their households from the ignominy of public aid but only at the cost of alienating their own labor.

When the choice that confronted a woman was between the hunger of her children, the never-sufficient benevolence of private charity or local relief, or the possibility of actually earning her own way, or at least part of her own way, the question of who would control her labor did not figure very significantly. For women of the elite, who had grown in public stature through their voluntary associations, grounded in the organization and direction of precisely this type of domestic labor, the turn toward bureaucratically managed, governmentally controlled methods of military provisioning had no such redeeming aspect. Class divisions among women in the town served to bifurcate women's domestic pursuits, as elite women's directive function was increasingly truncated and severed from the actual labor, which was increasingly taken up by poor women, not to clothe their husbands, but to support their families with a wage.

Once again, the class differences among Confederate women in the town limited the extent to which they could organize as a group and gain control over both their own labor and their larger social interests. For while initially the departure of troops to the front had the effect of empowering elite women, rendering their domestic labor of central public concern, ultimately the impoverished state of poor women and children led to the removal of domestic labor not only from the privatized locus of the household, as in the case of the ladies' aid societies, but from the control and direction of women altogether. The immediate and unalienated relationship between women and their labor within the domestic arena was therefore severed, subverting one basis of their patriotic fervor and the image of devotion to domestic duty that such offerings called forth in the troops. On the other hand, this organizational shift served to increase the efficiency of the Confederacy's war machine by establishing a central direction over clothing the troops and therefore a more equitable distribution of goods.

Perhaps of equal importance, it served to promote the well-being of the soldiers' families. As much as the voluntary outpouring of domestic labor and attachments on the part of Confederate women may have reinforced patriotism among the troops in the early years of the war, the balance began to shift as the war went badly and enthusiasm both at home and on the front began to wane. Rising levels of desertion were frequently attributed to the departure of men who could no longer bear the thought of the destitution their wives and children were likely to face. Catherine Rowland recorded the story of one such man who deserted to "go home and provide for his wife and five children who were in a destitute condition." He was recaptured and executed to deter his comrades-in-arms from taking a similar course. She was herself in the camp visiting her husband when this man met his fate. She wrote in her journal, "I heard the guns when they were fired & it was awful to my ears & saddened me the rest of the day. . . . The whole division was out to witness it and were marched by his grave after he was buried."[38]

For the common soldier, as for men of the elite, a simple and direct relationship between their public roles as citizens and their private roles as husbands and fathers was now beginning to come apart under the strain of protracted war and deprivation. The Confederacy, while employing whatever negative deterrents were at its command to stop this evaporation of men from the ranks, was forced to recognize the necessity of stepping in and supporting soldiers' families. For this reason alone the state and Confederate governments were moved to find ways to help soldiers' families support themselves. As Governor Brown stated as early as July 31, 1863:

> While those who are their natural protectors are required to leave them, and confront the enemy on the battlefield, those who remain at home, and especially those in authority, must do all in their power to relieve their wants, and prevent distress for the necessaries of life. Considering the state as the natural guardian of the helpless families of absent soldiers, I have, as its executive, done all in my power to contribute to their comfort.[39]

Along with providing employment for women and children in the state manufactories, the state government endeavored to promote the economic viability of what were now in effect female-headed households through the distribution of various necessities, especially cotton yarn for making their own clothing. "This admirable and philanthropic movement will place many a destitute family above want in the way of clothing; and the fact that such kindness has been shown their dear ones at home will make the soldiers on the field fight with renewed courage."[40] In exchange, the government hoped that women would support the war effort and in particular discourage desertion on the part of their men. As Jefferson Davis concluded his speech granting all deserters pardon in the summer of 1863 if they returned to their command,

> Finally, I conjure my country women—the wives, mothers, sisters and daughters of the Confederacy—to use their all powerful influence in aid of this call, to add one crowning sacrifice to those which their patriotism has so freely and constantly afforded on their country's altar, and to

take care that none who owe service in the field should be sheltered at home from the disgrace of having deserted their duty to their families, to their country and to their God.[41]

Only by stepping in as the "natural protectors" of poor women and children could the state hope to argue that the common soldier's duty to his family remained one with his duty to his country. Insofar as the government did this by rendering women and children more economically independent, it inadvertently contributed to the economic autonomy of lower-class women. In taking on the employment of women as its own responsibility, the state itself took up the role of the absent father or husband to support dependent families. The expansion of child and female labor thus became a sort of state charity.

This understanding of the employment of women, especially married and widowed women, as a form of domestic charity—rather than as a manifestation of their independent and autonomous integration into public market relations—was not new to the town, but the reliance of these women upon state-sponsored employment was. As we have seen in the case of seamstresses, employing women had frequently been undertaken as a benevolent gesture during the antebellum era. More significantly, the largest single employer of white women in the town, the Augusta Manufacturing Company (which during the war employed some seven hundred individuals, the vast majority of them women and children), consistently depicted its employment of poor women and children as a form of benevolence.[42] The context of the war only intensified the ability of the factory to cloak its exploitation of female and child labor with the claim to buttress domesticity. Despite the fact that the overwhelming majority of its workers were women and children, the factory had long been regarded with some suspicion as a potential threat to the independence and autonomy of white men. As one writer to the local press argued in defense of the company,

It may be said that they have realized immense profits, and can afford to be thus liberal. Their profits have been the legitimate result of well directed enterprise, and while there has been much clamor about market price, they were as much entitled to it as the farmer, mechanic or merchant, and in not availing themselves of it they deserve at least exemption from the popular clamor against "extorting corporations."

They furnish a conspicuous exception to the rule that "corporations have no souls."[43]

In particular, the factory deserved a reputation for being "charitable" and "patriotic" for the role that it played in employing poor women and children. This employment was made even more desirable by the mill's policy of exchanging some of its goods for produce, which it then sold to its workers at fixed prices. As a result, mill workers and their families were "well supplied with the necessaries of life, and really are able to live better than any other portion of the community, for much that they can get in exchange for cloth cannot be bought for money."[44] Factory employment, then, contributed more to an independence for poor women and their children than any other opportunity in the town. Even here, however, the produce of the mill was not sold on the open market, and the very employment of these women, however profitable for the firm, was viewed as a charitable and philanthropic endeavor on the part of the mill owners, as an extension of their war efforts to sell cloth to the poor or donate funds to the Augusta Purveying Association.

As much then as the war had the effect of increasing women's opportunities for wage labor and thereby bringing domestic labor into the market, the integration of women into the marketplace under these conditions altered the nature of employment itself, serving to play down the servile character of factory employment, which prior to the war had given factories the reputation of "having no souls." Now the status of factory work was enhanced as it was regarded, even more than in the past, as a special kind of charity for poor women and their children. Perhaps even more significantly, in substituting for the absent soldier and making a critical contribution to the economic support of his household, the factory could present itself as the supporter of all men's position as "free men," rather than as the creator of wage slaves. By contributing to the independence and autonomy of some soldiers' families, the factory was thus seen as making an invaluable contribution to the independence of the Confederacy as a whole.

While the production of clothing increasingly came under the control and direction of the Confederate and state governments, the organizational efforts of elite women to support the war effort did not simply abate, but rather began to shift their focus. As the rigors of war placed ever-greater strains on the resources of both individual households and the nation as a whole, public organization began to penetrate even more deeply into hitherto privatized aspects of Confederate women's domestic roles. Of all forms of domestic labor, the production of cloth and the sewing of clothing had long been the aspects of women's labor most subject to being organized outside the family circle and women's direction. On the other hand, labor more directly associated with social reproduction, the labor of bearing, rearing, and nursing the living as well as burying the dead, stood at the heart of women's privatized status. In the last years of the war, this labor increasingly became the basis and focus of elite women's organizational efforts.[45]

Just when the government established sewing manufactories in the town beginning in the fall of 1862, the ladies opened the doors of their soldiers' wayside home. Here they labored to nurse and feed the increasing numbers of sick and wounded men returning from the front. They estimated that between mid-August and mid-September of 1862, they cared for 365 wounded and sick soldiers. They also "entertained" 81 family members and attendants of the sick and wounded.[46] By the end of the war, as Catherine Rowland concluded, "Our very home has become a perfect Wayside Home & there is scarcely a meal but what some soldier stops."[47] Here the normally privatized domestic order was literally turned inside out and women not only went out to nurse the sick and wounded but took those who had nowhere else to go into their own homes. As Rowland noted, "We have two soldiers with us now, Mr. Milwood and Mr. Ruph and as neither of them had homes to go to [her mother] begged them to come & stay with us & they came up this morning from Millen [Wayside Home]."[48]

As the increasing role of the state in the production of uniforms worked to loosen the immediacy of the domestic tie between the soldiers and the women who served them, the ever expanding role of women in the care and nursing of returning troops reinforced that connection in an even more dramatic and immediate way. Calling for financial support for the wayside home, the town newspaper extolled the mediatory function the institutionalization of this domestic tie served. Many in the army from "neglect and inattention" had become "complaining and despondent," especially when they compared their lot to those who had remained at home and who had "traded and amassed a fortune." The wayside home, however, served to dissipate this resentment with a "kind look and a welcome reception."

The soldier's mood brightens as he "thinks of his own mother, wife or sister, anxiously awaiting his return, and he only blesses these country-women of his who have met him on the way and offered him food and nourishment."[49]

By being reminded that his participation in the war was the highest manifestation of his role as manly protector of his family and that women, at least, appreciated his sacrifice, the common soldier could, according to this writer, be made to feel that his efforts were not in vain. Men who had not sacrificed their lives and labor to the cause but instead had grown wealthy could at least defuse resentment on the part of those who had fought the battles for them by devoting some of their profits to the wayside home. As in the earlier case of the Ladies' Aid Society, elite men were encouraged to promote social mothering—the development of ties between their own wives, mothers, and daughters and the soldiery at large—in order to sustain the cause on which their own economic interests now depended.

For those women who participated in the wayside homes or worked in the hospitals, participation in nursing and caring for the returning soldiers signaled a shift in the nature of their wartime contribution away from the positive role of clothing frontline troops at a distance to the more familiar one of tending the sick and dying who turned up at their own doorsteps. Gertrude Thomas described in gripping detail the raw exposure to domestic loss that her experiences with the wounded and dying in the town's hospitals gave her.

Laying on the floor upon beds hastily filled with straw were wounded men, wounded in every manner. Some with their arms and legs cut off, others with flesh wounds, two men in a dying state another poor fellow with the ever present thought of home mingling in his delirium as he sits up and gathering his coarse shoes proceeds to put them on saying, "I am going home, I have a furlough to go home."[50]

Scattered about, poorly fed and half clothed, lay the products of some woman's love and care. Missing an arm, crawling with flies, some man was dying, unknown and unloved. When Thomas looked upon these men, she saw her brother or her own husband. When she looked upon these men the image of surrounding wives and children surfaced again and again in her consciousness. "There lay the man around whom had clustered all the endearing associations of home. A mother—a wife—a sister had loved him. Perhaps now around the family altar a group of children pray 'please bring Pa home safe and well,' happily unconscious of how he died. God grant they never may know."[51]

As women had initially sewed for the common soldier as an extension of their desire to protect their own sons and husbands, Confederate women now nursed the wounded, alleviating other women's disasters in an effort to ward off the prospect of their own. It was, however, in this common loss of their men that they finally found a lasting bond with the women of the common soldier. While their domestic labors may have been shot through with difference based on class, the loss of their men was direct and unmediated. Indeed, much of their attachment to their particular class position can be understood as an effort to protect the well-being of their own individual domestic ties, but in the final sundering of those ties in the loss of their male relations, all women were reduced to a similar position. Thus, as the dimensions of wartime losses mounted, Catherine Rowland was moved to record with increasing frequency the loss of local men and the plight of the widows they left behind. "I was truly sorry to hear today that Whitefoot Russel had been killed in Virginia, for though I have no acquaintance with him I feel very much for his poor wife, for they were much attached to each other & she has three little children to take care of."[52]

Gertrude Thomas also recorded her conversation with one "plain, respectable looking young woman," the mother of three children, the youngest of whom was six weeks old, who arrived at the hospital too late to see her husband, who had already died and been buried. "She was giving way to no outburst of sorrow," wrote Thomas, "She could not indulge in the luxury of Grief, but I knew what a desolate heart she must bear under that calm exterior and knowing the value of genuine sympathy I seated myself by her and told her how sorry I was for her—'that I too had a husband in the Army.' Her lip quivered and shaking her head she replied, 'You'll loose him I reckon.' "[53]

After one particularly costly battle, Gertrude Thomas commented on the streams of wounded and dying men that were reported to be pouring into Richmond. Confederate women were working night and day, nursing the living and burying the dead. " 'Burying their dead.' Oh how much untold agony is concentrated in those few words. Hope blasted—Joy destroyed. Life left blank—Hearts anguished—Wailing cries—and all the deep depths of despair. . . . Oh God hush the wailing cry and bind up the bruised heart of widow and orphan. . . . Give me Oh Heavenly father that spirit of humble faith which will enable me 'to trust thee, though thou slayest me.' " [54]

As much then as the initial outbreak of war drew Confederate women outside this realm of resignation and loss by linking their domestic labors to the cause of independence and autonomy, the death and destruction that mounted as the war continued served to reinforce their subordinate status with a new intensity far greater than they had experienced before. While women of the town, like two of its most prominent matrons, Mrs. Stovall, the wife of a general, and Mrs. Clayton, thought that "country, glory and patriotism" were great things, "to [their] bereaved hearts," wrote Gertrude Thomas in March of 1865, "each mourning for the death of their first born what bitter mockery there must be in the words." [55]

In supporting their men's drive for independence, these women had initially found a new autonomy and authoritative significance for their domestic concerns. However, with the death and approaching defeat of their men, they saw this independent role dissolving as domesticity once again became an exercise in subordination and resignation to a cruel and uncontrollable fate. These women found solace, as they had in the past, in an intensification of their faith, a faith that, as Thomas wrote, allowed them to "trust thee, though thou slayest me." Only through Christian resignation to the blind forces that would take one father or son but leave another, could these women survive the ever-mounting casualties of war. As Susan Cornwall concluded in the face of this wholesale sundering of the domestic tie, women had no alternative but to "suffer and grow strong." Strong that is, in their ability to bear the unbearable, in the resiliency and depth of their ability to resign themselves to personal loss.[56]

Although Gertrude Thomas had supported her husband's service in the army with the same commitment to independence and autonomy that he himself had voiced, the increasing domestic cost of the war very soon forced her to reconsider her views. When in the spring of 1862 her own husband returned to the front after one particularly costly battle, the plight of widowed women that she saw around her rose with an overwhelming force in her mind and she wrote, "never seeing him again occurred to me and it was almost impossible to suppress a shriek of Horror—Oh what a desolation must wring the hearts of widowed women of this country."[57] Fortunately for Gertrude Thomas, her own husband was wealthy enough to hire a substitute, and in the fall of 1862 he resigned from the regular service and enrolled instead in the Home Guard. "I shall never regret," she wrote, "the one year spent in service but I feel that he has escaped with his life—Oh when I think of the thousands and thousands of desolate homes and hearts, or the many bright intellects and manly forms hushed in death I turn to my husband and thank God that he is home again."[58]

Our whole world is demoralized—turned topsy turvy.

—Eliza Smith to her daughters, February 16, 1864

4

Defeated Men and Vulnerable Women

THE COLLAPSE OF THE CONFEDERACY

The successful invasion of Georgia by Union troops in the
spring of 1864 created a massive influx of wounded men and destitute
refugees into the city of Augusta. As the Confederate troops continued to
fall back in defeat toward Atlanta, more and more of the civilian population of northern Georgia chose to leave before the arrival of the enemy;
when Sherman's army eventually appeared, others were forced to flee by
the destruction of their property. One officer in the Confederate army,
General J. R. Simms, stationed outside Petersburg, Virginia, wrote to his

wife in July 1864 describing what she should expect from the advancing Union troops and advising her as to the course of action she should pursue.

> I want you to sell all my horses, mules & stock send off negro men and boys, & everything which they could steal, for when they go into a country they steal everything which they want & that which they don't want they destroy. You cannot trust to their honor in anything. I have seen enough of their brutish vandalism. If they should get there you can leave or stay as you may think best. I would prefer for you to keep outside their lines. I don't want you subjected to the insult which they inflict where they go.[1]

Sherman's march through Georgia was like a driving motor behind the collapse of the old patriarchal, slaveholding household structure. Already weakened and strained by the demands of fighting the war, the ability of individual men to protect and provide for their own was pushed to the point of total collapse by the final loss of life and property that accompanied enemy occupation.[2] Catherine Rowland's husband, Charles, wrote to her in late May from the Confederate front lines some seven miles north of Marietta. Retreating by moonlight, Charles described feeling "sick at heart" at the necessity of abandoning the fields green with wheat, oats, rye, and clover so desperately needed by the hungry Confederacy. Equally disturbing was the scene he witnessed on the highway: the road "filled with people moving and wagons piled with furniture and young children. . . . The poor women and children suffered[,] some by moving and some by facing the Yankees." In the face of this wholesale loss and suffering he could only conclude, "It almost seems sometimes as if Providence was against us."[3]

While some slaves went as refugees with their departing owners, others seized the opportunity to leave with the Yankee troops or to strike out on their own. As a result, just when the white household structure was most beleaguered from without by the advance of the Union troops, it was simultaneously threatened from within by the liberation of the slaves. Even the most powerful of white male household heads, like the slaveholding General Simms, could only advise their families to sell what goods they could before the enemy confiscated them and to try to retain as much control as possible. Left exposed to the will of the occupying Union forces by the defeat of their men, women like Mrs. Simms were best advised to leave their homes before the arrival of the enemy and to search for some safe haven behind Confederate lines.[4]

Homeless and frequently destitute white women and children, maimed and wounded Confederate men, slaves in the company of their owners, and newly freed men and women all turned their sights to Augusta in this last year of the war and poured into the city in hopes of finding sustenance and shelter. As a result, the urban population exploded, and by the time that Atlanta fell to Union forces in September 1864, Augusta had more than doubled its prewar size.[5] The number of wounded men at times outstripped the hospital capacity of twelve hundred beds and spilled over into private homes. Meanwhile, the black population tripled.[6] Catherine Rowland described the altered scene on the main street of the town that summer. "I went out for a little while this morning to attend to some business for Charlie & felt like a stranger in a strange land. Broad St was crowded with persons going up & down & I did not see more than half a dozen persons whose faces were familiar."[7]

While these strangers made up a disparate lot in terms of their economic position in the old social order, most of them shared the common characteristic of being household dependents: the very old, the very young, the disabled, white women and children, slaves.[8] As such they presented the city with a complex dilemma: how to shore up the failing power of white men to provide some form of protection and defense for the town as a whole and for the "deserving" household dependents that remained to these men as individual heads of household. As their hitherto dominant position in the household weakened to the point of final collapse, what ensued was a separating out of the relations of class, race, and gender, which had previously been contained together within the slaveholding household structure. As slaves left their owners in ever-growing numbers and even the loyalty of the common soldier to the Confederate cause was strained to the breaking point, relations of race and class became increasingly unstable, and town authorities attempted desperately to create substitute legal regulations to maintain as much of the old social order as possible. Only white women and children appeared to remain within the domination of the old household structure and as such were the only group worthy of continued "protection" by town authorities.

The need for such public protection by the town seemed to expand exponentially as the military power of the Confederacy weakened. By the fall of 1864, Mayor May claimed that over five hundred white families were entirely dependent upon the support of the Augusta Purveying Association, and by the following spring that number had increased to fifteen hundred.[9] While the services of this institution had originally been focused on the poor and the wives and children of soldiers without the necessary resources to support themselves, with the influx of refugees the class composition of the recipients began to change. Now even women and children of the elite found themselves thrown with the rest of the population upon the resources of the town. Some elite women like Gertrude Thomas were in an economic position that enabled their men to stay at home and hire substitutes; others, like Catherine Rowland, whose husbands were in the military, had always faced the same likelihood as any other woman that their men would be lost or wounded in battle. Now the defeat of the Confederate forces, whether or not their men were actually engaged in the battle, put the homes of all women at risk. According to the mayor, by October 1864 among the "very large class of our population dependent upon the contributions of the liberal for means of living" were now included "many . . . who, in ordinary times, were amply provided for by their husbands, fathers, and other relatives, and had no occasion to solicit assistance of any character; now, however, the claims of country have stripped them of their providers and friends, and they are reluctantly forced to accept the aid we cheerfully tender."[10]

Eliza Mason Smith offers one example of how the refugee plight caught up women of all social strata. A member of a prominent planter-class family from the low country outside Charleston, she and her family were forced to flee when the area fell to Union troops in May and June of 1863. She came to Augusta in the winter of 1864 to stay with her sister, Emily Middleton Izard, who was a resident of the place and whose husband, Allen Izard, was a planter. Eliza Smith's son, William Mason Smith, had enlisted at eighteen at the outbreak of the war and by the summer of 1864 had been critically wounded. Eliza spent long hours that summer in an Augusta hospital nursing her failing son. She expressed her own immediate familial distress within the framework of the larger social disorder of the city in letters she wrote to her daughters. There was, she wrote, "nothing but trouble, heavy trouble all around." Prices in the market were high beyond belief, and many foodstuffs could not be bought at any price. No goods were secure even once acquired because of widespread theft. "Men & women are robbed on these streets daily, also in the cars. Clothes are stolen out of the tubs & off the ironing table." Nevertheless, she concluded that "cheerfulness and resignation" were duties. Although anxious about her son's health and the dispersed condition of her family, she wrote that "I know that God over-rules all things, & doeth all things well." [11]

Although hardly destitute even with the serious reverses in her family fortunes, Eliza Smith suffered domestic loss: of her home, of members of her family, and even of those basic necessities that no amount of money could then buy.[12] She found herself, for instance, dependent upon the local purveying association for that scarce commodity, cloth. Her description of acquiring a piece of homespun on a refugee ticket reflects her lack of familiarity with such experiences or the accompanying social contacts. "I had to get the ticket & then go to a dirty shop, wait an hour, fall into line with a dozen or so greasy women & men, paying down for the piece $43." [13] While the actual invasion of Georgia by Yankee troops in the last year of the war subjected white women across the class spectrum to a common experience of domestic distress and public dependency, this newfound commonality was not such as to create the basis for a positive unity among white women. Rather, it had the effect of reinforcing among elites an appreciation of the class privileges with which they had previously been afforded by virtue of their connection to wealthy men.

The fall of Atlanta and the imminent possibility of a similar fate for Augusta in the autumn of 1864 caused Gertrude Thomas to consider seriously how defeat would transform her own domestic position. While she reiterated her longstanding opposition to slavery for its "terribly demoralizing influence on our men and boys," the imminent likelihood that the slaves would be emancipated by a Yankee victory forced her to acknowledge her own economic stake in the institution. "I grant that I am not so philanthropic as to be willing voluntarily to give up all we own for the sake of principle." She could only wish that they had "invested in something else as a means of support." As it was, the possibility that Sherman would destroy their "planting interest" presented her with a "gaunt picture." [14]

Thomas tried to imagine herself in the position of the Atlanta refugees, their city reduced to rubble, the civilian population ordered to leave. "It is a singular sensation to try and realise how I would feel exiled from my home as the citizens of Atlanta have been, and compelled to realise the Adamic curse of earning my own livelihood." She had made "no arrangement whatever for such a contingency." The need to consider seriously the prospect of employment rather than evolving feelings of self-empowerment presented itself to Thomas as the outcome of the destruction of her own personal Eden. The possibility caused her to mourn the passing of her own dependent but protected domestic status and to cling more tightly to the benefits of white male authority even as she saw that authority collapse. "In these troublous times how soothing the idea of a place of refuge— To a womans nature how inexpressibly delightful the idea of safety and protection."[15]

While Catherine Rowland worried about her husband's safety at the front from the outset of her Civil War diary, as Sherman's troops advanced through the state her concern expanded to the safety of her female relations as well. Rumors of the destruction wrought by the Union troops gave, according to Rowland, "stronger evidence than ever of the vile, mean, treacherous, black hearts of our enemies." They regularly burnt all gin houses and cotton and destroyed all the corn and provisions and dwelling houses, leaving people in a "starving condition." "Worse than all," she wrote, was the way that the hostility of the troops caused them to "destroy women's wardrobes and to tear their clothes to pieces."[16] The Yankees emerge here not as the enemy in some abstract sense but as men who posed a real and immediate threat to her own and other women's domestic place. She wrote with particular concern for her Aunt Fanny, who found herself on an isolated plantation with only her own young children and the slaves as a possible source of defense. While her aunt's plantation was in fact pillaged by Sherman's troops in August 1864, she was fortunate in being able to convince the troops to leave some supplies for herself and her children. Her slaves were not so fortunate, however, as the troops robbed them of everything they had. Despite her aunt's close escape, or perhaps because of it, Rowland continued to live in "constant dread" of a repeated raid and was particularly worried about her young children.[17]

Rowland wrote that "strenuous efforts" should be made by the local militia to meet the enemy and to protect such women and children, or "there is no telling when they will end their work of desolation." Such protection did not appear to be forthcoming in any great strength, however, and those left in the line of Sherman's march were frequently forced to fend for themselves as best they could. As the troops advanced in the direction of Atlanta, reports continued to filter in of the "many outrages" committed while "laying waste to the whole country." Even the cities appeared to be without sufficient defense, and Emily Izard wrote to her sister in July 1864, "Providence protects Charleston; I trust to Him for Augusta; there seems no human army ready for either." [18]

Despite repeated calls for volunteers for the local Augusta militia that summer, many of the white men who remained in the town and the county failed to enlist. In August the city council was forced to take action. They passed an ordinance requiring the registration of all white males in the city and the surrounding county between the ages of sixteen and sixty and empowered the local police to compel military service from all registered men. Although they commended those citizens who were enrolled in the local militia, they concluded that the legislation was still required because of those men who despite the imminent threat to their property and families refused to serve in defense of the city. They found such behavior in the very face of "imminent peril" to be "unworthy of the character of Freemen and Southerners" and "calculated to produce, (if it has not already produced), dissatisfaction, insubordination, and neglect of duty in the Corps now enrolled in the service." [19]

In fact, many of the local men who had enlisted early in the war were stationed far from home when Sherman began his assault and could only wonder from a distance at the reluctance of their fellow citizens to come forward for home defense. James Verdery wrote to his sister of the state of concern among his fellow Georgians from their winter quarters outside Petersburg, Virginia. He described the camp as "very dull & nothing at all going on." In fact, the scene of action had shifted to Georgia, and the troops were awaiting news of Sherman's progress with "great anxiety," fearing for the safety of their own homes and families. Rumors were widespread in the camp that Georgians would simply capitulate in the face of Sherman's assault. Verdery dismissed these rumors and wrote that although he thought the Union advance would bring great suffering, "I entertain but little fears that Georgia will accede to any propositions of peace with the enemy shorter than her complete & separate independence. . . . If all will but do their whole duty I see no possible way of Sherman ever extricating himself from the bold & hazardous situation in which he has put himself." [20]

As Augusta was a center critical to the production of war materiel, it seemed likely that Sherman would take it after the fall of Atlanta in September 1864, compelling the active service of all able-bodied adult white men to defend the city. Catherine Rowland wrote in that month that the Yankees were busy repairing the Atlanta-Augusta road, preparing the way to attack the city. In November 1864, she noted that Sherman was marching on Macon and that Augusta would certainly be next. Emily Izard described the frantic activity in the city. Troops were constantly coming and going and government stores and machinery had been removed to a more secure location. "We are certainly in a dreadful situation," wrote Catherine Rowland "but I trust God will soon smile upon us."[21]

Both she and Emily Izard made plans to become refugees should the city actually be attacked, following a course already taken by many of their relations who had departed for Athens or Savannah. Emily Izard was torn by the necessity of leaving. "I'm going to do what seems best—I hate to leave Allen, & am yet unwilling to be shelled—painful position—out of wh. God help us!" Catherine Rowland also looked to divine intervention. "It is an unspeakable comfort to know that God overrules all things & will do what is best for us. . . . He will not give us more than we can bear." Yet while much as she hoped that God would give her the strength to face her fate, she also called down His wrath on the enemy who stooped so low as to pillage women and children. "I trust they will be overtaken in their wickedness & will be punished for what they have done to us, but if God does not punish them in this world He certainly will in the next."[22]

On November 27 enemy troops did arrive at Catherine Rowland's family plantation, Ivanhoe, in Burke County. Some ten thousand troops proceeded to make camp on the property, only to be driven off by the arrival of Confederate forces. Before they left, however, they took all the draft animals and the meat and burned the gin and all the cotton. What they did not take, they destroyed, "pouring the syrup all over the floor & sprinkled the flour sugar all over the yard, filled the lard with trash & did every thing that was mean and vile." Witnessing this wholesale destruction, Catherine Rowland could only stand by and watch, concluding with impotent rage that "they are certainly the vilest wretches that ever lived & must be overtaken in their wickedness."[23] She also recognized how fortunate she was in the speedy arrival of Wheeler's troops, which forestalled the imminent pillaging of their house. Other friends and relations who found themselves in Sherman's path were not so lucky, and those who abandoned their property in the face of the invasion frequently returned to find their homes burned to the ground.

From her plantation in nearby Richmond County, Gertrude Thomas heard of the advance of the Union forces through Burke County. "The enemy are near us. While I write they may be approaching the city in large force—all day I have been engaged packing until late this evening." Preparing to take shelter in nearby Augusta, she described working harder in her haste to escape their arrival than she had ever worked before in her life. She also wrote of experiencing fear, an emotion that she could only recall having faced once before in her life, on the night that her father died, the greatest previous breach in her experience of patriarchal protection.

> I look back to that Sunday night Nov the 27th and can compare it to only one night in my lifes experience. The night . . . I came up home during Pa's illness and went to bed fearing that the summons would come during the night, as come it did, to tell me that he was worse. Just so that Sunday night I went to bed, not knowing but that during the night the bell would toll and the alarm that the enemy were upon us would be given.[24]

The enemy never arrived at the Thomas's Richmond County plantation, and Gertrude Thomas, although forced to flee, was spared the pillaging of her home. The next day their plantation, Cotton Town, located in Burke County, met with the same treatment as that of Catherine Rowland's. One of their slaves, Henry, left the plantation the night before and joined up with the Yankees. The next day he brought them to the plantation and showed them where the horses and mules were hidden. "They took such as they wished and having dressed Henry in a suit of uniform they stole Melnott a valuable horse of ours and mounted Henry upon it." They then set the gin house on fire and broke into the overseer's house. As with Rowland's plantation, they were interrupted in their work of destruction by the arrival of Wheeler's troops and departed hastily, leaving only one man to finish the destruction of the gin. "This man (the slaves say) our men killed."[25]

Rowland's response to the ever-mounting toll of domestic destruction on the one hand and the maiming and loss of men on the other was to intensify her commitment to the Confederate cause and to express a mounting rage against the Yankees in her diary. While marching through Burke County, these men not only pillaged her family's plantation, they also burnt to the ground the Millen wayside home, which the women of her family had supported. The wayside home was a particular target of the Union troops because a rumor was widespread that Union prisoners being taken south on the railroad had been denied food and water by the women there. In retribution, the home was destroyed and the superintendent was grilled by Union officers. She was charged with denying sustenance to Union soldiers, and her defense echoed Rowland's own sentiments. She replied that she had always given the prisoners water to drink, but because of the scarcity of supplies, she thought that giving them food would have been tantamount to taking bread from the mouths of their own soldiers. Moreover, she saw no reason to treat Yankee men better than they treated Confederate prisoners. Her own brother was a prisoner in a Union prison, and as he was reduced to "living on rats . . . she thought they could live on rats too."[26]

While the demands of fighting the war had created a widening fissure between white men's pursuit of their public position as free men and their private responsibility to protect their household dependents, particularly their own women and children, the actual experience of defeat brought forth another group of men who constituted a clear-cut threat to white women's domestic place. While the ladies of Augusta had publicly charged the white male leadership of the town with threatening to destroy their homes when they planned to burn the cotton in the summer of 1862, the Yankees, in their invasion of Georgia two years later, actually did burn Confederate women's homes to the ground. In the face of this outside threat from the soldiers of the enemy, the failure of the Confederate leaders to recognize elite women's domestic interests or lower-class women's material family needs paled before the depredations of the invading Yankees who, after maiming or killing the male enemy, went on to "make war on women and children."

While the onset of war may have endangered the domestic interests of Confederate women, now that they had sacrificed their brothers and sons to the effort and ultimately, in the case of the refugees, their homes as well, they expressed themselves as being unconditionally wedded to the cause. While Confederate men might hope to eventually recoup something like their lost place, their women could never hope to replace lost relations. They had, wrote Catherine Rowland in January 1865, "suffered too much to think of giving up now & it is a sacrilege to the dead to speak of such a thing." Thinking of her brother who died in the service, she wrote, "Reunion with such a foe can never be, there is a great gulf between us;

the blood of our noble dead & my noble brother cries out for vengeance & we ought to fight on as long as we have a man left, would that I were a man that I might raise my arm for the defence of my country."[27]

While secession and the war followed from the efforts of southern men to assert what they considered to be their proper position as freeborn male citizens in a slaveholding patriarchal republic, when that effort foundered and defeat appeared on the horizon in the concrete form of dead and wounded relatives and occupying Yankee troops, their women rose to claim the lost cause as their own. The greater and more irretrievable their domestic loss, the more committed they seemed to become to the righteousness of the cause for which it was suffered. For poor women who, in giving up a son or a husband, sacrificed not only domestic connections but the greater portion of their economic sustenance as well, the stakes were even higher in concluding that the sacrifice had been worthwhile. Thus, one poor woman addressed the local newspaper upon the "heart rending intelligence of the death of my son, the last one of three, who to serve their country, left me a disconsolate widowed mother." Although she could "assure you that the greater portion of the time since they left, myself and the little children left me have subsisted upon bread alone," she knew that "all this I feel like I could bear if, in the providence of God our country can be saved from the merciless grasp of cruel tyrants who are seeking our total ruin."[28]

For those southerners who increasingly talked of defeat Rowland had only contempt. In January of 1865 she wrote, "It is a burning shame for the people who stay at home to talk in this way while if they were in the field doing their duty, the enemy would never have gained the advantages they have." Howell Cobb, who was temporarily and somewhat unexpectedly assigned a command in Augusta in January 1865, wrote to his wife of his desire to get himself reassigned as quickly as possible. He found the city's population to be "depressed," "disaffected," and "too many of them disloyal." The supine attitude of much of the male population, combined with the virtual certainty of Sherman's attack on the city, made Cobb most eager to avoid being the military officer who was left in charge. "Whoever stays will have to abandon the place when Sherman comes and be well cursed for it. It would take an army to defend the place and there are not troops enough to make a respectable picket line."[29]

As early as the fall of 1864, Mayor May had addressed the rising desire for peace in his annual address to the city. "Our country wants peace—speedy, honorable, lasting peace." Peace that would, according to the mayor, allow for a return to the "magnificent prosperity" of the city, which the "blight of fanaticism" had all but destroyed. Yet he cautioned those who apparently desired prosperity at any price that whatever the cost of the conflict, it was the duty of all the people to "come manfully up to the requirements of the situation." He concluded his appeal by conjuring up the picture of women's sacrifice in order to stiffen the male citizens' flagging resolve.

> We have seen the mother bid farewell to her son, as, with streaming eyes, she strained him to her heart. . . . We have beheld the unutterable distress depicted in the countenance of the wife, as she gazed upon the receding form of the husband of her youth—that husband who is now waiting upon the eternal shore for the idol of his affections. . . . And in the day, when the sacrifices are made—when the noblest sentiments human life can utter are enunciated by those whose deeds follow fast upon their words . . . shall we not all prove ourselves worthy of a life of honor, or a death of fame? [30]

But a few months later the disparity between Augusta's "magnificent prosperity" and a "manful" loyalty to the cause reappeared, as the town authorities had once again to make a decision on the disposition of the cotton that constituted the economic lifeblood of the town. As the enemy approached, it became increasingly obvious that unless the cotton were burned it would fall into their hands. The Confederate military authorities complained vociferously to the city council of the large number of cotton holders who were doing all in their power to conceal their stores. Many were hiding it in cellars and outhouses, and some were even going so far as to float it down the river in hopes that it would "fall into the hands of the enemy rather than be burned." The commanding general appealed to the "well known patriotism" of the city fathers to take the lead in "draining this fountain of evil" and support them in their efforts to "remove to a distance a source of temptation to the enemy, of danger to the community, and of boundless corruption to the country." [31]

Increasingly there seemed to be two sorts of Confederate men: those who would fight for the cause that had taken so many southern homes and brave soldiers and those who would look only to their own narrow economic self-interest, which now stood to lose from further support for the war. As the *Augusta Constitutionalist* concluded, "this Revolution has produced some of the meanest and most grovelling of mankind, it has held an even balance by the example of some of the most exalted and aspiring souls—the true lords of creation. The grub worms who prosper now, bloated with profit . . . these earth bugs, we say, shall be blotted from the record book of memory, or recollected only with infamy, while the annointed names of a thousand heroes shine in perpetual spendor." James Verdery, who was so certain that Georgians would cleave to the cause of independence in the face of Sherman's advance in November, wrote with some contempt of the attitudes of his fellow Georgians by January of the following year. "From all the news I hear from Georgia it seems likely as if she intended to return to Father Abraham & beg his pardon for her past rebellious conduct & humbly submit to any punishment that he deems proper to inflict—('provided you leave our property alone')."[32]

By February, Georgia soldiers in Evans's Brigade, hearing of the mounting sentiment for capitulation at the home front, sent a letter to the *Augusta Constitutionalist*, hoping to encourage the population to persist in their support for the cause. While they sympathized with those citizens who had lost their property and livelihoods to Sherman's "ruffian soldiery," they pointed out that they too had lost their homes in his advance across the state. Unlike many of their fellow citizens at home, however, they were not inclined by this loss to call the Yankees their "brethren," much less had it "influenced us to degrade ourselves, shame our posterity, forfeit our honor, and submit to be 'hewers of wood and drawers of water' to the miserable race we have chased from so many battlefields." They had only to recall the three long years they had already given to the cause, and fellow soldiers who had given their very lives in the course of the conflict rose up before them. "The pale faces of our slain comrades would rebuke us! The empty sleeve, the crippled limb, the broken frame of our wounded brothers . . . would be to us the keenest reproach and disgrace." Those citizens at home who increasingly demanded capitulation, whose "love of self" had prevailed over their "love of country," were, according to these soldiers, those who had "never fired a gun, and never suffered in this cause." "You have not the power to make us slaves also!" the letter concluded. "You shall wait until we, the soldiers in the field, until our crippled brothers, until the widows and orphans of our slain comrades, until all these, with our aged fathers and mothers are ready to bow down to Yankee task masters."[33]

In the normal course of things the pursuit of men's economic self-interest was also to the domestic interest of their women. The war, however, had intervened to sever this relationship. Women had been asked to submit to domestic loss in order to promote their men's independence, an independence in the political realm which once achieved would presumably redound to the domestic benefit of their women by reinforcing the power of their men as household heads. The war also created an immediate economic prosperity for some of the men in the town who chose to stay behind. Now these men, who had hitherto supported the war only with words or financial contributions, were being asked to risk their lives and property to defend what was left of domestic life in general. In shirking this emergency service, they raised the ire of women who had already sacrificed their men and contributed their domestic labor to the cause. As Emily Izard wrote to her sister, who was burdened down by her labors to save her critically wounded son, "We are so much with you in spirit, Lili, over that cot of pain & peril. War is a cruel condition of liberty. Nothing else requires such sacrifices & I, weak woman, shd. prefer bondage, if it were silken. I have no heroism. But I shd. hate a *man* who would flinch, even from martyrdom for his country."[34]

Some women went beyond mere expressions of resentment toward the slackers and layabouts. One wrote to the *Constitutionalist* to suggest that if Confederate men could not be counted on for protection, black men should be armed. If that proved insufficient, white women should arm to join in their own defense. "Do not start at this proposal," she wrote. "I tell you that if I have not misunderstood Southern women there are thousands in this state this day whose heroism and fearlessness would put to shame those poor apologies for men who are besieging the doors of the surgeon for 'certificates of disability,' or making petitions for 'soft places.'" While such extraordinary circumstances required extraordinary measures, the white male population appeared to be eviscerated, "valor oozing out their finger ends." Although all local troops had supposedly been ordered off to confront Sherman, "no one unacquainted with the real state of affairs would have suspected such to be the case from the crowds of the male gender to be found on our streets." The men needed to make up their minds either to strike the heroic blows necessary for victory or "give up masquerading in the guise of patriots and freemen. Throw down our arms, humbly lay down our necks for the foot that will not be slow to tread upon it."[35]

Although this writer drew the line at actually forming Confederate women into regiments, she did suggest that they be armed to defend their own homes. "Let each one put her mark on one at least of the foe, as they put their brutal feet on our streets or with doors defended by faithful servants, from the windows make her feeble arm felt." It was true that they would risk a degree of "malignity" that "the foul fiend himself could not exceed" if they should fail. However, Sherman had already demonstrated the truth of his adage that "war is hell." What fate, she queried, could be worse than the misery he had already inflicted upon a defenceless civilian population?[36]

The editor of the paper applauded this bold effort, describing it as an effort to shame Georgia's "shrinking sons into manhood and independence." It was, he wrote, "one of the cheering signs of the times that the women are unsubdued and hopeful. When the men of Georgia give up all as lost, when they cease to be really *men*, the women of the old State will still uphold the arms of the soldier in his struggle and hold the foe at distance."[37]

Augusta's white male citizens were spared the necessity of this final test of their role as protectors. Although the fighting came within sight of Augusta, the city itself was miraculously spared, and Sherman's troops swept on into South Carolina, "where they intend," wrote Thomas, "to leave no house standing, so they say." In fact, Columbia provided a picture similar to that of Atlanta, as large portions of the city were burnt to the ground in February 1865 and much of the population was left destitute. Their march through Carolina, wrote Rowland, "has been a repetition of their march through Georgia, a war upon women and children and stealing everything from us as they go."[38]

By escaping actual destruction by Union forces, however, Augusta was transformed into a mirror image of the decline wrought in the social order elsewhere. As the Confederate forces fell back in defeat, wounded soldiers arrived at the city's hospitals. As plantations were overrun and whole cities fell before the Yankees, dispossessed women and children and newly freed slaves swelled the city's population. The very growth of this population, cut adrift from its social moorings, reflected not only the decline of the power of the slaveholding patriarchal household to defend, protect, and order its own elsewhere, it also undercut the very foundation of the city's social structure as well.

While the growing number of dependent white women and children taxed the resources of the city, the social order was further stressed by signs of disaffection among the burgeoning population of common soldiers and newly freed blacks. What white women of the elite, like Eliza Mason Smith, experienced as a disturbing and unaccustomed contact with the lower classes was in fact the consequence of the erosion of the power of the white town fathers not only to "protect" white women, but also to contain and direct class and racial forces within the system of white, patriarchal households as they had in the past. As Mrs. Smith described it, "Our whole world is demoralized—turned topsy turvy."[39] Whether as recipients of the public benevolence of the Augusta Purveying Association or as victims of the mounting incidents of theft, white women of the elite found themselves directly exposed to an unaccustomed class and racial interface, from which they had hitherto been protected by their men and by the old social order.

The wounded soldiers flooding the town played an ambiguous role in the decline of the old social order. When they had served on the battlefield, their loyalty to the cause had been a bulwark for the social order and a critically important defense against the depredations of Union troops. However, their arrival in the town, maimed and wounded, graphically reflected the declining power of the old order to protect. While elite women, who were called upon to nurse these soldiers in the city's hospitals or in the wayside home, experienced a bond with lower-class white women in the common loss, direct contact with lower-class men was a disturbing experience to them. Gertrude Thomas attempted to reconcile the disparate emotions that arose in her at the bedsides of these dying men. For the dying man of her own class, the man with "very much such a face as Stonewall Jackson's," she could immediately conjure up the image of someone "around whom had clustered all the endearing associations of home." For the "common looking man" who died alongside him, however, she felt an instinctive aversion, which she had to overcome by reminding herself that although "not the same refinement of the other had been bestowed upon him," he also had a wife or mother who loved him and "perhaps the ties which bound him to earth were equally as strong."[40]

While the common soldier was the mainstay of the old social order as long as he was fighting at the front, he presented an equivocal figure when he was dying in the hospital. The threat posed by class distance could be neutralized, however, by envisioning the poor man within a common domestic frame. The soldiers only became truly dangerous when they survived their wounds and began to congregate on the city streets and in the local saloons. "There were," wrote Mrs. Irby Morgan, herself a refugee to the city in the summer of 1864, "crowds of sick and wounded soldiers in Augusta, and going up Green and Broad Streets any pleasant day you would see the sidewalks thronged with them." Unlike the wounded soldiers who were dependent upon the domestic ministrations the women of the town, the soldiers who massed on the city streets constituted a large group of lower-class men free, at least for the moment, of any domestic strictures. The resultant erosion of class distance was noted humorously by Mrs. Morgan, who recounted an exchange between "a noted belle" of "magnificent form and graceful carriage" and "a pale, cadaverous, ragged soldier" on the city streets. The soldier, lounging against the side of a building with several companions, was "looking eagerly" at the belle as she promenaded down the street with her "stately walk." "The lady had on a dress with a very long train to it, and as she turned the corner she looked back, and gave her skirt a slight pull. The soldier, still looking intently at her or the train, now said: Go on, marm, it's a comin'. It's jest turnin' the corner. She blushed and hurried on. Of course there was a hearty laugh."[41]

This piece of apparently innocent effrontery had, however, a more serious underside, as it reflected the general erosion of class distance on the public streets. Kate Cumming described a similar scene in Chattanooga, where she was visiting her husband. Like Augusta, the city was crowded with sick and wounded men, whom she described as "the roughest of soldiers." Although the soldiers were much in evidence, no women "of any description" were to be seen on the city's streets. "I suppose, she wrote to her mother-in-law, "they are kept at home by the numbers of rowdy men on the street."[42]

From the beginning of the influx of wounded men into the city, the Augusta City Council had endeavored to maintain social order by limiting the manner in which the troops could occupy public spaces. Beginning as early as the winter of 1863, there was a protracted struggle between the city authorities and the military over the location of expanded hospital facilities. The military authorities wanted to occupy the town hall and other central buildings, like the nearby boy's academy. The city council struggled to convince them that the race course, which was located on the edge of town, would provide an excellent location for the construction of a new hospital. It would also have had the advantage of keeping the soldiers outside the town. The military refused this option, and the city fathers were left to attempt to regulate the behavior of the growing mass of soldiers in the city through prohibitive legislation.[43]

Whenever the soldier population boomed, as with the influx of wounded in the last year of the war, the council made efforts to close down the city's saloons, as it was ostensibly "their duty to promote by every means within our control" the soldiers' "recovery to health and active usefulness." The Grand Jury was perhaps more forthright when they noted that "the peace and good order of our community demands that something be done to save our youth and our noble brave defenders from the drunkards grave." The mayor explained the action of the city council in closing down the saloons in the local press. "At the request of the General Commanding this post, I issue this Proclamation requiring the closing of all barrooms in the city for the present. . . . Large numbers of troops are in the neighborhood of Augusta, and passing through, and it is a matter of indispensible necessity that places where spiritous liquor is sold remain closed."[44]

In some cases the behavior of individual men was so reprehensible as to prompt local citizens to protest to the military authorities. One B. Willis was removed from duty in the office of the Provost Marshal at the request of several citizens of "the highest standing and influence." Although Willis was a member of a family of "respectability and good social position," he was also a "gambler, a drunkard, and a man of infamous character," who was "in the highest degree offensive & reprehensible." His removal was therefore called for by the "best interests of the community and the service" and his commanding officer declined to "reinflict" his presence on the community when requested to reassign him to the town at a later date. By January 1865 conditions had deteriorated to such an extent that the Grand Jury made a special appeal for better regulation of the troops. "We also desire to call the attention of the military power to the fact that our Citizens are frequently subject to indignities from members of the Provost Guard and others evincing unwarranted authority. Scenes occur daily in our streets of violence and abuse."[45]

Even if the majority of the troops comported themselves better, the size of the soldiering population alone was sufficient to insure that some abuses would occur. In the last year of the war the basic problem of introducing large numbers of footloose adult men into a civilian population composed largely of women and children was compounded by rising levels of active disaffection among the troops. James Verdery wrote to his sister describing conditions among the Georgia troops. He feared that unless their rations were increased and their wages paid, there would be an increase in the rate of desertion, which already averaged about ten men per day. "This army is becoming more despondent every day some say that we are whipped and havn't got sense enough to know it."[46]

In his annual address of October 1864, Mayor May announced that Augusta's police had joined forces with the military authorities to apprehend the growing number of deserters taking refuge in anonymous corners of the city. Officers in charge of the local hospitals even began to oppose the placement of wounded soldiers in individual homes for fear that once the men were outside their watchful care they would malinger to avoid returning to the front. Mrs. Morgan discovered this policy much to her distress when she endeavored to take a personal friend, a wounded officer suffering from gangrene, into her home to give him better care than the hospital could provide. "The officers had given orders that none should be taken to private houses, as many were already scattered in different directions, and some tarried longer than the officials thought necessary." After some heavy negotiations, she was able to secure her officer, but she had to agree to report his condition to the appropriate military authorities every morning at nine.[47]

While the presence of wounded, maimed, or disaffected soldiers on the city streets or in the public saloons constituted a disturbingly concrete and visible sign of the weakened state of the Confederate war effort, the rising incidence of theft against private households indicated the possibility that this disaffection was, at least among some, being transformed into active class hostility. The Grand Jury described the state of the social order in the town in January 1865 as "appalling," revealing a disregard for the law so widespread that "it is seriously to be apprehended that if a better spirit is not exhibited we shall be in danger of falling into anarchy." Catherine Rowland recorded several incidents of theft or attempted theft within her own circle of acquaintances during the last few months of the war. In the case of at least one of these robberies, the theft was perpetrated by a soldier.[48]

Support for the Confederate cause was grounded in the perception of common interest among all white men, regardless of their disparate class position. Respect for the sanctity of other men's household goods reflected a perception and expectation of a like respect for one's own. The rising incidence of theft against Augusta's wealthy indicated that this sense of solidarity in the common cause was being replaced by an understanding of the extent to which class inequalities divided those who had continued to prosper even during wartime and those who had lost, if not their lives, perhaps their health or their economic assets. The unity of all white men based on their common position as heads of households was ceasing to unite Confederate men as a shared ideology, as it became increasingly shot through with distinctions based on class.

Even more threatening to the social order than lower-class white disaffection was the decline of the elite patriarchal household structure from within, as a consequence of the growing autonomy of the slave population. The increasing possibilities for more diverse employment for the city's slaves outside the white household and the growth of that portion of the black community living apart from it were fueled by the departure of adult white men to the front, as well as by the influx of refugees into the city. As in the case of the common soldier, the war created a situation in which the white population of the town was forced to depend even more upon black slave loyalty at the very moment when conditions were offering blacks new possibilities for autonomy. One need only consider the manner in which black refugees arrived in the city to see that their presence reflected their owners', especially their mistresses', increased dependence on their labor just when white control over that labor was becoming ever more tenuous.

From the perspective of the white town residents and the city authorities, the most desirable black refugees were those who arrived in the company of fleeing Confederate women and children, just as the most desirable soldiers were those duty-bound to the domestic ministrations of the town's Confederate women. Such was the case with Joe, a manservant and jack-of-all-trades, who accompanied his wounded master, Irby Morgan, along with Morgan's wife and children and several of his owner's nieces to Augusta in the summer of 1864. Before the Morgans arrived in Augusta, they had been refugees once before in Marietta, after fleeing their home in Memphis. Joe was the only slave who still accompanied them, and his many talents were consequently even more essential to their well-being than they would have been before the war.[49]

But for every slave that arrived in the company of his refugee owners, others arrived alone or in groups, impressed by the military authorities from the surrounding countryside to labor on the city's fortifications or in the hospitals. As in the case of those slaves who arrived in the company of their owners, impressed slaves also served an increasingly critical role in the defense of the beleaguered white household through their labors for the flagging Confederate cause. While many civilian white men could not be induced to drill for the militia, black men were impressed to do the backbreaking labor of building the fortifications necessary to any final stand in defense of the city. While the ladies nursed, fed, and offered spiritual succor to the wounded and dying soldiers, their impressed slaves did the hardest and dirtiest labor associated with hospital care.[50]

While most slaves who arrived in the city were under the direct authority of their owners or of the military and continued to serve these masters, others arrived on their own as free men and women. Whether actually liberated by the advancing federal troops or simply able to make their escape in the confusion of owners' efforts to relocate, increasing numbers of freed men and women also found shelter in Augusta's burgeoning black community. For these men and women, the last year of the war offered them their first experience of freedom, and they seized the opportunity to exercise this new found autonomy within the anonymity afforded by a settlement of thousands of African Americans living on their own.[51]

Even before the outbreak of the war, the extent to which the Augusta slave community managed to live as though they were free elicited comment from outside observers. William Pritchard, in explaining the difficulties of acquiring an accurate estimate of the size of the black population, remarked upon the condition of many of the city's slaves. "There are so many superannuated—so many as free as the laws will allow—so many who are eroding the ordinances regulating negroes living out separate and apart to themselves—so many who hire their own time—so many whose owners are in other localities that there are many difficulties in the way of counting or enumerating them." Despite these problems Pritchard estimated that twelve hundred of the city's slaves, roughly 25 percent of the total black population, were essentially acting as free agents.[52] The tripling of the black population in the last year of the war, composed as it was largely of slaves without masters, whether impressed, runaways, or attached to female-headed households, must have further reduced the already tenuous authority of white masters in such an environment.

Changes in the gender composition of the town's white population also contributed possibilities for more autonomy among slave men by creating a demand for male labor that the white population could no longer supply. In fact, as the number of resident adult white men declined and the number of adult white women rose precipitously through the influx of a primarily female white refugee population, the situation within the black community was, if anything, reversed. Increase in the town's black population was more likely to be male than female, as those impressed to work by the military were customarily able-bodied men, and adult men were also the most likely to escape from the surrounding plantations and take shelter in the city. On a purely functional level, the demands on white manpower to fight the war created the necessity to impress black men. Slaveowners were not pleased with the necessity of sacrificing their labor, but given the reduced state of the local white labor market, no alternative existed.[53]

While this impressment of hundreds of male slaves created one new avenue for expanded laboring opportunities, the expanded demand for all kinds of consumption goods also provided new possibilities for advancement outside the immediate control of the white household, opportunities that the city's black community was quick to grasp, as hack drivers or hucksters, or by preparing and selling foodstuffs to the passing troops.

From the outset of the conflict, the local authorities recognized the threat that wartime conditions posed to the security of slavery and saw how that threat was exacerbated by the scarcity of able-bodied adult white men in the town. This scarcity meant that those who remained in the town had to band together more rigorously in order to maintain their position of authority. White men were required to participate in nightly patrols to help maintain racial order. As early as June 1861, however, the Grand Jury complained of the neglect of the Patrol Laws; in the face of the clear "exigencies of the time," such neglect was doubly reprehensible. Disregard for their collective responsibility for maintaining order was opening the way for the violation of other laws as well, particularly those laws that governed slaves hiring their own time and living apart from their masters. Confronting the structural problem created by the absence of many men otherwise liable for patrol duty, the Grand Jury called for the appointment of special detectives empowered to "take any secret measures necessary" to apprehend slaves now living outside the law.[54]

In stark contrast to their repressive approach to the black population of the town, the same Grand Jury reported on the situation of white women as well. The difference in their approach to these household dependents reflected a basic split occurring in the household structure and in the authority of white men to hold those households together: increasing repression applied to the black community, increased "protection" extended to white women and children.

They advocated continued efforts to extend the protective face of the white male household head to these "loyal" members of the old household structure, urging that a special tax be levied to support the women and children of "our fellow citizens who have entered the military service." A year later, the grand jury called even more emphatically for the defense of the interests of dependent soldiers' families. In particular they attacked those who "exact the highest possible price for any purchasable commodity," a practice that "bears the hardest upon the families of those who having sacrificed the comforts and allurements of home are engaged at distant points in defending the rights of those remaining." At the same time they made an even stronger statement urging the enforcement of the Patrol Laws. "These laws are important at all times but now rendered doubly necessary by the absence of so many of our citizens in defense of our homes and Country."[55]

As Sherman's troops actually came within sight of the city in February 1865, the significance of these patrols expanded as the growing number of slaves escaping to the town from the surrounding farms and plantations rose precipitously. In a letter in the local paper in February 1865, the mayor described the situation from the perspective of the city authorities. "I wish to call your attention to the fact that there is at this time within our limits, and in our vicinity, a large number of runaway negroes who are nightly engaged in depredating upon the property of our citizens, and committing other outrages against the peace and good order of our city." The mayor urged the white citizenry to exercise some vigilance and to "examine their kitchens, outhouses and other localities where negroes can be concealed, every night." He also urged those white men who were exempt from military duty and still at home to form a night patrol. Only through the organization of what remained of white male authority could the old social order be upheld. As the mayor concluded, through this "small service," men on the patrol could rest easier "with the knowledge . . . that in so doing they are protecting their their own families and property, as well as the families and property of their neighbors and friends."[56]

Here the difference in the public treatment of the two forms of household dependents, white women and children and ex-slaves, diverged even further than it had in the past. While the town fathers had routinely attempted to provide substitute support for white women and children and substitute authority (in the form of repression) for the black population, now those white men who remained in the town were urged to "protect" these women *against* the growing autonomy of the black population. The two groups were actively pitted against each other. Thus while they made efforts to arouse what remained of the adult white male population to "protect" white women and children, the local authorities endeavored to limit the extent to which this "protection" was actually necessary by tightening legal regulation of the black community.

Of particular concern to city authorities was the ever-increasing cohesion and mobility of blacks, and the council passed tighter laws strictly limiting the number who could congregate at any one time in the public streets or elsewhere. Hack drivers, who were ostensibly always under the supervision of white owners, were particularly worrisome to the council, which charged that they used their vehicles not only on "legitimate" white business but to secure their own interests and those of the black community. In one case that both the city council and the Grand Jury singled out for notice, hacks were used to rob a city merchant of a large amount of sugar. Undoubtedly this case was especially alarming, not only because it demonstrated the possibilities inherent in uncontrolled black mobility, but because the black hack drivers in question appear to have been aided by white accomplices. As a result, in January of 1864, a renewed effort was made to limit the use of hacks to "legitimate white business and under the observation of whites."[57]

Perhaps the most difficult to limit though legislation were the black hucksters, who congregated in the lower market and bartered their masters' or their own agricultural produce. City police were detailed to arrest "all speculators in the necessaries of life" but apparently to no avail, as the complaint of "extortion" by these hucksters continued to appear frequently in the press. One woman, signing herself "a housekeeper," claimed to have paid two dollars for one turnip and described the black population's eager pursuit of this avenue of advancement as "a vim bordering on mania." It was, the housekeeper asserted, "to their exertions that we are indebted for the high prices provisions have reached." Not only was her larder empty because of this "extortion in the market," but she also found it almost impossible to obtain domestic help, as black women were increasingly able to find employment outside the white domicile. "It is with great difficulty that a house servant can be obtained at any price—for the blacks are above work as long as they can speculate and extort from the hungry soldiers in the camp or at the railroad stations, by the sale of musty ginger bread, bullet-biscuit or sour beer." [58]

The influx of refugees and soldiers created an ever-growing demand for basic commodities, and black hucksters were quick to make what they could of the gap between this rising demand and inadequate official supply. While the local press had debated the question of speculation among the merchants in the early years of the war, in the last years of the conflict black hucksters were squarely blamed for rising prices by the local press.

The irony, of course, was that it was the very needs of the white community that created not just the opportunity, but the very necessity of this flowering of enterprise within the black community. Even the housekeeper, while calling on the local authorities to put an end to black "extortion" in the name of white domestic interests, recognized that the root of the problem lay elsewhere. For as the influx of refugees to the city drove up prices and created new opportunities for black enterprise, it simultaneously rendered these same refugees ever more strapped for sources of support. Women and children of the slaveowning elite found their slaves' ability to labor for their support to be increasingly critical to their own survival. Take for instance the case of Joseph and Caroline Jones. With Joseph Jones receiving only military pay, the Joneses found themselves in increasing economic difficulties as the war progressed. They counted heavily upon the ability of the one male slave they had with them in the city to bring in an income through the hire of his own time. As Joseph Jones wrote to his wife, "I think that Titus had best put down the carpets, & do any thing else that you may wish before he goes to work. It would add greatly to your comfort to receive his wages every day—far more I think than if you retained him at home. I will tell him to try & make one Dollar a day for you. his services are *honestly* worth this. He had best work with his old employer. It is not well for him to change about any more than necessary." [59]

To reconcile their own increasing economic dependence upon their slaves' wages or entrepreneurial initiative, with the apparent threat black autonomy posed to the domestic welfare and security of white women and children as a whole, a line was drawn between the "loyal" slave, presumably one's own, or one who directly served the household, and the "disloyal" slave, who had become detached from the white household, who had the temerity to serve his own interests or those of the black community, and whose increasingly autonomous, unsupervised existence was presumably responsible for high prices in the market and rising incidents of theft and general social disorder. Mrs. Irby Morgan clearly made this distinction with reference to her own slave, Joe, whom she always described as "our faithful servant." [60] Living just outside the city, she was dependent upon Joe to make almost daily trips there for her. As an able-bodied black man, he was liable to impressment by the Confederate agents, and he engaged in constant tricks in order to elude them, such as binding up his leg and hobbling along on crutches so as to appear disabled for heavy labor.

Viewing the matter from the perspective of her own immediate domestic interests, Mrs. Morgan wrote that she was "uneasy," not because her slave was subverting Confederate authority, but rather because she feared that he would be caught and "forced to work on the fortifications or to move cotton, for they were stacking it in the streets preparing to burn it several times." According to Mrs. Morgan, the military authorities were generally suffering from a shortage of hands as a result of the widespread ingenuity of the black population in eluding them. "They would," she wrote, "hide in the day, but at night the churches would be crowded." Mrs. Morgan described a raid on one such evening church meeting, itself proscribed, which the ever-wily Joe was once again able to escape. "One night the officers heard of this meeting, and made a raid on the male portion, and got a good many hands for their work, but Joe jumped out the window and made his escape. The next morning he laughed and told me about it, and said he was too smart: they couldn't 'ketch' him." [61]

Joe, the "faithful servant," was described by his owner as "invaluable" in enabling her to "get on very comfortably" despite wartime difficulties. "Joe was the quickest, smartest negro I ever saw—always ready and willing for any emergency." While this very cleverness and ingenuity was invaluable to their owners, who relied ever more heavily upon their slaves' ability to improve living standards for whites, this very same ingenuity created the basis for charges of "extortion" by white housekeepers when it was turned to the pursuit of the black community's own interests. While Mrs. Morgan was pleased that Joe escaped and was therefore spared for her own service, Mrs. Izard had a different story to tell concerning the same incident. As she wrote, "Col. Rains is impressing negros to work on the fortifications of Augusta. Seized a number in Church last night. Augusta will be the better for their absence from the corners."[62]

From their location as dependent members of the slaveowning elite, women like Mrs. Morgan and Mrs. Izard defined the loyalty of their slaves from the myopic perspective of the interests of their own households. Those slaves who labored for their owners they understood to be both industrious and faithful. However, as a growing number of blacks were enabled to turn their energies toward the clothing of their own households and driving hacks to serve their own community, the fact that they may have labored more diligently than ever before in their lives only condemned them. From the perspective of these elite white women, they had now become "idle."

If urban opportunities for black autonomy outside the white household taxed the insularity of the white owner's vision, the arrival of the Union armies on their plantations engendered a far more decisive crisis, which their hegemony as slaveowners could not survive. Although Catherine Rowland was well aware that slaves on other plantations were taking advantage of the appearance of the Yankees to make their escape, she continued to believe that the benevolence of her own family's rule would be reflected in the loyalty of their newly liberated slaves. It apparently did not occur to her that slaves might remain on the plantation for reasons of their own, and she concluded with some satisfaction that "all of the negroes remained faithful & though they were offered every inducement to go off with the Yankees not one of them left except Alfred."[63]

Rowland clung tenaciously to the belief that the slaves in their household could not function successfully outside it anymore than she could herself. For a brief moment she had actually considered the possibility that the Union army might present an alternative white authority structure that could compete with the "loyalty" of the slaves to the household, and it was with some relief that she recorded the way in which Yankee behavior precluded this possibility. Thus when the occupation army arrived on her family's plantation, Rowland wrote with grim satisfaction that the troops not only destroyed her possessions but "took everything from the negroes, at which I am much surprised as they profess to love them so much."[64]

Nevertheless, as she heard reports of slaves leaving owners she considered benevolent, such as members of her own extended family, it became increasingly difficult for Rowland to sustain her belief in the integrity of her own household. When, for instance, fifteen of her aunt's slaves left with the Yankees, she could only record that the event "surprised me very much." Even her own family's slaves refused to work after the Union raid, although they remained on the plantation. This behavior she tried to attribute to the destructive influence of the Yankees, who had left the slaves so "frightened & so demoralized . . . that they do nothing at all, [as] the Yankees told them they were coming back again & if they found them working they would kill them. . . . I am not surprised at the negroes being frightened & suppose when every thing is quiet the feeling will pass off & they will go to work again."[65]

Gertrude Thomas described a similar scene on her plantation. In her case, she claimed that the slaves not only declined to leave with the invading troops, but that they even killed the Yankee soldier who had been left behind to finish off the job of destroying the gin house. As for Henry, the one slave who ran off the night before the troops arrived and who led them to the plantation the next day, Gertrude Thomas had a ready rationale. "Henry has no ties to bind him to the plantation and has been a runaway from childhood." Here Thomas recognized that the ties that bound the slaves to the plantation might have more to do with loyalty to their own families than to her own. When, however, John Boss, their driver of several years, who had a wife and child on the plantation, left several days later, she was harder pressed to explain his departure. Whatever his reasons, however, she was convinced that his chances of surviving outside the plantation were slim. She concluded "I have kindly feelings toward him and I *hope* he may do well while I *doubt it*."[66]

While the war rendered women like Gertrude Thomas and Catherine Rowland increasingly aware of their dependent status and the desirability of "protection," it simultaneously created the possibility, even the necessity, of increased autonomy and independence among their slaves. While autonomy from their husbands and brothers also came as a wartime necessity to white women and children across the class spectrum, it cut deeply into their standard of living, forcing them to make constant sacrifices and to increase their labors without any real prospect of a fundamental alteration in their dependent status over the long run. For the slaves, on the other hand, autonomy from the master promised new long-term opportunities that clearly outweighed whatever it might cost in immediate economic hardship and personal duress. While the war drove home the lesson that white women and children could survive independently only at great cost, it demonstrated both the necessity and the viability of independence to an ever-growing proportion of Augusta's black slaves.

At the beginning of 1865 a critical moment in the conjuncture of race and gender relations in Augusta presented itself. The patriarchal slave-holding household structure of the cotton-producing plantation of the region, which had hitherto dominated social relations, had been turned topsy-turvy, broken apart, and, uprooted from its traditional base in the countryside, its fragments seemed to be converging in desperation on the beleaguered town. By the spring, fifteen hundred white, largely female-headed families were encamped within the city, dependent on the good offices of the Augusta Purveying Association to subsist. At the same time, the wave of black refugees arriving in tandem found in the same chaotic circumstances that reduced their white counterparts to charity new opportunities for economic independence and domestic autonomy, absent under the plantation regime. As the Confederacy buckled under the combined force of military defeat, economic hardship, and slave disaffection, a more egalitarian social structure seemed momentarily to emerge. One correspondent to the local newspaper argued that the "sudden and unexpected development" of the "intellectual, moral and industrious capacity" of the black population "is the astounding fact of the war." This incipient black autonomy was, in his view, nothing less than "a miracle," particularly as it had occurred "so rapidly, so thoroughly without disturbance to our organic system." The only question in his mind was whether slaveowners would recognize the altered state of their relationship to their slaves with sufficient alacrity to turn their newfound energies to their own ends. "I cannot urge upon you too emphatically," he argued, that the master must recognize this new "quickness of thought and feeling" in his slave and "not allow him to get control of it but must direct it for the benefit of all parties involved."[67]

The time had come, according to this writer, to integrate the black population into the transformed economy and social structure that four long years of war had wrought. Rather than struggling to force blacks back into slavery, their new status should be officially recognized. In particular, black men should be legally granted the power to protect and defend that they were spontaneously assuming. Indeed, insofar as white men had defaulted in their defense of independence, perhaps black men could enable them to recover their place. This writer argued that in granting the slave the status of a free man, his energies could be turned to support the Confederate cause. "All can see that our only resource remaining are our slaves—the choice is no longer negro as slave or soldier, but whether they will be soldiers for us or the Yankees."[68]

The choice presented here was apparently a clear-cut one. White men could accept the decline in their authority within their households or they could insist on that authority at the cost of their their public position as free men in an independent nation. Yet in practice, this choice was really no choice at all, for the public position of the Confederate man as citizen was dependent upon his private position within the patriarchal, potentially slaveholding household structure. To abandon the Confederacy was to abandon the socioeconomic foundations on which it had been based. To lose public, political power was to be weakened in one's private authority to direct as well as to protect, whereas to reduce one's power over subordinate members of the household was to undercut the very economic and social basis of one's public political position in the first place.

For several weeks correspondents to the *Constitutionalist* argued vehemently on both sides of the issue. One slaveholder, recently returned from military service, including a stint in a Northern prison, argued for the primacy of preserving political independence. "Everything that makes life worth having is wrapped up in our struggle for independence . . . if necessary for its achievement, free every negro in the Confederacy and put a musket on the shoulder of every one able to bear arms." But others argued just as passionately that to abolish slavery was to undermine the very foundation on which the Confederacy stood. Slavery, one writer concluded, must be preserved because of its "intimate connection with our domestic and social relations: Our habits, our manners, our feelings, our character, our social life, all grew out of it; habits, manners, feelings, character, social life, which we considered worth the preservation."[69]

The editor of the *Augusta Daily Constitutionalist*, James Garner, himself a large slaveholder, made it clear to his readers that as far as he was concerned support for emancipation was a foolhardy as well as a minority view. To try to "improve" the black population would, he wrote, lead to a "decline in virtue—an immense decline." If any portion of the male community was to be further empowered, he argued that it ought to be poor white men. "Better to raise up those of our race, as Wm. Greg [a prominent mill owner in the region] has done. He has quickened the torpid existences about him into energy."[70] By improving the position of poor white men, the Confederacy could hope to renew a vast reservoir of support for the cause while avoiding the necessity of reducing the position of slaveholding men both within their own households and in the society as a whole.

The passage of the Negro Soldier Bill in March of 1865 removed the issue from the realm of debate and presented it as a fait accompli. As a last desperate effort, this legislation came too late to save the foundering Confederacy. It did, however, effectively serve to foreshadow the gendered meaning that emancipation would take on in the context of military defeat. Black men would be granted the status of free men, but only because white men had failed to protect their own domestic space. The emancipation of the slaves would, under any circumstances, have entailed a radical restructuring of white men's understanding of the scope and meaning of their own manhood, but in the context of impending military defeat, this loss of their household dependents was imbued with a particularly intense emasculating meaning. As a son of one of the town's leading residents, who had himself fought for four years, wrote in response to the passage of the bill, "ample opportunity will soon be given the patriotic negroes to set an example to the sticking cowards of Georgia especially to the 'purchasing agents and the bomb-proof militia' who give balls for the ladies while the army is starving, and the country is almost ruined for the want of men."[71]

In reality, his prediction would never be tested since by the time the bill passed it was already too late to save the Confederate war effort. By March the inevitability of defeat was already apparent to Gertrude Thomas, and she began to prepare for the end. The emancipation of her family's slaves along with the decline in her husband's ability to make a sufficient income opened the possibility that she would be required to seek paid employment herself. She realized that her only job possibility was as a school teacher and then only if she remained in Augusta. She began to learn French, something she had once planned to do in order to "while away many leisure moments," but "now when I study I think it may probably aid me some day in the only plan I can form for gaining a support." She also tried to acquire some minimal domestic skills, turning her hand to baking. Still she could not envision the final outcome, and she wished that the resolution, however difficult, would come. "At times I feel as if I was drifting on, on ever onward to be at last dashed against some rock and I shut my eyes and almost wish it was over, the shock encountered and I prepared to know what destiny awaits me."[72]

Gertrude Thomas did not have long to wait. On May 1 the official news of the fall of the Confederacy and the imminent arrival of occupying troops was greeted by the outbreak of a riot in the city. "An event," wrote Thomas, "often dreaded but never experienced before!" Confederate soldiers broke into the stores on the main street of the city and carried off whatever they could. Gertrude Thomas described a scene of great confusion and disorder as the bell tolled one o'clock, the traditional reminder to pray for the soldiers who were "alas by so many of us neglected." She saw numerous men running down the street carrying their booty in bags and bundles over their shoulders. Confederate officers struggled to gain the attention of the crowd and, by appealing to their "better nature," managed to convince some to join them in quelling the riot. Rumors of the burning of private homes were rampant, and a large crowd of black rioters appeared before the home of George Jackson, one of the city's prominent merchants and a large slaveholder, intent upon burning his house to the ground. They were met, however, by an equally large force of mounted militia and dissuaded from their course. Infantry were also called out to guard the factory, and by the end of the day two men lay dead, one black and the other white.[73]

Despite the obvious disaffection of the soldiery, Thomas could not bring herself to call this "excitement" a "rebellion." "I had like to have said rebellion but rebel is a sacred word now, worthy to be ranked with such words as Home, Heart & Heaven." Safely ensconced in the domestic pantheon, even the disturbingly disorderly among the soldiery were to be forgiven for their revolt against the rebel regime. Like James Garner, the newspaper editor, Thomas saw these lower-class white men as the keystone to the future of the white household, especially in the face of the imminent emancipation of the slaves. The black rioters, on the other hand, were in Thomas's mind an entirely different story, and upon receiving the official news that they were in fact emancipated, she wrote, "Tonight the impression is general that *slavery* is *abolished* that *the negroes are free*—that is free to plunder and starve." [74]

With the slaves cut off from the discipline of the white household, Thomas could only envision that they would be reduced to starvation or to stealing what they could no longer earn through labor for whites. Unable to recognize the viability of a separate black household, Thomas thought emancipation a legal fiction. She persisted in her belief that survival was impossible for blacks outside the framework of the white household and the authority of the white master. Mrs. Irby Morgan betrayed the same one-sided vision in the way she and her husband received the official news of Lee's surrender. "We both wept like children." By contrast, for her slaves the arrival of the Yankee troops to take the local arsenal was a moment of joyous celebration. "In the course of the day I heard a noise, and on looking out, saw sure enough a long line of blue coats, drums beating, banners waving, negroes running, shouting, yelling, looking like lunatics just escaped from the asylum. Among the number my cook ran by me, with her white apron tied to the end of a broomstick, shouting and cheering at the highest pitch of her voice, jumped the fence and was gone." [75]

After dark the cook, Celia, returned "utterly exhausted and said she was tired almost to death"; she immediately began to pack up her things in order to leave for Virginia, where she hoped to find her children. Mrs. Morgan dissuaded her from going by pointing to the difficulties she would face, especially with the railroad lines destroyed. "I did not want," wrote Mrs. Morgan, "to see her start and maybe die in a fence corner by herself." Nor did she want to face life without a cook, particularly as "no negro could be got for love or money." She offered to pay her cook's fare to Virginia if she would remain with the Morgan household until they were able to return to their home in Nashville. Celia, she wrote, "looked undecided" at this offer, and Mrs. Morgan asked her, "Don't you believe me? Did I ever tell you anything but the truth?" She said "No ma'am, but, missus, is I free?" [76]

Although Mrs. Morgan was able to retain the services of her cook, she was unable to acquire those of a laundress, and her nieces were forced to do the laundry for the first time in their lives. Slaves who had remained when Sherman's troops swept through the region now proceeded to depart en masse. They crowded into the city from the surrounding plantations, as Gertrude Thomas wrote, "loafing around the camps and corners of the streets." By the end of May, Thomas herself retained only two of her slaves, one a young boy and the other a house servant named Patsy. She struggled to hide the way in which her ex-slaves hasty departure undermined her previous worldview. "If any expression of surprise or sorrow was expected by the servants," she wrote defensively, "they were disappointed for none was made by Mr. Thomas or I." The departure of all of her mother's domestic slaves distressed her even more than the departure of her own, as they were longer with the family. This cut more clearly the illusion of one united household.

> Susan . . . Ma's most trusty servant, her advisor, right hand woman and best liked house servant has left her. I am under too many obligations to Susan to have harsh feelings towards her. During six confinements Susan has been with me, the best of servants, rendering the most efficient help. To Ma she has always been invaluable and in case of sickness there was no one like Susan. Her husband Anthony was one of the first to leave the Cumming Plantation and incited others to do the same. I expect he, influenced Susan. . . . She was the first to leave Ma's yard and without a word of warning.[77]

Thomas tried to avoid employing the newly emancipated freedmen and women and made an effort to secure white servants instead. She was successful in finding one girl in the town orphanage to replace one of her children's nurses, Milly, who had left. She wrote of her new white servant, "I am thus far very much pleased with her and Cora Lu gets on admirably with her. I very much prefer her to Milly."[78] Despite her apparent success in finding a nurse, these efforts on her part to replace her former slaves with white help were on the whole a failure. Despite several trips to Dublin, the Irish neighborhood of the city, she was not able to secure any more white servants.

Gertrude Thomas remained dependent upon the services of the freed men and women and tried with little success to perpetuate the kind of control she was accustomed to having under slavery. She described her struggles over the laundry. Whenever the ironing piled up, her servant, Nancy, was now always "sick." This led to a final confrontation with Nancy. Coming into the ironing room to discover "the clothes all piled upon a table, the flies swarming over them," Thomas said, "Nancy do you expect I can afford to pay you wages in your situation, support your two children and then have you sick as much as you are?" Nancy made no reply, but the next day she and her children were gone for good and as a consequence Thomas wrote, "I was again engaged in housework most of the morning."[79]

In a vain effort to resist this wholesale departure of freedpeople from their previous owners, Thomas attempted to require a note of discharge from her new employees. When, however, she requested such a note from a woman she hoped to hire as a cook, the woman simply departed to find more congenial employment elsewhere. Thomas was forced to recognize that she could not hope to exercise such controls over a workforce in such high demand. She told her husband that the effort was like "fighting shadows." "I certainly sacrificed a good deal to principle for I lost an opportunity to get an excellent cook at $5 dollars per month. . . . The fact is that all the best servants belonging to families we know will be engaged by the low class of people and we will have to take inexperienced servants."[80]

Ultimately, despite her best efforts to perpetuate the old order under the altered conditions of the new, Thomas found that she was herself forced to take up ever-increasing amounts of domestic labor. After Nancy departed with her children she wrote, "I have done a good deal of housework and today startled Frank by saying that I intended ironing—it was amusing to see his look of astonishment but indeed the necessity for it appeared quite imminent." The following month, Eliza Izard described a similar situation in a letter to her sister. "We are tired to death, scratching to keep ends together and doing our own work. . . . It is all dreadful, universal misery."[81]

Just as the increased autonomy of black men was understood to mirror the decline in the independence and power of white men, the increased control that black women gained over their own labor was directly reflected in the necessity of white women taking up the work formerly done by slaves. As white men were called upon to transform their understanding of their own manhood, white women were forced to confront a massive change in the meaning of their womanhood, in Thomas's particular case, in the meaning of her "ladyhood." After describing the manner in which her mother's household was shattered by the departure of her female slaves, Thomas sketched her image of these new freedwomen as they appeared in the town. "Yesterday numbers of the negro women some of them quite *black* were promenading up the streets with black lace veils shading them from the embrowning rays of the sun, under whose influence they have worked all their lives."[82]

Much as black men would shortly acquire the vote, that fundamental symbol of political independence, black women were appropriating the veil. For Thomas this was a vision of gender similitude that was inconceivable until she saw it before her very eyes. She was, for the first time, forced by the actions of these women to see *them* within the context of *her* own experience of womanhood. It was a vision of likeness, however, that in its very origins undercut the patriarchal ground of her previous benevolent feelings toward her slaves. When she finally had to see these black women as women like herself, she also had to confront the decline of the patriarchal power of her slaveowning husband and of the protected status that she derived from him. Where they had once been united, however antagonistically, as dependents within the same household, black and white women now stood divided by the interests of their separate households and their respective men. As Thomas wrote in June of 1865, "I must confess to you my journal that I do most heartily despise Yankees, Negroes and everything connected with them. . . . I positively instinctively shut my ears when I hear the hated subject mentioned and right gladly would I be willing never to place my eyes upon another as long as I live. Everything is entirely reversed. I feel no interest in them whatever and I hope I never will."[83]

> Forgetting that he had ever led heroes, [he] contended to make
> bread for his wife and little ones. This marks the true man.
>
> —*Augusta Daily Constitutionalist*, June 14, 1865

5

The Domestic Reconstruction of Southern White Men

Early on the morning of May 10, 1865, Jefferson Davis was camped outside Macon, Georgia, with a small entourage. Although a ship was waiting for him at Pensacola, he had delayed his own escape from the country in order to rejoin his wife and children, hoping to secure their safety as well. Hearing the approach of Union cavalry, Davis made one last effort to escape capture and hastily donned what turned out to be his wife's waterproof. As he fled their tent in the misting half light, Varina Davis threw her shawl over her husband's head as well. Taken by Union officers before he could mount his horse, Jefferson Davis appeared to the world as a man dressed in his wife's clothes in a last desperate effort to elude his fate.[1]

Taken to Macon under heavy guard, Davis and his family were transported by rail to Augusta, where they were transferred to a light craft that carried them down the Savannah River to a waiting oceangoing steamer. News of the president's capture preceded him to Augusta, and as heavily armed troops lined the thoroughfare citizens thronged the main street of the town on the day of his arrival to catch a last glimpse of their fallen leader. Hearing the news that Jefferson Davis was in Augusta a prisoner, Gertrude Thomas buried her face in a pillow and wept bitterly. "This was indeed," she wrote, "the climax of our downfall." Turning to her young son, she urged him to go out and try to catch a glimpse of Davis as he passed by. "Perhaps you may be allowed to get near enough to him to speak," she counseled her son. "If you can, go up to him and say, Mr. Davis will you permit a little southern boy to shake your hand?"[2]

Out on the street, the Federal troops were in no temper to humor a young boy, but were in fact quick to arrest any members of the crowd who engaged in such acts of disloyalty to their newly established power. Indeed, the assembled crowd stood by silently as the entourage passed, except for Henry Harford Cumming, one of the town's leading citizens, who insisted upon honoring Jefferson Davis. As his son, Joseph Cumming, recounted years later, Henry Cumming, "in the sight of all men, stepped forward, lifted his hat and remained uncovered until the prisoner had passed." Addressing Jefferson Davis he said, "Mr. President, I salute you." Commanding Cumming to "Halt," the leader of the guard demanded his name and his place of residence. Cumming stalwartly replied, "My name is Henry H. Cumming. I reside just here, sir." Within the year, however, Henry Cumming was no longer a resident of Augusta. Burdened down by the loss of one of his sons in the war and plagued by postwar economic difficulties, he was thrown into a deep melancholy. Haunted by the fear that his economic decline would render him unable to provide for his family, he was beset by the fear that his wife would be brought to "poverty and want." Finally, on April 14, 1866, he committed suicide.[3]

Thus passed the President of the Confederacy and one of the most prominent citizens of the town. What began as an effort on the part of these men to defend a particular construction of manhood—a construction that at its most extreme was grounded in the right of at least some men to be the masters of slaveholding households—had ended in death and defeat. Like their captured president, the white male citizens of Augusta were now stripped of their political independence, even as the town itself was put under military control. At the same time, the arrival of the occupying troops underscored the official emancipation of the slaves. This abolition of the system of slavery, which so many of them had originally gone to war to defend, undercut the social and economic power of the white male household head from the inside as surely as political defeat subverted his position from the outside. These men had staked their sense of themselves as free men upon their successful founding of an independent nation; the defeat of the Confederacy now presented them with an overwhelming threat to the very deepest level of their masculine identity.[4]

The most fundamental change confronted them in the alteration of the basic structure of their households. They could, after all, hope eventually to regain control over their political affairs. The domination by northern troops was humiliating, but it was not likely to last forever. The wealth that the war and emancipation cost them could conceivably be replaced. The loss of their position as slaveowners, however, was permanent. Henceforth they could never again be empowered by holding other human beings as a form of property, by treating them as a simple extension of their own interest and their will. While the white elite might endeavor to replace the control that slave ownership had given them through both legal and extralegal means, such attempts were poor substitutes for the direct and organic grasp of power that slave ownership had conferred upon them.[5]

The fate of the remainder of the household dependents, in particular that of their female dependents, was also called into question by this sundering of the master-slave relationship in the context of defeat by the North. Paternalistic claims in relation to their slaves might lie in shards around their feet, but in relation to their own family they might hope for a persistence of their dominant position as household head. While their public position in relation to other men, whether those men were the occupying Yankees or the freedmen, might now be largely outside their ability to control, their domestic relationship to their wives and children remained as one arena of both responsibility and self-identification. Here was the one apparently nonantagonistic relationship of domination that remained to southern white men, the one arena in which they could hope to persist as "men," in the original antebellum sense of the word.[6]

Rather than looking out to the exterior construction of manhood, however, to their relationships with other men in the public arena, these men were now called upon to alter their self-concept by attaching themselves more firmly to the domestic arena, as *the* location of self-realization. The striking fluidity of female gender roles that the war had unleashed was now matched in the postwar period by a striking transformation in the proper forms of manly behavior. The underlying thread that remained constant was the attachment of both men and women to the material necessities associated with the reproduction of life. While the war served to turn women's gendered roles inside out in the pursuit of their domestic attachments, the political and economic repercussions of defeat required that men should now turn theirs outside in.

The privileged position of antebellum white men had enabled them to assume that a singleminded pursuit of their own individual interests as "free men" would necessarily benefit their familial dependents. In the aftermath of defeat this assumption could no longer be made. The question that now confronted them was simply this: To what extent had the loss of their public and political position reduced them so far that in addition to being unable to "protect" their women they had been reduced to a position that was actually *like* that of their women? The demands of fighting the war had already served to reveal that the cotton-producing South, and by extension the southern white men who ran it, was no longer sovereign. Those qualities associated with sovereignty, the power to command and the power to dominate, appeared dysfunctional with the fall of the Confederacy, which placed them at the mercy of the North. On the other hand, those hard-bought qualities that their women had acquired in the trials of the struggle, the ability to accept loss and to carry on, the ability to submit to forces outside one's control, appeared to offer a better ground for the reconstruction of defeated southern white manhood and for southern gender relations more generally.

The northern press certainly seized upon the image of the defeated Confederate president dressed in female garb to press home the point that in defeat Confederate men had indeed become *like* their women. Just as the southern press had lauded those women who dressed as men to follow their men into the battle for southern independence, the northern press now reveled in the retreat of the vanquished leader of the Confederacy in woman's attire. As the war had promoted a generalized masculinization of the entire culture, drawing even women into activities previously limited to men, the northern press gloated over the female costume of Jefferson Davis, implying that defeat had indeed pushed Confederate men into a subordinate status previously appropriate only to their wives and daughters. If the war had constituted the ultimate test of their manhood, what could they be in defeat but women? At least, concluded the northern press, they were no longer really men.[7]

From the northern context, where victory was a sign of manhood, the subjected Confederates now did indeed appear to be "unmanned." Only by shifting their line of vision from the public arena could southern white men hope to reclaim their identity. Ironically, it was only through their attachment to their families, by placing greater significance on the sphere of domestic life, that they could recover their sense of manhood anew. But would they be able to accomplish this shift without being reduced to the same subordinate status as their women? This was the critical question. Only the persistence of their authority over their women could protect them against such a fate. As a result, the perpetuation and persistence of gender difference and hierarchy in postbellum white society became absolutely pivotal.[8]

Somehow, white men's private relationships to their women had to be made to compensate for their public losses at the hands of other men. As one local editorial concluded in the face of imminent Confederate defeat, it was as though "the mighty oak" was "hit by lightning" and only the "clinging vine now kept it erect." Fortunately for the fate of the stricken oak, it was apparently "ordained by providence" that woman, the "ornament and dependent of man in his happier hours," would in defeat become his "stay and solace when smitten with dire and sudden calamities winding herself into the rugged recesses of his nature and binding up the broken heart."[9]

Under these circumstances gendered relations became highly politicized. Confederate men looked to the domestic arena as their one remaining location of legitimate domination just as the same war that had defeated them on all other terrains had increased, however painfully, the autonomy of their women. The very absence of men at the front had served to erode gendered difference; as many women were forced to take over the management of their own households, others were called upon to take up wage labor for the first time. As the war effort itself became dependent upon the public organization of the previously privatized domestic labors of women, women's efforts to clothe, feed, and nurse the troops had served to reveal the way in which their own domestic labors literally created, or at least underpinned, the public position of their men. Women themselves became public figures, and their work became visible through the formation of their own autonomous organizations to support the war effort, like that of the wayside home or the Ladies' Aid Society.[10]

It was not possible simply to return to the antebellum quid pro quo, where, as George Fitzhugh argued, a woman's only right was to "protection" and her primary duty was to "obey."[11] In practical terms alone, the weakened economic condition of southern white men, whether as a result of wartime destruction or of the loss of their slaves, meant that they were hard-pressed to provide the same standard of "protection" for their family. Unable to "protect his wife" in the face of political defeat and economic loss, Henry Cumming escaped the impending challenge by ending his own life.

For most of the defeated Confederate men of Augusta, however, life, of necessity, did go on. The only way to survive was to transform the proper location and content of their manhood. While the local citizenry resented the northern newspapers treatment of their fallen leader, their own press had, in fact, made the same association between defeat and emasculation even more stridently and forthrightly during the final months of the war. Questions of men's gendered identity were discussed at some length because the looming possibility of defeat undercut southern men's *own* assumptions about the basis of their gendered identity. They worked desperately to hang on to their antebellum conception of themselves that they had gone to war in order to defend. However, as the prospects of victory grew increasingly dim and disaffection from the cause rose to new heights, the local press could only attempt to shame the town's male citizens into a continued support of the war effort by accusing them of actually *being* women. The country was being ruined "for want of men." Instead the town was filling up with "the croaking and carping of pantalooned 'stay at homes.' "[12]

One writer to the paper, signing himself a "Border State Man," contrasted the militant behavior of the men of the deep South upon the outset of the conflict with what he characterized as their increasingly craven behavior in the last year of the war. When the border states had initially urged caution they had insisted upon their right to "fly out of the Union like bounding bucks" and "haughtily replied that [they] were free men and had the nobility of spirit to dare maintain your right or to die in their defense." Now when truly called to the test these same men were apparently willing to "slip back into the Union like crouching spaniels." The ultimate questioning of these men's gendered status, however, occurred when he asserted it inconceivable that southern women could find any man to love in such cowards. How could women who had sent their men women's pantaloons when they failed to enlist at the outset of the war now regard their men's craven behavior with anything but contempt? How could such a woman bring herself to "clasp her arms around her husband's neck," knowing all the while that the "Yankee collar is considered by him worth quite as much." [13]

In an article entitled "True Manhood," the *Augusta Daily Constitutionalist* offered up the antithesis of this unmanly conduct in the behavior of one Marcus Jerome Clark, a young man who died heroically on the battlefield. As a true exemplar of masculine behavior, he chose death in the service of his ideals before dishonor. His last words were, "I die before my manhood, and yet I have been a man to my country." If, the editorial concluded, the men out skulking in the swamps would only emulate young Marcus Clark and "BE A MAN," their collective independence could be defended and even the Yankees, those "imps of Satan," could not rob them of it. [14]

Although the press lambasted male shirkers for their increasing reluctance to defend what now appeared to be a thoroughly lost cause, they rarely criticized the dedication of Augusta's women to the war effort. While some of the men appeared to falter in their commitment to their independence when that commitment demanded their willingness actually to fight and die, women were rarely criticized for failure to live up to their own gendered responsibilities. Until the end, Confederate women of the town continued to nurse the sick and wounded, care for the returning soldiers at the wayside home, and scrape together what little they had for the soldiers at the front. In victory or defeat, the domestic tie persisted. For the men, their defeat on the battlefield signaled the failure of political independence and cast their masculinity into doubt. Victory or defeat, however, had no effect on the attachment of women to the domestic needs of their men, which remained constant regardless of the war's outcome. As a result, the local press concluded that women were in reality of a "two fold nature." During periods of social crisis and revolution, they were capable of acts of "adamantine strength," the "shocks" of which were such as to "topple over poor, frail men who are by a figure of speech supposed to be made of 'sterner stuff.'" [15]

Seen from this domestic perspective of Confederate wives, mothers, and daughters, the failure of the Confederate war effort itself was not an unmitigated loss. The end of the war meant not only defeat of the Confederate drive for independence, but also an end to the destruction of human lives, of women's sons, husbands, and fathers, that had hitherto been sacrificed in the quest for independence. Thus Gertrude Thomas's initial response to the news that the Confederacy had fallen was to weep for joy as she realized that her brother at the front had "come home to stay— had not fallen a sacrifice to the Moloch of war. I burst into tears and wept for joy—Mr. Thomas said 'why, what are you crying for?' and could not understand it, but any woman will." For her husband, the end of the war signaled not only the defeat of Confederate hopes for independence, but also of his own position as a slaveholding male citizen. Gertrude Thomas described him as being "cast down, utterly spirit broken" at the official news of defeat. She found him to be "particularly sensitive upon the subject, expects *no good times*." And although her brother was glad to be home once again, he "like *every true man* and soldier deeply feels the humiliation of our surrender." [16]

If Gertrude Thomas's first response to the news of defeat was to rejoice that her brother was spared, her second thought was to sympathize with those women who had lost their male relations in the war and now had nothing to show for it. "Oh how unutterably sad how bereaved must those families feel who have lost some dear member in the effort to accomplish a Confederacy. Valuable lives lost and nothing accomplished!" [17] For these women, who had taken the cause of their men's liberty as their own, the consolation of national independence was also gone. "For thee, oh my country," wrote Susan Cornwell, "how many mothers have ceased their wailing for the first born left lying cold and naked on the battlefield, or stark and stiff in the dreary hospital? For thee how many a loving wife hath stilled the heart yearning for him who but lately was its cherished idol, how many a sister hath quited her agony . . . and silently resolved to 'suffer and grow strong.'" [18]

Those men who failed to return home, Cornwell continued, had fallen "victims of their love of liberty." [19] The truest of men, those like Marcus

Clark, had died with their independence. For those who returned without their liberty, defeat was indeed a new sort of trial, which could prove to be an unbearable humiliation.

In order to carry on, they had to struggle to find a greater sense of self-worth in a different kind of love, concluded Cornwall, the love of their wives and children. To do so would require that they learn to "obey those who so late were in deadly array against us" but who now "control our minutest affairs." This was the bitterest lesson that the defeat of the Confederacy had to teach the "proud Southron," to learn to subordinate themselves to the very same men they had fought four long years to be independent of. "Now," wrote Cornwall, "chafe as you may under the yoke, you must submit—how hard." As both the slaves and the women of the planter class had recognized in the antebellum period, the way to accept such subordination to another man's will and yet retain some sense of self-respect was to acknowledge a master above the master, to believe that subordination on this earth was but a prelude to some ultimate self-realization in another. "Teach us, Oh, Father," wrote Cornwall, "those lessons of patience and resignation which hitherto we have refused to learn and grant that once more we may lift our hearts to thee and cry *Our* Father!"[20]

During the war itself, Cornwall frequently drew a connection between Confederate victories and the religiosity of the troops. Victories she welcomed as a sign that the Confederates were the true children of God; failure on the battlefield, she concluded, was a direct reflection of the lack of a proper faith and humility among the soldiers. Joseph Jones wrote to his wife early in the war that the rampant destruction wrought by the Union troops of what he described as the "wealth of a century" served to reveal the "futility of earthly possessions with their engrossing cares and sordid affections." Defeat and destruction on the battlefield constituted a sign that Confederate men had indeed overstepped themselves, that they had lost sight of their proper place in the divine order of things. As Charles Rowland wrote to his wife upon one crushing defeat toward the war's close, such total failure of Confederate forces on the battlefield could only indicate that "God was against us."[21]

The struggle to accept postwar defeat engendered humiliation and depression among these men. It forced them to confront the depth of their own religious convictions in the process. For only through relinquishing their own authority to a higher one could they find consolation in their faith. Only by reconceiving their own proper place among men and accepting some newfound limits to their authority could they make peace. As the *Augusta Chronicle* concluded upon the final defeat of the Confederacy, "We have become an overpowered and armless people . . . powerless to resist . . . let us be orderly and peaceful, obeying the laws prescribed for our government, and leave the rest to the wise dispensations of HIM, who, had we better served, might have given to the South that victory which he has withheld from it and too surely bestowed upon another." [22]

The struggle to reconcile themselves to the loss of public power through an acknowledgement of their ultimate subordination to the workings of an almighty force outside their ken absorbed the energies of some of the town's citizens. Gertrude Thomas wrote of the response of one prominent Augusta minister, J. E. Evans, to the defeat. He confessed to her in the course of a Sunday dinner at her house that the necessity of reconciling himself to defeat was "the greatest trial to his Christian grace that he had ever had to contend with." For other men, the problems and possibilities associated with a return to family life absorbed their energies. Whatever their public and political losses, there was, after all, what remained of the family circle. If anything, argued Susan Cornwall, the family should be more valued in the name of those members who were lost in the war and would never return. Beyond that, she offered the family and domestic ties as a substitute for the independence and public power that men of her class had held before defeat. She painted a bleak picture of the fate of their president, Jefferson Davis, forced to languish in prison, stripped of all security, even of his own dwelling and the comfort of his family. By contrast, she advised the depressed men of her class and race, "You have still your homes, your wives and children are around you, sharing your sorrows as well as your joys. Though you may not have as many luxuries as in former days, you still have enough to eat and wear, and can repose in security." [23] Like their women, these men would now have to find meaning and self-fulfillment within the narrower confines of a subordinated domestic place.

During the war, women's domestic interests had been turned toward supporting their men's struggle for independence. Now with the defeat of the war effort, domestic life could at least regain some integrity, however attenuated by war losses. A defeat in all other regards, the end of the war could at least be viewed as a domestic victory. Charles Rowland wrote to his wife from the front to describe the terms of the armistice. "Our government is destroyed, our money of no value and we have to go back in the Union." There was some consolation to be taken in the restoration of domestic order, however. "You can," he wrote to his wife, "take up your silver and be easy once more." While he worried about the economic difficulties to come, he assured his wife that if they could get "pure water and corn meal, we can survive." [24]

Here, in their role as fathers, husbands, and sons, defeated Confederate men found an avenue of opportunity as well as responsibility. Faced with the loss of their political autonomy as well as their power to own slaves, ex-Confederate men could at least hope to return to their old position as the protectors and providers of their women and children. Rather than "yield to despair" in the face of their diminished power relative to northern men or of the possible consequences of emancipation, the local press repeatedly urged defeated Confederate men to turn their emotional energies toward their own families and to once again take up their domestic duty to "feed the women and children whom we are bound to support." [25]

The same newspaper that had in the closing months of the war described some of its male citizens as "pantalooned stay at homes," inclined to give up the struggle like "crouching spaniels," now asserted that acquiescence to Federal authority would not constitute the emasculation of the town's white male citizenry, as they had so vociferously claimed only a few months before. On the contrary, the local citizenry was advised to accept the imposition of military authority precisely *because* it would allow them to carry out their manly responsibilities—now defined in domestic terms rather than as the public pursuit of their rights as "free" men. The failure of this pursuit was in fact made tolerable by expanded recognition of the import of men's domestic role. Their first priority should now be to turn their energies toward the difficult task of supporting their wives and children. "It is neither unwise nor unmanly to thus acquiesce in the logic of existing facts," one editorial concluded, "and thus cheerfully pursue the only path left to regain the position lost to us by the 'fortunes of war.'" [26]

Making such an about-face was no easy matter. It was no longer possible to assume that simply by pursuing their public status as "free men" the interests of their dependents would automatically follow. Defeat sheared apart these two aspects of men's gendered role and forced them back upon their domestic responsibilities without any corresponding public position. In his annual speech in the fall of 1865, Mayor R. H. May tried to shake the citizens out of the demoralization that had ensued. "Let us not brood over our losses," he urged his listeners, but rather "profit by the experience of the past." The region, he argued, was blessed with immense natural resources that were only partially developed. The war had served to reveal Augusta's possibilities as an industrial center. Her experience as one of the Confederacy's most critical workshops for the production of military goods could now stand her citizens in good stead. While only time could "heal the humiliation of defeat and heal the gaping wounds which man has made," the mayor concluded, by their own labors they could hope to support their families and to develop the economic resources of the town as well. Only through their "own exertions" could they hope to "retrieve our disasters."[27]

The local press concurred with the mayor, arguing that a manly course of behavior now demanded submission to northern political domination so that the business of life might go on. "True chivalry" required the citizenry to "yield gracefully when fairly vanquished." This was no less man's duty than to "fight manfully while he has the power." Who, after all, was the true exemplar of southern manhood, General Lee in his surrender to General Grant or the assassin of Abraham Lincoln? In surrendering to forces beyond his control, Lee had evidenced the greater courage. As Mrs. Irby Morgan wrote of Lee in her postwar recollections, although "crushed and broken-hearted" at the defeat of the Confederacy, he at least never gave way to despondency after the war. He refused to give up the "battle of life" simply because he had lost the military encounter. Instead he "went to work again and died in harness."[28]

This was an image that both the press and the mayor worked to reinforce. The "battle of life" had moved to the forefront of the postbellum construction of manhood. The essential manliness of labor, no matter how humble, was assured if that labor were undertaken in the support of family life. And if the example of Lee himself were not sufficient to convince depressed citizens, stories of "Lee's gallant captains" also appeared on the pages of the local press. One such officer was described as ploughing a small field with what had been his war horse. "Forgetting that he had ever led heroes, [he] contended to make bread for his wife and little ones. This marks the true man." As long as a year after the war, the press was still recording such stories, describing young men around the city still wearing their "faded jackets of grey," while industriously tilling the soil. "These men are heroes, as much to be commended in private life," concluded one editorial, "as they were deserving of praise on the battle-field."[29]

From this domestic perspective, acceptance of a newly subordinate public and political status not only did not constitute a violation of masculinity, it was in fact critical in promoting what was most fundamental to it, the well-being of a man's wife and children. For only in accepting their loss of power in relation to other men, whether these were Yankees or freedmen, could ex-Confederates hope to thrive in their private role as fathers and husbands. Having dedicated all of his energies to the Confederate cause, Joseph Jones found himself with "nothing left, but a wife, three children, my profession & an indomitable will to labor." He was grateful, however, to find a support for his family through his own efforts as a doctor, and a year after the war's close he wrote with some pride that "we have great cause for gratitude . . . I have been able to make both ends meet and have provided a comfortable support for the family."[30]

Many men of the town were not as fortunate as Joseph Jones. Although commerce boomed briefly after the end of the war, the state of trade in the town declined precipitously a few months later. The depressed state of the economy meant that the kind of positions elite men were accustomed to filling were frequently not to be had. Allen Izard's nephew wrote from Augusta in the summer following defeat of being "restive & anxious to do some thing, never mind how little." And Paul Verdery, a member of the local planter elite, returned home from the war to find work, but only of a manual sort on his father's plantation. "It is pretty humiliating," he wrote to his sister in the fall of 1865, "for a Parlor Gentleman like myself to be seen stripping fodder in the field, and doing all sorts of rough work about a farm, but I don't mind for it contributes to my health." It also contributed to his sister's education, and he urged her to remain with her aunt in Athens and continue to attend school as long as her aunt was able to keep her. "Don't trouble yourself about our work," he concluded, "for we get along very well."[31]

Paul Verdery's labors in the fields were matched by the expansion of housework among the women of the family. They were all, as he put it, "busy as Bees." Paul Verdery was, in fact, delegated the responsibility of writing to his sister because the women of the family, who would otherwise have written, found themselves without the time. Not that they were entirely without hired domestic help even in their reduced circumstances, but much of the housework that prior to emancipation would have been done by their slaves they were now forced to take up themselves. They continued to hire the labor of one woman, a "Negro girl (Julia)," who was however, employed both as their laundress and as a farm laborer. With this exception of the laundry, the women of the family were now apparently called upon to perform all their own housework.[32]

In taking up the housework, the Verdery women experienced a class fall that mirrored the experience of their men, who were reduced to laboring in the fields. Both were a reflection of their loss of control over black labor. However, the women of the family remained on the plantation, immersed in their daily domestic tasks, long after Paul Verdery was able to find a position clerking in Augusta. Writing to his sister in the fall of 1865, he expressed his pleasure at his new position. Although he received "a mere trifle" for his labors, he concluded that it was considerably "better than nothing." In fact, his position as a clerk represented a decided advance over farm labor. Still, it did not provide a wage sufficient to maintain what he considered to be a proper appearance. He wrote to his sister in October 1865 describing himself as being in "desperate need" of a new coat and appealed to her to make one for him as he could not afford to have it made in town. She did so, and upon receipt of the garment, he described himself as being "highly pleased" with her effort and promised to "return the favor" if the opportunity ever presented itself.[33] Paul Verdery remained dependent upon the domestic labors of the women of his family to make up the difference between the appearances appropriate to his public position and his ability to earn in a sluggish postwar economy.

In exchange for the contribution that his sister made toward his keeping up an appearance appropriate to his newfound position as clerk, Paul Verdery expressed a heightened recognition of his dependence and indebtedness to the domestic labors of his female relations. This was not a new recognition on his part, however, for he had previously acknowledged such indebtedness during the war itself. In the same vein the local press argued that the wartime contributions of the Ladies' Aid Society actually offered a model for women to follow in the economic difficulties of the postwar period. "Ladies," concluded one such editorial, "there were heroines among you in the crowded hospitals, on the bloody battlefields, wherever there was pain to be alleviated, or fainting hearts to be strengthened . . . and we feel assured that there is no emergency you cannot meet, no exigency for which you are not provided."[34] Such women could surely be relied upon to serve their men's best interests in peace, as they had so generously served them in war.

The distinguishing characteristic of women's wartime labors was apparently not their public or independent organization, but rather what they indicated of the lengths to which these women had been willing to go to maintain their domestic relationship to their men. Rather than reflecting a fundamental break with their independent and public wartime activities, their redoubled domestic labors were therefore understood as a simple reflection of the persistence of this domestic attachment, now under the altered circumstances created by defeat. Now that their men's interests were directed inward, toward the family rather than outward, toward the assertion of their status as free men in an independent nation, women's labors were expected to follow suit and to return to a privatized domestic focus.[35]

As in the case of Confederate men, their women were now being called upon to find their sense of self-worth in the expansion of their domestic roles within the family. Through an intensification of their gendered consciousness, they too could cushion themselves against the implications of their economic decline. They could even hope to find in the very labors that had previously been the lot of their slaves an increased self-esteem. Women who had rarely known such labor before the war could take pride in the contribution that they now made to the viability of their households, much as during the war they had taken pride in the contribution that their domestic labors made to the struggle for Confederate independence.

During the war, however, the intensification of Confederate women's labors was assumed to be temporary and to make up a vital part of an effort to underwrite and even expand their privileged class and racial position through the establishment of the political and economic position of their men. While their wartime labors did indeed constitute a reflection of their love and concern for the health and well-being of their families, as the local press asserted, they also served to increase these women's individual autonomy within the household as well as in the public arena.

By contrast, the defeat of the Confederate war effort and the emancipation of the slaves created an apparently permanent structural change within the elite household that was entirely uncompensated by any public advance for the ex-Confederates of either sex. For this reason, the local press labored as hard to stress the inherent dignity of domestic labor for elite women as it worked to promote the acceptability of field labor on the part of elite men. In parallel fashion, elite women were urged to recognize that although they might not empower themselves as individuals through their labors, their families as a whole would benefit. One editorial actually went so far as to conclude that with the "plethora of labor saving devices," the loss of slave labor really would not create much of an added burden for their previous owners. In fact, for those families with more than one adult woman, the increase in domestic labor would be inconsiderable. Slaveowning women had long complained of the difficulties in running a household with unwilling slave labor. Now through the presumably willing labor of mothers, wives, and daughters, some even anticipated that the household might actually function more efficiently than it had under the old order.[36]

The economic decline of elite women could therefore actually create the basis for an improved domestic life. Although as individuals they might be required to labor more diligently at unaccustomed tasks, they could take heart in the knowledge that their individual sacrifice contributed not only to the economic recovery of their families, but also to the improvement of their household's domestic life. According to the local press, the postwar situation offered women an avenue of opportunity that was, in its own way, even more substantial than that provided by the war itself. While Confederate women had seized the opportunity to make a public and recognized contribution to the war effort, the war was grounded in the defense of individual male rights and prerogatives that as women they could not personally share. Although the war promised to empower their men, in reality it had also torn their families apart and threatened their children, the most precious of their fruits. Now the postwar situation offered to empower women in a different way, not through the increased power of their men in the public arena, not even by their own opportunities to be "like" their men. Rather, it was by drawing men more closely into their own domestic location that they would empower and exalt their feminized place. As the local press concluded, if "every woman" in a southern household would only accept her changed economic circumstances, as necessity would force her to in any case, she could then make a critical contribution to the "happiness, energy and usefulness of the whole land."[37]

The gendered location of elite women thus emerged as the critical position from which to supply the energy that would be necessary for the postwar recovery of their class as a whole. As the local press pointed out, these women were much better able to sustain their spirits in the face of "overwhelming reverses of fortunes" than were their men. They more easily accepted defeat. Women took the decline of their race and class in stride with more "quiet uncomplaining dignity" than their men were able to muster. Among the women "there has been no outcry or complaint, no impatient railing against the adverse destiny, no eating dust and rending of garments under the feet of the conquerors." Disasters that broke men's spirits and left them "prostrate in the dust" appeared only to call forth new-found energies among the local women, giving a previously unsuspected "elevation" to their characters.[38]

Women were better able to accept their own reduced position with dignity, as their status had always been defined not simply by their dominant race or class position, but by their subordinated gender position as well. As a result, they had no public status in their *own* right to lose; although they certainly felt the loss of the Confederacy they did not, in contrast to their menfolk, experience it in so direct and personal a sense. Insofar as they existed as *individuals* in their own right, they were accustomed to subordination and lack of public power. This did not mean, however, that they easily or willingly accepted the defeat of their men. Indeed, in some ways, they were more unforgiving of the loss of manhood that defeat entailed than were their men. While ex-Confederate men fell into depression upon defeat and questioned whether their being vanquished on the battlefield did not indeed indicate a failure of masculinity, their women had no such *personally* sobering experiences.[39]

Having identified with men's belligerence during the war, they could not so easily give up this identity. The Confederate cause had cost many women their husbands, sons, and brothers, and women could not easily accept that they had died in vain. The local press, which complimented women on their ability to accept their own subordination, also complained about their "unladylike" treatment of the Yankees. "We are told that a large number of ladies are heard almost daily uttering oaths in the Provost Marshal's office." This behavior could apparently be attributed to an excess of enthusiasm generated by sermons that local clergymen had preached during the war. The editorial concluded that "We trust our divines will preach more religion and less belligerent doctrines hereafter. Then the fair sex, at least, can obey the scriptures and 'swear not at all.' "[40]

Even at the turn of the century, Joseph B. Cumming Jr. recalled that "sentiments and loyalties were still strong" among the women he knew in Augusta. He wrote of his cousin, Anna Montgomery, who refused to attend the wedding of his future father-in-law since it was to the daughter of the commandant of the U.S. Arsenal and therefore required that she attend a ceremony over which the United States flag was flying. "Extreme case, yes," concluded Cumming, "but not unique." Another "aged relative" cried when he came to say good-bye before leaving to fight overseas in World War I. She "became tearful," however, "not because I might be killed in battle, but because it distressed her to see a kinsman wearing a Yankee uniform."[41]

Such women never faced the possibility of losing their life or their limbs in order to truly "BE A MAN." They indentified with their men's public position, a position upon which they were dependent but which they did not, themselves, occupy. As a result they could maintain an ideal that sober reality may have forced their male relations to abandon. Identifying with the position of their men, but lacking the concrete experience of life within the male realm, women could persist undaunted in their conviction of their superiority over the foes who had triumphed over them. On the other hand, with their own discrete location and practice, they could offer men an alternative arena for the reconstruction of self-worth in the face of the very real public defeat they had suffered.

With the tables turned and the centrality of domesticity correspondingly heightened, women were now in a position to be "heroic" in their defense of the "fortunes of a hapless husband." This shift to domesticity, however, offered these women no more autonomy as individuals. In fact it demanded a further relinquishment of their own sense of self in the name of the "larger" interests of their men and their families. It was out of their own intensified subordination to the needs of their men's egos that these women found the power to hold up their husbands, "crushed under the weight of defeat." With "words of comfort and patience," they could lead men to "peace and resignation." Against the crushing weight of men's defeat in the public arena, they could offer up themselves as a last legitimate terrain of domination. Through their very submergence of self, they could continue to provide the foundation for a renewed male sense of masculinity. As one editorial concluded, "I have noticed that a married man falling into misfortunes is more apt to retrieve his situation in the world than a single one, chiefly because his spirits are soothed and relieved by domestic endearments and self respect, kept alive by finding that, although abroad may be darkness and humiliation, yet there is still a little world of love at home of which he is monarch."[42]

Thus, men and women could both realize themselves through an intensification of their original gendered identities, while order could be established in an otherwise disorderly world through the one arena in which some white elite control was still retained. The gendered relation could expand in its significance for men's self-esteem at the same time as women's lack of self could create the material basis for it. As a result of this willing subordination on the part of women, "a spirit of independence" would come to replace the "inertness which has hitherto paralyzed all of our efforts."[43]

Nevertheless, simply reestablishing domestic relations on their traditional footing was not possible when the economic underpinnings of these traditional relations had so precipitously collapsed. Men's inability to provide meant that women's position within the family was not as hermetically sealed as it had been prior to the war. Just as the postwar economic situation meant that providing for their families became increasingly problematic at precisely the moment in which defeat and political occupation caused men to look inward, the expansion of women's economic role during the war and the continued necessity of their economic contribution in some form could run directly counter to their men's heightened need to provide in order to affirm their manhood. The most obvious way to reconcile the necessity to supplement men's ability to provide with the appearance of depending on male labors alone was to be found in the act of "economizing." Rather than earning money, women could contribute to improving family living standards by cutting back on domestic costs. In particular, by expanding and intensifying their own unpaid labors, women could make smaller incomes go farther. This recalls the position of GEF on the contribution that she had hoped to make to the war effort itself: "If I can't make money by my work, I can save what little I have." Women "might not be able to earn, but they could save." The straitened condition of the postwar economy served only to intensify the wisdom of that advice. By reducing their expenditures as well as taking up more domestic labor, women could enable their men to support the household on their "meagre earnings" and thereby bolster their sense of self-worth.[44]

The local press labored to encourage ex-Confederate women to accept their decline in class position, to economize with grace. Some were able to do so with apparent equanimity. For others, however, the consequences of defeat and the postwar economic difficulties were not so easily negotiated. One man wrote to Charles Colcock Jones describing how the economic decline of his family was such as to threaten his wife and daughters' physical well-being. "My eldest daughter has been quite ill and is now at the North with her Mother, hoping to find health in the change of climate and relief from all household duties which are now dreadfully onerous at the South, and will with the climate break down all ladies unless we can make a change in the labour both in and out of doors."[45]

Other women eventually made the transition, but only after an intense and bitter struggle. Some women, not unlike men such as Henry Cumming, were simply unable to adapt themselves. Nor was it, as the press implied, an inherent characteristic of women's nature to "adhere to the fortunes of a fallen husband" with self-abnegating good grace. Gertrude Thomas and her husband, Jefferson Thomas, found their marriage stressed almost to the breaking point by economic and social strains of household life in the postwar period.[46]

While the Thomases were among the wealthiest members of the antebellum planter class in the Augusta region, in the sluggish postwar economy Jefferson Thomas found that his efforts to work both his store in town and his various plantations only drove him further into debt. He soon came to regret that he had abandoned his youthful medical studies at the Augusta Medical College. When he had married Gertrude Clanton, a member of one of the largest slaveowning families in Georgia, his future as a planter seemed to be assured, and such professional training had seemed superfluous. Under postwar conditions, however, the economic prospects of a planter were proving to be more uncertain than he could ever have envisioned as a young man.[47] A year after defeat, his wife wrote of the way in which the "unsettled state of the times," the unstable price of cotton on the one hand and the uncertain nature of his control over the labor of the freedmen on the other, worked together to make her husband "worried in mind as well as body." As he sank further into debt each year, his irritability and depression increased. He described himself as being "run to death," and his wife worried that the strain of repeated bankruptcies and forced sales of their properties at public auction was more than his nervous and physical systems could bear.[48]

Gertrude Thomas was also humiliated at the public sale of their property year after year. Finally, in 1868, they were forced to give up their house in Augusta and move out to their plantation, Belmont, in order to economize. With her own economic circumstances in such disarray, she was taken aback by a visit from a friend, who complimented her on her good spirits and who noted that, by contrast, "everyone in Augusta is so depressed." Gertrude Thomas strove diligently to at least keep up the appearance of good spirits, but privately she was as disturbed as the rest of Augusta's defeated white citizenry. The very knowledge of her family's decline, she wrote, "deepened the lines of my face . . . furrowed my brow & aged my heart." Gone forever was the ability of the men of her family to provide endlessly and apparently effortlessly for all that her heart might desire. Gone as well was the position in the world that her relationship to such men had afforded her. "My life, my glory, my honor has been so intimately blended with that of my husband and now to see him broken in fortune, health and spirits" was almost beyond bearing.[49]

Gertrude Thomas experienced her husband's decline as a fundamental severing of her identification with his self-interests as her own. The quid pro quo of her antebellum life, where he "protected" her and in exchange she "obeyed" him was apparently dissolved. Contrasting her antebellum attitude toward her husband to that of the postbellum period, she wrote of her changed perception of his picture. "I shall never forget when Mr. Thomas left for Virginia. I looked forward to coming home and seeing his picture. I remember the awe, the reverence with which I approached the parlour and hesitated, with a similar feeling to that with which one advanced to drag aside the cover from the face of a dead friend. I expected a mournful pleasure." She contrasted her wartime attitude of awe and reverence with her current view of her husband, reduced to the position of mere father to her children. "I entered the room, and staring at me without one gleam of tenderness was the picture of my husband and it gave me no comfort . . . and since then I have only prized it as an excellent likeness to transmit to the children but I do not love and prize it as I did before." Gertrude Thomas seemingly could not recover from what she described as "the sepulchre of my buried pride, my high hopes, my woman's ambition in the success of my husband."[50]

The question for both Jefferson and Gertrude Thomas was how their relationship could be renegotiated. He did not turn easily to the consolation that religion or his family might have offered him, and she did not accept with magnanimity their economic decline or the increased demands placed upon her to sacrifice for her family. In fact, they both initially responded to their economic decline with feelings of humiliation and depression. Gertrude found that the "unaccustomed" necessity of doing her own sewing left her "very tired and impatient." No wonder, she concluded after one difficult bout with her children's clothing, that poor women were "so often cross." She was shamed by the social and economic decline that taking up such labor indicated, and she tried to console herself with the thought that at least her own family would understand. "My relatives are practical common sense *honest* people and they will approve of my trying to make my own dresses." Her husband, however, did not seem very supportive. He was not particularly appreciative of her efforts, as Paul Verdery was of those of his sister. He "never praises," she wrote, and did not appear to appreciate her "puny efforts" to arrest the "floodgates of debt with which I feel that we are contending." "I do not think," she concluded, "that he is that man to appreciate a wearied woman, wearing a faded calico until she can afford a better one, so much as a gay woman, fashionably dressed in clothing for which she is owing the money they cost."[51]

As her relationship with her husband deteriorated, Gertrude Thomas turned with increasing intensity to the comfort that her relationship with her children continued to afford her. "Indeed," she wrote a few short years after the war, "I love all my children more than I ever did before and they are a source of inexpressible comfort to me."[52] She urged her husband to find his own sense of self-worth and fulfillment in a similar intensification of his domestic attachments, but Jefferson Thomas's relationship to his children did not serve to compensate him for his lost public position in as straightforward a way as it did for his wife. In fact, it actually served to intensify his anguish, for as he pointed out to her, he could not hope to retreat entirely to the privacy of their familial life, as she could. His public position and responsibilities as a father could not be reconstructed in the same self-contained and privatized fashion as her own, even if he were so inclined.

Indeed, it was still Jefferson Thomas's responsibility to face the world and to negotiate their slow and painful economic decline, if only to wrest whatever could be saved for the future well-being of the family itself. Gertrude herself recorded what she considered to be the worst of their social humiliation, the frequent bankruptcy proceedings that required her husband's repeated appearances in court. On one such occasion, Jefferson Thomas described himself as the "worst broken man in the world." For all that Gertrude Thomas was mortified on that day, at least she could remain within the privacy of her home. Even so she clung to the power of the domestic tie to transform the meaning of the experience for her husband as well, writing that as he left the house he was "nerved (to try & do the best he can) by kisses upon dear little lips uplifted to his so utterly unconscious of what a weight was on his mind."[53]

For herself, Gertrude Thomas found that the intensification of her relationship to her children, what she described as her "mingled love and pride," served to develop an "energy I had not supposed to be latent in my character" in defense of their interests. For her husband, despite her best efforts, their postwar decline was such as to lead him to try to shed his attachments to children for whom he could no longer hope to carry out his paternal responsibilities.

As he came to realize that he could no longer protect and support his children as he had in the past, Jefferson Thomas began to regard with increasing dread the possibility that his wife might again become pregnant, looking upon more children as just "more mouths to feed and little feet to cover." This attitude on her husband's part, wrote Gertrude, "chills my womanly heart." Rather than feeling distance from her children, Gertrude found not only that her relationship to her children intensified with the family's deteriorating economic circumstances, but that she became ever more committed to protecting them as best as she could. "I have a source of comfort which Mr. Thomas has not. My children and my baby. I hold Julian clasped to my heart & I am nerved to courage—I look upon Turner and I take comfort and whatever happens I *must* do something for the children."[54]

As her energies and ambitions turned toward her children, she came to have a sense of herself as an *active* agent in their protection. Her husband, on the other hand, increasingly saw them not only as a burden he could ill afford, but also as a necessary factor in production. While Gertrude clung to her children's possibilities in life and grieved over their lost future, Jefferson Thomas appeared to think ever more narrowly of his own immediate economic problems. He was in fact soon moved to withdraw his eldest son from school and set him to work in the fields, an act that only served to further alienate his wife's affections. She wrote in her journal of her son's poor treatment by her husband, thinking perhaps of herself as well. "Dear brave good boy stands erect by his fathers side, his confidant, his friend, bearing on his young shoulders the weighty knowledge of our embarrassed situation. He never murmurs, never complains . . . of having no money or of being taken from school to assist in ploughing and other work."[55]

Despite the sacrifices of his son and his wife, Jefferson Thomas manifested only an "extreme depression of spirits," a depression that, according to Gertrude, "reacts upon us all." He had little compassion for his son's trials and responded with sharp irritation to his efforts to find some time to read between farm chores. For her own part, Gertrude was appalled at the ready willingness, not just of her husband but of his male peers in general, to sacrifice their sons' futures to their own immediate economic self-interest. She was not inclined to see the labor of her son in the field as heroic, never mind what Lee's gallant captains might be doing. On the contrary, she wrote that while it took three generations to make a gentlemen, the men of her class were now cavalierly allowing their sons to descend to the ranks of day laborers. "Boys who were born heirs to thousands plough daily side by side with the negro who perhaps works for his victuals and clothes." Such a boy would surely grow up to be "an ignoramus," wrote Thomas, unable to acquire even the most minimal of educations.[56]

It was the repeated failure of her husband to protect their children, even to the point of working her son in the fields, that forced Gertrude to develop individual initiative in her own right. As she put it, the postbellum economic decline of her family "nerved her to courage," causing her to consider with increasing frequency how she might protect her children herself. She began to question her husband's management of the family's financial affairs, at least in the privacy of her journal. She also began to wonder how she might actually *earn* money, tiring of the limited role of economizer. As she wrote in 1870, "Can I make money? At times I have thought I would try and get a situation with Miss Sedgwick or Mrs. Wrights [schools in Augusta]." Jefferson Thomas opposed this final affront to his role as household provider, and she concluded at that time that it was "better for me to content myself with my [sewing] machine and house-keeping."[57] Finally, in 1878 her neighbor who ran the local rural school died, and Gertrude Thomas managed to acquire the position. Jefferson Thomas's economic circumstances still did not improve, however, and when Gertrude wanted to quit school teaching several years later, he actually opposed this because the family had become dependent upon her earnings.

Over the years, both Gertrude and Jefferson Thomas's conception of their proper roles as mother and as father were gradually transformed. While Gertrude became more protective of her children, Jefferson eventually came to accept her expanded public role and to find more consolation in his own domestic duties and responsibilities. Religion played a critical role in this redefinition. Initially Jefferson Thomas found as little solace in his religious faith as he did in his family. He became, in fact, more irreligious after the war than before and began to swear freely, much to his wife's despair. She also found that the collapse of slavery, which she had come to rationalize in religious terms during the war, threw her entire belief system into question.[58]

However, she recovered from this religious crisis several months after the war and in the years that followed found in her religious faith a critical support in the face of the public humiliation of her family, her private trials with housework, and her difficult relations with her husband. Given the consolation she found in her faith, she found her husband's rejection of religion doubly difficult. It set them on a collision course, for rather than growing together as a couple in their common acceptance of a will outside their own, they instead grew ever more estranged as the experience of defeat actually intensified their gendered difference even as it bound them ever more closely in their common experience of decline.

Eventually, however, Jefferson Thomas did experience a religious conversion, and this contributed to his finding more consolation in his familial relations. It was at a camp meeting in August of 1870 that he evidenced a "sincere desire to become a christian." He responded to the minister's appeal to the congregation that those who wished to be "more faithful as parents" should come forward. Gertrude described how "crowds" assembled before the altar in response to the call. When she saw her husband among the rest of the supplicants, she was momentarily "blinded with tears." She saw in her husband's spiritual efforts the possibility for some healing in their own relationship and prayed for divine aid for them both, for she wrote, "I know how weak I am and I feel together we could be so much stronger." Her husband came up to the altar repeatedly and was apparently "locked in great struggle." Finally the minister came over to Gertrude Thomas and said that her husband was "much affected" and suggested that a few words from her might help him. She went over to where he was kneeling but found herself to be without words. "What could I say," she wrote in her journal, "I who was no better than he?" She stayed with him, saying finally, "I am going now. Pray on, and we will both try to be good."[59] She returned to her seat and raised her prayers with the rest of these seated around her. Her prayer was, "God be merciful to me, a sinner," for, as she wrote, "I knew that the best prayer I could make for my husband was to try and be better myself."

Ultimately, then, the rebalancing of the Thomas's relationship in the face of political defeat and economic decline was not dissimilar to that advocated so blithely by the local press. Both Jefferson and Gertrude Thomas found consolation in their renewed religious faith and in their expanded commitment to domestic life. Jefferson Thomas came to accept his wife as a more active "protector" both of their children and of himself. Gertrude Thomas learned in exchange to subordinate herself ever more firmly to her husband's self-empowerment, to make him "better," as she wrote, by being even "better" herself. This was not an equal exchange, however, but an exchange that continued to reflect the asymmetrical power of gender relations. So while Jefferson Thomas came to accept and even see the usefulness of his wife's empowerment, she continued to provide the actual basis for his own. She continued to bemoan the necessity of her exposure to economic forces previously the domain of her husband alone, but she moved with increasing strength toward a new conviction of what it meant to be a good wife and mother. "I console myself with the idea," she wrote several months after the camp meeting, "that I am what every good woman should be—his friend and counsellor, never loving him better than when the day seems darkest and the duty hardest."[60]

In May of 1871, Jefferson Davis finally returned to Augusta, this time as a free man. Gertrude Thomas, who had bitterly criticized

Davis for many of his policies during the war, wrote that he was "dearer, far dearer now in the hour of defeat than he was when chief magistrate of the Southern Confederacy." She recalled his previous march through the town and how she had sympathized with him, "our fallen chieftain in his degradation." It was at that moment, at what she had described at the time as the "climax of our downfall," that Gertrude Thomas found a deep and abiding commitment to the cause. She, like the rest of the defeated Confederate population of Augusta, had been powerless publicly to indicate her support as Davis was taken through the town a prisoner. "No woman daring to wave her handkerchief or make a sign of sympathy," wrote Thomas, "and men so crushed by defeat that the closed carriage passed by crowds who dared not cheer him for fear of sharing his fate." The Thomases had done something on that day, however; they named their young son after Davis. Over the years, she taught her children to preserve his memory and never fail to recite, "I pray God for the release of President Davis."[61]

With Jefferson Davis's return to the town in 1871, Gertrude Thomas, who had cried and remained indoors when Davis passed through the town a prisoner, finally had the occasion to make his acquaintance. She carefully recorded the event in her journal for, as she wrote, "I am writing history for you my children." And upon being introduced to Davis, she took the opportunity to present her son as well, and "drawing Jeff to me I introduced him as Jeff Davis Thomas." She described how Jefferson Davis took her son's hand in his own, drew him closer and placed his arm around him. "I cannot tell you Mrs. Thomas," he replied, "how highly I appreciate the compliment." Suffused with pride, Gertrude Thomas went on to explain the circumstances under which the boy had been named. "Perhaps you will understand Mr. Davis," she said, "how dear you are to the dear daughters of your people as you so gracefully termed us, when I explain that our little boy was named for you the afternoon you passed through Augusta a prisoner. We could do nothing else to express our sympathy and we honored ourselves in naming him for you." "My dear Madam," he replied. "I appreciate the compliment so much the more."[62]

Although the public arena was apparently lost to the members of the defeated white citizenry, or at least they would no longer dominate it as they had in the past, their power in the private arena of their households, however truncated those households were, persisted. In the face of the public humiliation and incarceration of their former leader, the private arena of the family remained to ex-Confederate men, not only as the residual ground for their sense of themselves, but as the ground out of which a new generation of southern men would emerge. Growing up under their mothers' influence, a younger generation of white men arose that could continue to live by the old social order even in the face of new circumstances—at least as long as their families, especially their women, continued to make up the shortfall that defeat to the North and the loss of their slaves had created. Through their own sacrifice and self-denial ex-Confederate women could at once work to ensure the persistence of some semblance of their men's antebellum sense of masculinity, while expanding the significance of the family and their own role as mothers as vital constituents of the new order. As Gertrude Thomas concluded in her account of her conversation with Jefferson Davis, the ex-president told her that he himself had "great faith in the Southern women, that they would train the boys right." Placing his hand on her son's head he concluded, "It will come out right. I may not live to see it, but it is not in the nature of God to allow the best people he ever made to remain permanently under the rule of the meanest people ever made." When she recorded this exchange with Jefferson Davis, Thomas took issue with Davis's castigation of the North, but not with his assertion that southern white women would make the next generation of southern white men into the region's "redeemers."[63]

When the smoke cleared away, where do we find the devoted
women? Where were Mary Magdalene and the other Mary after
the crucifixion?

—*A History of the Origins of Memorial Day*

6

The Politics of Domestic Loss

THE LADIES' MEMORIAL ASSOCIATION
AND THE CONFEDERATE DEAD

On April 26, 1875, almost ten years to the day after Jefferson
Davis was marched through Augusta in defeat, another procession assembled to cover the same ground. Never in the history of the town had
such a crowd gathered, pouring in from the surrounding countryside and
only recognizable to many of the town's citizens by their organizational
uniforms.[1] By 9:00 A.M. the streets were alive with preparation for the
day's events, and by 2:30 the various military and civic organizations that
had been invited to participate in the parade were in formation. Ten thousand people jammed the streets and crowded every available window of

the buildings lining the main street in anticipation of the day's events. Led off by the Richmond Hussars, the county's Confederate cavalry unit, the procession set out in veteran military formation. They were followed in close order by the United States Post Band in full regulation uniform, playing the Radeztky Quickstep, the Louise March, and the Not for Joe Quickstep. The first division was rounded out by the Augusta Volunteer Battalion, marching one hundred and ninety-nine strong, and the Schuet-zen Club, Augusta's German-American society, turning out seventy-seven men in a full uniform of gray jackets, black pants, and felt hats trimmed with green plumes.

Not to be outdone, the local fire companies, the police force, and various other societies of the town and the county filed by in their most splendid attire and proudest bearing. At the height of the procession, a group appeared that required no uniform to stir the crowd. They appeared on horseback in civilian dress, their identity marked only, as the local press reported the next day, "by their scars, crutches and empty sleeves." [2] Here were the Confederate veterans, turned out in full force to give their fallen comrades their due, for this was the day that the cornerstone of the town's Confederate Monument was to be laid.

At the very end of the procession, following the town's dignitaries and officials, the judges and the clergy, and the Augusta Medical College faculty, came the citizens of the town and the county who were the most responsible for the procession and the erection of the monument itself. Seated in carriages, the officers of the Ladies' Memorial Association rolled past the assembled crowd in dignified style. They disembarked at the home of the town's wealthiest widow, Mrs. Emily Tubman, whose spacious house commanded a prime location on the central square. As they took their seats of honor on her verandah, they surveyed the vast congregation arrayed before them. They were moved, according to the account in the local press, to contemplate with "joyful hearts" this physical manifestation of their ten years of organizational labors. The sentiment was returned by the assembled crowd, who with "one voice, blessed their work, and said it was good." [3]

Taking the stand, the Orator of the Day, the Reverend General C. A. Evans, began his dedicatory address by noting that any contemplation of the experience of the town in the ten years since the defeat of the Confederacy could only awaken "painful reflections" and revive the "many distressing humiliations which we have suffered." He proposed instead to discuss the brightening prospects for the coming decade. According to Evans, hope for sectional reunion was growing as a consequence of the rising national sentiment for the recognition of the "valor and virtue" of the individual soldier, whatever his section of origin. The animosities generated by the war were rapidly fading and only "the heroism, devotion and patriotism of all [was] remembered." As one concrete substantiation of his claim to this growing sectional unity, Evans pointed to the prominent role of the U.S. Post Band in the day's festivities. "We at least," he asserted, "are here to-day from all parts of the Nation—Confederates and Federals—native and foreign born, with our sons and daughters, to say with one united voice, 'let sectional strife cease!'"[4]

While the North and the South might always disagree about the cause of Confederate independence, Evans told his memorial audience, it was to be hoped that they were now of one mind when it came to the desirability of recognizing the nobility and self-sacrifice of the individual soldier. This recognition of the common soldier, regardless of the particular side on which he fought, was not only being espoused by ex-Confederates, according to Evans, it was also becoming increasingly common in the North as well. And here Evans made reference to a speech that had recently been given by a northern general, Bartlett, of Massachusetts, upon the occasion of the centennial of the American Revolution. "Men," General Bartlett asserted, "cannot always choose the right cause, but when, having chosen that which their conscience dictated, they are ready to die for it, if they justify not their cause, they at least ennoble themselves." On this basis, this northern general had concluded that the nation as a whole should be as proud of the southern men who fought at Bull Run as they were of those who fought at Bunker Hill.[5]

Certainly, Evans insisted, the citizenry of Augusta were present to lay the cornerstone of the town's Confederate Monument not in order to indicate their continued adherence to the legitimacy of the politics of secession, but instead to bear witness to the "honesty" of the motives and the "valor" of the service of the Confederate Dead. Anyone who thought the construction of Confederate monuments indicated the unregenerate character of ex-Confederates failed to understand the critical distinction between reviving the collective political cause of the Confederacy and honoring the individual conscience of the Confederate soldier. Indeed, in laying the cornerstone of the monument, the citizens of Augusta were not only ritually marking out the basis for sectional reunion, but also indicating a critical shift that had occurred in their own understanding of the meaning of the sectional crisis and the war itself. As Evans explained it, in the war's aftermath a "divorce" had occurred between white southerners' commitment to the Confederate cause, on the one hand, and their attachment to the Confederate Dead on the other. The construction of the monument constituted a symbolic acknowledgment of that divorce. Once completed, it would mark the death of the Confederate cause, even as it indicated that the Confederate Dead continued to live. Indeed as the bearers of a new tradition in the making, they would grow larger in memory than they had been in life.

Sectional reconciliation was therefore based on the abandonment of the causes of the war and focused instead on the common sacrifice of the individual soldier, whatever his political affiliation, whatever his "cause." There was, however, a hierarchy of cause abandonment here. The cause of Confederate independence could be articulated by the memorial movement as "lost," while the cause of the defense of the institution of slavery was either never mentioned or actively denied. The very silence and denial of the Confederate Memorial movement on the issue of slavery as a cause of sectional conflict revealed the way in which it was the cause that was truly lost. For although the Confederate nation was defeated, the political prerogatives of white men, which it had been designed to represent, were only lost insofar as ex-Confederates persisted in clinging to the particular political form that they had taken in the drive for Confederate nationalism, and perhaps more critically, as long as they persisted in asserting their rights to slaveownership or some legal replication of it, as in the Black Codes.[6]

What sectional reconciliation required of ex-Confederates was nothing less than a reconstructed understanding of what it meant to be a free white man. When they "divorced" themselves from the "causes" of the war, they were actually divorcing themselves from the antebellum construction of their manhood as heads of independent, potentially slaveholding households. Their vehicle for doing this was the veneration of the Confederate Dead. Thus, Evans asserted in his Memorial Day address that far from being a testament to war, Confederate monuments actually laid the groundwork for peace. Rather than inflaming sectional conflict, their recognition of the valor of the Confederate war dead would actually act as a "conservator of popular patriotism." They would indicate that all men who served their country out of the integrity of their own personal convictions, whatever the substance of those convictions, would be commended by their fellow citizens, whatever the outcome of the struggle. At least on Confederate Memorial Day, Evans concluded, the dead and the survivors were still one in spirit. "You will suffer me to say without reserve," he asserted in his speech, "that my heart is to-day in the graves of my fellow-comrades. This is the time of my trist, when I give myself to them in tender recollection."[7]

Here Evans understood the survivors' bond with the Confederate Dead as being a fundamentally personal and domestic one, whereas he acknowledged the Confederate cause to have been a public and political matter. He had himself served in the war, and when he talked of his "fellow-comrades" he meant, in the first instance, those men whom he had personally known in the ranks. For his audience as a whole, he assumed that the basis for their continued attachment to the Confederate Dead was also in the first instance an overwhelmingly personal and domestic one. It was in fact an attachment constructed out of their own domestic loss, and as such it acted as a sort of mirror, reflecting their own emotional and economic distress, the familial cost of the loss of so many fathers, husbands, brothers, and sons who had fallen in pursuit of the Confederate cause.[8]

In his annual address to the citizenry of the town in the last year of the war, Mayor R. H. May had himself indicated the manner in which the devastating domestic cost of the war had come to overshadow the initially aggressive stance of the citizenry in their pursuit of political independence. "The heart," he informed his fellow citizens, "sickens in contemplation." For while they had all witnessed the "friends of our youth go forth from among us, strong in the justice of their cause," they had all too often seen them return "with the calmness of death upon their features," accompanied only by the "wailing notes of woe" from their women. While the male citizenry had set out to war to "win glory," the mayor asserted, those who remained behind now knew only too well that they were just as likely to be "swept unheeded away upon that dark sea of blood," leaving behind their bereft women and their orphaned children. It was in this bond between the town's women and their lost male relations that the mayor found the vortex of their collective loss. "We have seen the mother bid farewell to her son, as, with streaming eyes, she strained him to her heart," he told the assembled citizenry. They had all witnessed the "unutterable distress" on the face of the wife as she contemplated the retreating back of her soldier husband, a husband who was now in too many instances waiting for her "upon the eternal shore."[9]

Here the mayor indicated the way in which the Confederate Memorial movement carried a reconception of the basis on which white manhood could be constructed. The cause of slavery was rendered mute, as slavery was lost from the white household structure. Instead the relationship between white men and the household dependents that legitimately remained to them, their own women and children, was understood to stand at the core of the war's meaning. A war that began grounded in the right to own slaves was thereby transformed in retrospect into a war grounded in the first instance in familial defense and familial loss. As C. A. Evans put it in his address, "God gave me no brother, but my sacrificed country has given me thousands." The Confederate Memorial tradition was the public manifestation of the fraternal bond that had first arisen during the war and which persisted in the war's aftermath in the context of death and defeat. Evans acknowledged that there were already many benevolent associations in the town to "help the needy and to dispense alms in practical good will to men," but he contended that there was still something critical lacking in the public institutional structure of the town, no matter how "public and efficient" such existing charities might be.[10]

The erection of Confederate monuments in Augusta and across the Southland would fill this void. The large crowds that such events attracted reflected the extent of the "popular sentiment" seeking public means of expression. "It must," argued Evans, "have a language to make itself understood." Indeed, according to him, the "shaft which shall spring from this spot will be the tongue of popular sentiment." This new language, this "voice" that was called forth into the public organizational structure of the town, was none other than the organized presence of ex-Confederate women of the town. "We assemble at woman's call," Evans told the assembled crowd, "a call that men may gladly obey," to lay the cornerstone of the Confederate Monument. For it was "not man's privilege, but woman's to raise these monuments throughout the land."[11]

What was empowered in the persistence of the bond between the Confederate dead and the war's survivors were the remnants not only of the white man's domestic arena, most particularly his women and children, as opposed to masculine, public arenas of loss, whether of region, class, or race; it was the particularly *female* experience of the white familial bond. Of course, during the war itself women in the soldiers' aid societies of the town had already made similar public claims to the centrality of their previously privatized relationship to their men and, by extension, to all the men in service to the Confederacy. Confederate women, whose labor had been dedicated to the well-being of the men of their own immediate families, became public figures in the service of the Confederate cause. Even during the war, they had responded by attempting to give the unknown soldier a familiar domestic face. At that time, however, their efforts were thwarted, both by the "male" orientation of the Confederate cause itself and by the reality of the actual class distance between many of the women who participated in voluntary work and many of the soldiers who filled the ranks.[12]

Indeed, the ladies of Augusta discovered during the war that the ordinary Confederate soldier was frequently disturbingly unlike the men of their own families. As much as they had tried to view these men through a unifying white lens, they were disconcerted to find that the common soldier was frequently difficult to envision as a member of their own familial circle. The Confederate Dead, however, proved to be much more easily homogenized domestically than the actual Confederate soldier had been in the flesh. Separated from the disturbing reality of their actual presence, class difference could be conveniently expunged in the Confederate Dead. So too, in the defeat of the Confederacy their commitment to the cause as an extension of their own prerogatives as free white men died with them. Instead, the familial bond with the Confederate Dead, which persisted in the lives of the survivors as well, could now become not just the primary concern of Confederate women but the critical basis for the continued recognition and honor of the individual men who served in the war, both the living and the dead.[13]

Thus, while ex-Confederate men found their public political power at least temporarily truncated and their economic position, particularly their right to black labor, seriously compromised, ex-Confederate women found a continued and even expanded basis for their own public organization in this very same decline in the position of their men. Certainly, the defeat of the Confederacy had been devastating to the class and racial privileges of both white men and white women, but unlike their male relations, white women had few public, political prerogatives of their own to defend or to lose. They had no need for a "divorce" from the prerogatives of "free men"; they had never possessed these in the first place. In fact, Confederate women's specifically gendered contribution to the war had never known a "cause" of its own; rather it had been constructed as a mirror of the cause that had belonged in the first instance to their men. Indeed, Confederate women's greatest contribution to the war had been the willingness to *sacrifice* their own domestic relations, their husbands, their sons, and their fathers, whom they had given up in the name of empowering these same men collectively in class, race, and regional terms. These women's specifically gendered contribution had therefore been marked precisely by their own readiness to sacrifice that which they most valued, that is, their own individual "cause" of their domestic relations, to the "larger" causes of their men.[14]

As intensely as the war had elicited the male struggle in defense of their "manhood" as they understood it, so it had called forth a public female energy to mother their men. It was this domestic relationship, beginning with the construction of garments when the troops first left and moving on to feeding and nursing the troops in wayside homes and hospitals, that culminated ultimately in the care for the graves of the fallen and the Memorial Day tradition itself that was at the core of the Confederate Memorial movement. In the postwar period, however, this politics of domestic sacrifice, hitherto occupied in the first instance by Confederate women, increasingly became the experience of their men as well.[15] Having been forced to give up the political and economic causes of the war, Confederate men were pushed back onto the very sacrifice of themselves, or as they memorialized it, of the Confederate Dead. Having given up their claims to slaveownership and regional dominance, they retained uncontested dominance only over their own bodies and the "makers" of those bodies, that is their mothers, wives, and daughters. They could "reconstruct" themselves then through the vehicle of the Confederate Memorial movement, because it offered a way to valorize themselves by honoring the greater sacrifice of the Confederate Dead. As a result, the act of mothering the dead emerged now as *the* basis upon which a viable post-Confederate tradition could be built. And so appropriately enough, the Memorial Day ceremonies of 1875, which began with the laying of the cornerstone of the Confederate Monument, closed with a sojourn to the "City of the Dead."

Here, in the Confederate soldiers' section of the city cemetary, the women and children of the Ladies' Memorial Association had decorated the graves not only of Augusta's own Confederate Dead but of unknown Confederate and Federal soldiers as well. The inscriptions on the wreaths laid upon the graves expressed the persistence of the domestic bond even in death, as in the case of the wreath that read "For His Mother" and was placed on the grave by the local Augusta ladies at the request of a mother who was unable herself to visit the site of her son's grave. Here we see the continued extension of the domestic relation, as during the war-time when one woman had "mothered" the wounded in hopes that some other woman elsewhere would mother her own. Now that the Confederate soldiers were safely buried, they could be transformed into reflections of their women's idealized images of them, untarnished by the realities of their lives and deaths. They could be reconstructed as a simple extension of their commitment, their relationship to their women and children. The self-asserting warrior of the war's outset, militant in defense of his pre-rogatives in relation to other men, white and black, could reemerge in the postwar memorialization of the Confederate Dead as a dutiful husband or son who sacrificed his life for the defense of his home and motherland, or as one grave decoration put it, "A Martyr for a Noble Cause." [16]

This victory of the domestic face of ex-Confederate men's "masculinity" was paralleled by a gendered shift in the institutional struc-ture of the town in the war's aftermath as well. What the white "fathers" of the town lost in political power and economic wealth, the white "mothers" gained in the persistence and even expansion of their own public orga-nizations dedicated to the politics of domestic loss. In the face of their husbands' and fathers' inability to act as "social fathers" in the public arena, women responded by redoubling the work that they had initiated during the war as "social mothers." In the face of the decline of the white male citizenry's public power to "protect and defend," they organized the Ladies' Memorial Association in order to continue to support their men. It was not only the Confederate Dead that begged vindication, but the white male survivors who remained in need.

In his annual message of October 1865, Mayor May explained the political and economic crisis that military defeat had brought upon the town in terms that echoed the experience of the defeated Confederate survivors as individual men. He began by acknowledging that the town was fortunate, for unlike her neighboring cities of Atlanta or Columbia, she had been spared direct military destruction. Both in their individual status as survivors and in their collective position as citizens, ex-Confederate men of the town had been spared the ultimate price of war. They had that much to be grateful for. Nonetheless, they were gravely wounded. Just as they were not the men they had once been as individuals, so the town was no longer the political or economic entity that it had been before the war. It would, according to the mayor, require many years of hard labor in order to "retrieve our disasters" and close the "gaping wounds" that the town had incurred as a result of the conflict and its aftermath.[17]

While ex-Confederate men struggled, often unsuccessfully, as individual heads of household to support their families in some semblance of their antebellum economic position, the town fathers struggled with equally little success to fill their old public institutional positions as "social fathers." In the face of the postwar occupation of the city by northern troops and the emancipation of the slaves, the white male citizenry of Augusta found themselves stripped of much of their previous economic and political position. They found themselves unable to exercise even the most basic municipal functions of maintaining social order and supporting the dependent poor. In their governmental, no less than their individual capacity, they experienced a massive erosion of their ability to "protect" those they deemed worthy of protection.

Perhaps the most deeply galling public "humiliation" that the town fathers experienced was the difficulty they faced in maintaining what they understood to be good social order, that is, a social order that reflected their continued dominance. They could no longer control activity on public streets and consequently "protect" their own as in they had in past. In the year following the war, the town was plagued by particularly high levels of petty theft and other criminal activity that the city fathers were unable to repress. As Gertrude Thomas wrote, "We live in troublous times. Lawless acts are being committed every day and the papers are filled with the robberies that are constantly taking place."[18] She attributed this thievery to a partnership of sorts between some of the occupying troops and some of the newly freedpeople, precisely the groups whom the white town fathers had lost the ability to control. Although Thomas reasserted her belief that emancipation, in the end, would be the best for all, she confided to her journal that she was deeply troubled by the decline of the old order and the social disruption that would have to be endured before a new one took shape. James Verdery wrote in the same vein to a friend. In describing the state of the town in the winter of 1866, he admitted that he was hard pressed to ward off feeling "blue." "We still have the abominable Yankees among us," he wrote. "They are the vilest set of that *detestable* race I have ever seen. 'Plunder' is their watchword at present. You never heard the like of so many robberies being committed, as is now carried on in this city, principally the Yankees in connexion with some of the lowest classes in the city. It is really dangerous to walk the streets after dark, for in a moment you may be knocked down and robbed." [19]

James Verdery's friend, identified only as "Blanche," left for Europe shortly after the collapse of the Confederacy, apparently in order to avoid confronting the decline of what for elite white women of the town constituted "protection," the institutionalized public power of the men of their race and class. Voluntary exile was not an option open to Verdery himself or to the majority of the white citizenry. James Verdery counted himself fortunate simply to have found a position as a clerk. He, at least, could hope to earn a living, even if he did not feel personally secure in walking down the street at night. No matter how depressing he or other ex-Confederates might find such circumstances, they had no alternative but to remain in spite of their inability to maintain local control.

In the face of the widespread social disorder, the members of the county's grand jury were appalled when they convened in the winter of 1866 to find that the court docket was virtually empty. Although the town was, from their perspective at least, racked with crime, almost no criminals had been apprehended. Rather than resigning themselves to the shift in power that underlay both the increase in crime, apparently directed largely against ex-Confederate property holders, and their inability to contain it, the citizens of the grand jury turned on the city council, charging the municipality with incompetence. "The condition of our county," the grand jury concluded, "is incompatible with the claims of her citizens, to be considered a civilized and law abiding people." [20] In its efforts to defend itself against these allegations, the city council only further revealed the real root of the problem. The council, its members complained, lacked the power to govern as it had in the past. With slavery abolished, the freedpeople now emerged as public figures in their own right, and much of the legal power to govern the black population rested in the hands of the occupying northern troops. An administrative center of the Freedmen's Bureau had been established in Augusta at the close of the war. Among its duties were to adjudicate labor disputes between the area's planters and the freedpeople. In general, the bureau's courts found that rather than being "robbed," white employers of the region were "robbing" their newly freed black laborers.[21]

The city council ultimately could only plead for sympathy for what it experienced as a powerless condition. "No one who has not experienced the difficulties of the position," they informed the grand jury and the citizenry at large through the local press, "can form an adequate idea of the trials and mortifications to which members of this Council have been subjected." The members of the city council might have been spared some of these "trials and mortifications" if they had been able to take the mayor's advice upon the fall of the Confederacy more to heart. Mayor May advised his fellow ex-Confederates to strive to accept the arrival of the occupying Federal troops and the consequent decline of their power to direct the life of the town as they had in the past. According to Mayor May, the best course of action available to the white male citizenry would be to turn their energies toward recouping the individual and collective economic losses they had incurred during the struggle. As the mayor noted in his annual message of October 1865, "Let us not brood over our losses but rather profit by the experience of the past. Let us trust to time to heal the gaping wounds which man has made, and to our own exertions to retrieve our disasters." He urged ex-Confederate Augustans to willingly relinquish the political power that was largely lost to them in any case; they would at least be freed to turn their energies to the pressing economic problems that they faced, not only as individuals but in collective, municipal terms. Only in this way could they hope to protect their own families from economic need and perhaps be enabled to meet the needs of the town's dependent poor as well.[22]

Here the economic difficulties of the white male citizenry in their capacity as town fathers echoed their personal and domestic dilemmas as individual heads of households. The town, like so many of the individual male citizens of Augusta, found itself seriously in debt in the war's aftermath, a direct consequence of the Confederacy's defeat. Even as late as the spring of 1865, despite ever increasing demands to support the war effort and ever growing numbers of public dependents at home, the town government was still less in debt than it had been when the war began. At the time of surrender, however, virtually every bank note then in circulation was rendered worthless. All the town's banks promptly collapsed. Even patriotic local merchants were inclined to refuse to accept the town's notes. This situation was further exacerbated when emancipation reduced the town's taxable property base. At the same time, the sudden influx of freedpeople into the town necessitated greatly increased expenditures, if only to confront the epidemic levels of smallpox that accompanied this migration. "Heavy expenditures," concluded the city council in the winter of 1866, "have been met and the government of the city enabled to move on under circumstances that would appear to furnish nothing but discouragement."[23]

While the economic solvency of the town had collapsed in the wake of military defeat, the increased municipal responsibilities that had come with the war persisted and, in some ways, actually increased. The mayor urged his fellow citizens to remember their debt to those white women and children who found themselves dependent upon the town's charity. Confederate war widows and their children represented a permanent public obligation, according to the mayor, as the totally "unprotected" dependents of those who were lost in a cause that they presumably continued to honor. Among all the Confederate survivors, it was these dependents of the Confederate Dead who had paid the highest price for the war and who found themselves most exposed to economic hardship in the disrupted postwar economy. They had little alternative but to continue to look to the town fathers to act, at least in terms of material support, as substitutes for their lost male relations.

With the war over and the ex-Confederates' political power in eclipse, their economic responsibility to support these public dependents expanded almost inversely in proportion to their declining ability to fill it. Indeed, the very same defeat that had rendered them politically powerless and economically bankrupt had also killed male household heads and vastly increased the ranks of the dependent and poor. The number of poor demanding relief would have been staggering under the best of circumstances. At the time of Confederate surrender, there were some fifteen hundred such families dependent on the Augusta Purveying Association for their daily sustenance. By the following fall, this number had declined substantially, to some five hundred families, but the mayor offered little encouragement that their ranks would undergo any further decline given the depressed economic condition of the town.[24]

High outlays for charitable relief and ever-rising levels of indebtedness seemed to be the probable long-term fate of the town in the years immediately following the war. In 1867 the city council discussed the possibility of enlarging the Augusta Canal, which might stimulate further investment in textile manufacturing and thereby increase municipal revenue while simultaneously augmenting the main form of wage labor available for white women and children.[25] The town fathers recognized, however, that they were caught in a vicious circle. While the high cost of supporting the town's dependent poor continued to drive up the town's indebtedness, the ever-rising level of the debt itself made it virtually impossible to borrow more money to make improvements. Yet without the increase in water-power that would come from an enlargement of the canal, it would not be possible to attract the sort of industry that would enable poor white women and children to become self-supporting and allow the town to finally dig itself out of debt. The mayor could only advocate patience and diligent labor at this juncture.

> Having but recently emerged from a terrible and desolating war, the political difficulties of which are still unsettled, leaving us in a state of more than embarassing anxiety and solicitude, it could not be expected that the affairs of our city government should at once assume a bright and promising aspect, or a flourishing and healthy condition. On the contrary, corporations, like individuals, have suffered much, and it will take years of patient and laborious industry and economy . . . to restore them.[26]

As in the case of their own families, the town's citizenry found themselves called upon to support public dependents when the town's resources had shrunk dramatically. In terms of public relief, the white male citizens who sat on the city council drew an uneasy racial line between the worthy and the unworthy poor. Although the council at times recognized a responsibility to support all the dependent poor regardless of race, it was at the same time obvious that they really only perceived one social group in the town as legitimately entitled to their support, and that was white widows and orphans, especially those who had lost their male relations in the war effort. It was after all during the war that the city council had committed itself to support the women and children who were widowed and orphaned by it. In the postwar era, the mayor reiterated the council's commitment to act, in an economic sense, as substitute fathers and husbands.[27]

At the same time, the needs of the newly emancipated black citizenry were viewed by the city council as a form of encroachment upon the limited resources of the city. The council's attitude was similar to that of individual property owners, who concluded that emancipation had severed all ties to their ex-slaves. Unless these newly freed people made the requisite gestures of deference and apparently continued to acknowledge the primacy of the white household, they were to be cast adrift. Along the same lines, the town fathers were inclined to view the needs of the freedpeople for town support not, as in the case of the dependent white poor, as calling for a public extension of their private role as fathers and husbands, but rather as the demands of an undeserving group which only caused them trouble and drained resources that they needed in order to protect their own.[28]

Basically, for all that defeated Confederate men might endeavor to shift their focus of self-definition from the political to the economic arena and from the public to the domestic realm, they found both transformations ultimately impossible to make. The economic power of white male elites had always been fused with their political hegemony. Their public lives had always been viewed as an extension of their individual position as heads of household. Thus while their postwar losses might incline them to retreat into what remained of their households and private economic efforts to promote it, this very heightened domestic economic focus pushed them back outward into the public and political arenas, if only to meet somehow the needs of impoverished white women and children in the town.

Thus while Mayor May encouraged Augusta's white male citizenry to accept the decline of their public political authority in the town and the region in the name of their economic responsibility to provide for the members of their own households and the impoverished Confederate poor more generally, even this strategy offered limited relief. In aspiring to become providers when they had failed to be protectors, elite white men could succeed only minimally. As the grand jury reflected in 1866 in light of Augusta's economic plight, "We staked our all on the war, our lives, our fortunes and our sacred honor." In the war's aftermath, they found little left to work with, as they were "threatened with absolute want" without the success of the crop then in the fields.[29]

Unfortunately, in the year following the war, even the weather seemed dedicated to contributing to the continued travails of the ex-Confederates. Much of the crop on which the members of the grand jury pinned their hopes was destroyed by drought. Consequently, the city council braced itself for even more hardship among the poor. At this juncture, one white farmer was moved to write to the *Augusta Chronicle and Sentinel* to describe the situation to which hinterland farmers like himself found themselves reduced. According to this farmer, uncertain economic conditions generated by defeat and emancipation, combined with a year of serious drought, had rendered them unable to provide an adequate living for their immediate families. They could not possibly also provide for the town's dependent poor. The effort to discharge their primary private responsibilities now consumed "at all times our thoughts, to the exclusion of every other consideration." Acquiring a mere subsistence for their own families now required their "most earnest effort," he wrote, and constituted their "greatest trouble."[30]

The lament of this farmer might seem to reinforce the wisdom of the mayor's advice that political defeat be stoically accepted and energies devoted to economic recovery instead. Nevertheless, the farmer also complained that his straitened familial circumstances rendered the "arrogance" of the occupying northern troops even harder for him to bear. They appeared to him to be determined to "rub salt" in the wounds of his political impotence. They conducted themselves, he wrote, as though they thought the defeated white male southerner should consider himself as "blessed" if merely allowed to "breathe the free air of heaven." It was indeed true, this farmer concluded, that this "blessing" was virtually the only privilege that remained to them in their reduced postwar circumstances. Ultimately this farmer concluded after some struggle that, even in the face of the "arrogance" of northern occupation, the region's ex-Confederate farmers only desired to "shield from want the suffering and helpless ones dependent upon us."[31]

In publicly relinquishing his former claims, this farmer indicated the extent to which his own conception of his proper place had been given a more domestic focus in the postwar context of military defeat. It was now sufficient, according to this writer, that white southern men be honored for the personal and individual valor that they exhibited exclusively in their private capacity as fathers, sons, and brothers. Southern farmers were now "subdued, patient, submissive and faithful" to the laws and "obedient" to the newly established authorities, however much the "arrogance" of the latter might rankle.[32] Gone was the militant posturing that accompanied the first blush of secessionist sentiment and the early years of the war. Gone were the impassioned assertions of their intention aggressively to defend their rights and prerogatives as "free" men, as they had defined them, in the form of an independent slaveholding Confederacy.

Of course there were some men of Augusta who had opposed secession from the outset and others who at the time had participated in the war effort only out of their commitment to domestic self-defense. Perhaps even more of the region's ex-Confederates were like Jefferson Thomas, who entered the war out of a militant commitment to the "cause," served a year before joining the home guard, and by the end served in the name of domestic self-defense.[33] But it was only in the war's aftermath, in the face of the failure of their political drive for independence and the loss of their right to hold property in slaves, that the commitment to do their domestic duty and sacrifice their own lives for home defense emerged as such a universal explanation for why white southern men had risked the hazards of war.

The anonymous farmer now drew the logical conclusion of this position when he asserted that only one command of the northern authorities could arouse ex-Confederates like himself to lift their shoulders from the domestic grindstone and incite their anger and self-assertiveness to return, and that was when they were "ordered" to "forget our dead." Only then, he wrote, did a "fitful gleam" of the "old fire" light up. Although white southern men would keep their heads bowed in relation to the victorious Yankees, this yoke was borne in the name of their primary responsibility to provide for their dependent women and children. The newfound primacy of their domestic masculinity compelled them to accept the death of the Confederate cause but the very preservation of their honor in its new domesticated form necessitated that they defend the memory of their fallen comrades who were no longer able to defend themselves. Hence the farmer, who began his letter by asserting that his "greatest effort" was to provide for his dependents, concluded it by noting that "the only thought that is left us" is our "cherished remembrance of our kindred and friends whose bones lie scattered all over our fair land."[34]

It was as though ex-Confederate men were being chased in an ever constricting circle, retreating from the political front to the domestic arena, only to discover their inability to maintain even this more circumscribed definition of themselves. Indeed, the loss of the cause necessitated an intensified attachment to an ever more abstracted and "unreconstructed" Confederate Dead. As a result, there was generated a reciprocal and apparently intensifying relationship between their renunciation of the Confederate cause, with all its attendant political and economic consequences for the actual domestic reconstruction of southern white men's sense of self, and their compensatory glorification of the Confederate Dead. If the living ex-Confederate man could no longer defend his dependents, either those of his own family or the town's Confederate widows and orphans, he could at least honor the death of that power in the form of a movement to recognize the valor of the Confederate Dead. The more ex-Confederates were domestically "reconstructed" and the more they were made painfully aware of their shortcomings even within that more limited domestic construction, the more attached they grew to the apparently "unreconstructed" dead.

The institutionalization of the Confederate Memorial tradition in the town thus reflected the extent of the collapse of white men's political and economic mastery both on the public and the private front. So important did the defense of the Confederate Dead become that even ex-Confederate men's inability to protect and provide for their living families could be displaced psychologically through the memorial campaign. Consider the case of Joseph Cumming, who along with his three brothers served in the Confederate army for the duration of the war. While one brother was lost during the war to dysentery, it was his own father, Henry Harford Cumming, who had risked the wrath of Union troops to recognize Jefferson Davis when he had been brought through Augusta a prisoner. Shortly thereafter, Henry Cumming took his own life, having constructed himself as much a war casualty as the son who had recently succumbed in a northern prison. Joseph Cumming's own story, however, took a happier turn.

Returning from the war physically unscathed, he applied himself to his profession and became a prominent local lawyer, as his father had been before him. At the same time, he also became an ardent supporter of the memorial movement, giving annual memorial day speeches, dedicating memorial tablets, and supporting the work of the Ladies' Memorial Association. When the Confederate Survivors Association was first organized in Augusta in 1878, he was among the charter members.[35]

Even before the ceremonies to lay the cornerstone of the Augusta Confederate Monument in 1875, Joseph Cumming had emerged as an important spokesperson for the memorial movement. In 1873, he gave the dedicatory speech for a memorial tablet erected in the town, in which he remarked on the "strange spectacle" that such tablets presented. "What other conquered people," he queried his audience, "had worked to erect monuments to perpetuate the memory of their own conquest?" This apparently "strange spectacle" was not so strange as it might initially appear, he went on to claim, for while white southern men were defeated, their motives, according to Cumming, were pure.[36]

If these monuments had simply been a question of "mournful pride," Cumming asserted, they never would have been built in the first place. Their very construction was the result of the manner in which simple grieving over the war dead had been transformed by the catalyst of public defeat into a private determination to preserve their memory. In the first instance, the presence of occupying troops had necessitated this transformation of mourning the dead from a private family obligation of individual women into a politicized public ritual that was normally the terrain of men. Denied the power to tell the story in the public and political "male" arena by official history, ex-Confederate men had no choice but to fall back upon the domestic terrain of their women and children, for the northerners were not content to simply occupy the South. According to Cumming, they also insisted on covering it with monuments to their own fallen soldiers. Had these Yankee monuments been merely depoliticized memorials they might have elicited little reaction but, according to Cumming, they had emblazoned on them, for every southern child to read, mottoes in which the "just cause" was dismissed as a "rebellion" and "true men" were "branded" as "traitors." Such monuments would impose upon southern "children and their children's children" a historical version of the conflict that damned their own fathers and grandfathers as less than honorable men. It was therefore the ultimate necessity of defending manly integrity that transformed what had been a "sentiment for the dead" into a "high duty to the living and the unborn; and what had been intended only as a memorial to heroism became also a protest against calumny."[37]

Here Cumming's position is similar to that of the anonymous farmer who wrote to the local press in the year after the war. Both men claimed to be able to accept their loss of power in the public arena as the consequence of their defeat in battle. However, when they saw that "public" domination carried to the point of violating their own private domestic integrity, teaching their own children and grandchildren to think in the former enemy's terms, they felt compelled to register a protest. To dishonor the Confederate Dead constituted for both men an *incursion* into what remained of the basis for white southern men's perception of themselves as honorable, in the only arena in which such a self-perception remained viable, in relation to their own women and children.

It was this necessity of defending their own manhood, in their *own* land, to their own children, that transformed private mourning into public monuments, according to Cumming. The terrain of domestic relations became the only ground they could still legitimately claim and reclaim for posterity, if not for themselves. Here Joseph Cumming's memorial politics can be seen as a kind of extension of that to which his father had been committed. Both men claimed the right to define some public space in which Confederate heroes might be seen as having dignity and honor. While his father insisted upon the right to at least indicate his respect for his fallen president, despite the occupation of the city streets by hostile northern troops, Joseph Cummings insisted some eight years later upon his right to publicly honor the Confederate Dead.[38]

Here, however, the similarity ends, for Joseph Cumming, unlike his father, found the basis for a reconciliation with the postwar environment by fusing his "male" public role as provider and protector with an attenuated, hitherto "female" private domestic space. As Joseph Cumming explained it, now it was the "task of love" to preserve that manhood where it still stood undefeated, in domestic honor, and to raise up the next generation to hear the "true" story.[39] Ex-Confederate men could continue to be honored in public space, but in a public space that would of necessity be a feminized one.

Twenty years later, Joseph Cumming was still giving memorial addresses in Augusta and had by then so far extended his argument as to claim for white southerners a sort of victory that the northerners in their apparent domination had failed to achieve. By 1895, the Civil War had become, according to Cumming's Memorial Day presentation of that year, a war motivated more by "sentiment" than any other war in all of recorded history. Forced upon the "female" terrain of subordinate characteristics, the dead had been resurrected as "martyrs" to the cause, recognizable primarily by the "purity" of their motives. As a result, Cumming now argued, southern men had proven the extent of their commitment to their manhood and were revealed to be even more "manly" than men of the North. Southern men had, after all, been animated by a "true love" of their prerogatives, willing even to die for them. Northern men, by contrast, had been fired by self-interested, mercenary motives, and in the long run they had been unmanned by their honorless pursuit of material gain. "We went to war not for conquest," Cumming asserted to his memorial day audience, "not for glory, not to escape oppression. But a proud and high-spirited people flew to arms to defend what they considered their sacred right, from high handed and presumptuous interference, albeit the right itself was little better than an abstraction." [40]

Industrial might may have won northern victory in battle, but southerners' dedication to their honor had given them the war in the long run. However, this was a triumph that had, in the last analysis, less to do with restoring the Confederate Dead to their proper place in the telling of the history of the war than with the domestic reconstruction of the surviving men. So while Joseph Cumming's father responded to economic loss with a fear of his inability to support and protect his wife as in the past, through the feminine memorial tradition Joseph Cumming was able to turn this very economic decline of ex-Confederate men into a virtue, literally into domestic virtue. In the memorial tradition, men's commitment to their honor was conveniently disembodied. The stainless Confederate Dead were thereby divorced from any sordid, failed "causes" like the material base of their antebellum construction as free men, their right to hold black slaves.

It is in this light that we must reconsider General Evans's claim in his address of 1875 that the aim of the memorial tradition was to divorce the Confederate soldier from the cause and to strip the Confederate legacy of any political significance beyond creating good will between the sections.

In actuality, once severed from one another, neither the cause nor the Confederate Dead could persist as they had in real life. Indeed in the very act of "divorcing" the Confederate cause from the Confederate Dead, the citizens of Augusta fundamentally transformed both. It was precisely the link between the individual soldier and the Confederate cause that underwrote the basis of the antebellum construction of southern white manhood as economically independent, politically empowered heads of potentially slaveholding households. Once the dead were no longer attached to any political cause they could be redefined to reflect the feminized experience of the survivors. Shorn of their identity as inherently political beings, as the actual or potential "heads" of economically independent households, they could be reconstituted as empowered, but to a much greater extent by virtue of their private, personal roles than they had been in life. Viewed as an extension and a confirmation of the more domestically identified masculinity of postwar white men, the Confederate cause could be redefined as a cause without a cause, no longer embodying the "larger" class and racial interests of these men but instead symbolizing their own now relatively depoliticized and domesticized understanding of themselves.

The reconceptualization of the cause of the Confederacy itself as a defensive, domestic struggle was thus integral to the efforts of ex-Confederate men to find some honor in their circumscribed postwar status. They too now had to follow the path first carved before the war by their women, who were called upon to sacrifice their potential for self-realization in the name of their family's greater good. Much as their female relations had earlier sacrificed sons, their substance and their product, to the war effort so that their men might be individually self-empowered, the Confederate soldier was now recast as an extension of that sacrifice, as a consequence of the domestic commitments of the dutiful brother, son, or husband. The focus was on that which could continue to empower men, the enduring gendered subordination of their women and children, not on that which had been irrevocably lost, their right to the ownership of black slaves. This, at least, was the underlying race and gender politics of the Confederate memorial movement as it emerged in the town in the years immediately following the war.

This focus on the domestic arena reflected an underlying shift in gender relations themselves. Under postwar economic conditions and the politics of memorialization that followed upon them, relations between white men and women were altered because domestic concerns could not return to a strictly private status in the war's aftermath. As male gender roles shifted in a domestic direction, the entire domestic arena itself was given a more public and increasingly institutionalized face. So it was at precisely the same moment when the political and economic condition of southern white men appeared to be at its nadir, in the winter of 1866, that a series of editorials first appeared in the local press urging the ladies of the town to form a regularly constituted organization that would formalize rituals for honoring the Confederate Dead. Modeled along the same lines as the wartime ladies' aid societies, the first duty of such an organization would be to tend the graves of the Confederate Dead located in the city cemetery. Here the writer envisioned an organization with a chief directress and regularly constituted committees to visit the cemetery and to decorate the soldiers' graves every Saturday afternoon. The newspaper also suggested that the organization meet on a regular weekly basis and that a secretary be chosen to keep a record of the proceedings, for while the activities of such an organization might appear to be a "small matter now . . . if acted upon, it will form a part of the history of the country." [41]

In a further editorial the local paper also urged the Augusta ladies to follow the example of other southern towns and set aside April 25 as a day of general memorial. Here the editorial sketched out that distinction between the politics of the "cause" and the survivors' "depoliticized" domestic attachment to the Confederate Dead that General Evans elaborated more fully in his memorial speech a decade later. "To enshrine the memories of the dead in the hearts of the people is not to adhere to the political tenets of their and our faith in the past, it is not to revive and keep alive the feelings of bitter hatred which controlled both sections of this great country in the late war." Instead, this editorial appealed to the ladies as mothers, while the soldiers were presented as their collective sons. "The majority of them were young, had just attained that period in life, when, if possible, one more wholly monopolizes the affections of a mother than any other." They pointed to the line of domestic continuity that memorial activity in fact constituted. The unknown Confederate Dead in the city cemetery died in a "strange city," according to one editorial, and would have remained among "strangers" except that they had been taken into the universalized domestic affections of the town's "earth angels," as the editorial described those women who worked in the city's hospitals. At the time, these women had eased their final passing, speaking to them of "the promises of the Bible, and, what is grander still, of the sacrificial offering of Christ." The women who did this work, according to the press, acted "kindly—like true women. They shall not lose their reward."[42]

Now another challenge confronted the town's ex-Confederate women. Through their continued homage to the Confederate soldier, now reincarnated as the Confederate Dead, they could give all honor not only to the soldier's aggressive valor as he marched off to the front, but to his "Christlike" demeanor in sacrificing his life to the cause. Here was the opportunity not only to memorialize that which was lost but to create a "rebirth" among the living as well. The town's ex-Confederate women were thus in a position both to rescue the lost public persona of the Confederate soldier and to affirm the "self-sacrifice" of the survivors. From the perspective of the Georgia Ladies' Memorial Association, it was more than simply convenient that Confederate defeat had occurred in the spring, when flowers would be readily available for grave decoration. As they noted in their history of the origins of Confederate Memorial Day some thirty years later, in establishing April 26 as the day of remembrance they had hoped to encourage the citizenry to draw the connection between their own Confederate Dead and the resurrection and ascension of Christ. "Like the hope that spread over the earth on the morning of the Resurrection," they recorded in their account, "so the soft light of this sentiment shone over Dixie, and when April came, love wreathed her roses where the soldiers sleep." Wrapping themselves in this domesticized Christian rhetoric, these ladies went on to assert the primacy of their own role in this resurrection. "Whose task," they queried, "had this been even in Biblical times? . . . When the smoke cleared away, where do we find the devoted women? Where were Mary Magdalene and the other Mary after the crucifixion?[43]

Mother love could, according to the Georgia Ladies' Memorial Association, work a transformation of the Confederate soldier similar to the Biblical one. Confederate men would indeed rise again, if the Georgia Ladies' Memorial Association had anything to say about it, if only on the top of monuments of stone. And if this were not a sufficiently militant domestic reconstruction, the ladies concluded their history of Confederate Memorial Day with an explanation for their continued organizational existence in the postwar era that located the very impetus for the war in their own shadow. "No one," they asserted, "could refuse us the simple privilege of paying honor to those who died defending the life, honor and happiness of southern women." [44]

Not only would this recognition of the Confederate Dead serve to preserve the "lost cause" of their men's economic and political position while simultaneously legitimizing their domestic "reconstruction." It would also serve to console the widow and orphan, who could look to few other comforts in this world. As one editorial in the Augusta press concluded in its appeal for the organization of the Ladies' Memorial Association, "Trouble hovers over them as a storm cloud, lingering long. The vacant chair, the empty larder, the cries of hungry children, all combine to bring a mighty weight of sorrow upon their hearts." The consolation of their fathers, husbands, and sons in departing for the front, according to this editorial, was the knowledge that even if the war cost them their lives, they could at least rest assured that their wives and children would be cared for by a grateful populace. But as during war itself, when support for soldiers' wives and children was in critically short supply, the amount of actual aid the charitable resources of the town could provide was clearly insufficient. What the town's ex-Confederate population could continue to offer was public recognition and appreciation for their domestic sacrifice. As the newspaper editorial concluded in its appeal to the women of the town to form a Ladies' Memorial Association, "The knowledge of sympathy is to an afflicted soul, what curatives are to the sick, and it was never more so than with this great class [widows and orphans]. . . . To know that their husbands or sons live in the hearts of the people, is to wives and mothers almost a sufficiency in life." [45]

During the war itself, Confederate women had taken some consolation in the knowledge that if their men were to be wounded far from home, they might find some care in the hands of other women. If ex-Confederate men, either in their private capacity as fathers, husbands, or sons or in their public position as town fathers, were incapable of providing for white women and children as they had in the past, such women and children could at least receive some public recognition of the cost that their domestic sacrifice continued to entail. Support for the continued organizational activity by ex-Confederate women in Augusta was the least that ex-Confederate men could offer under the circumstances, for in preserving and expanding the domestic bond across the chasm of death, such women's organizations could now ease the pain of separation. They could do so by maintaining the domestic bond that they had so militantly pursued in the initial formation of ladies' aid societies to assist the soldiers during the war. Now in the face of death and defeat, they could continue to render service and thereby honor the dead. This memorialization would not only cast dignity upon the wartime contributions of the Confederate Dead, but would serve to dignify the wartime contribution of the living as well and thus aid them in their domestic self-reconstruction. Finally, through their efforts to at least uphold the personal honor of all ex-Confederate men, the organization could offer some consolation to those women and children who felt their loss most keenly, the widows and orphans of the Confederate Dead.

Thus when editorials in the local press encouraged the women of the town to form a Ladies' Memorial Association in the winter of 1866, they were responding to social changes few white Augustans had envisioned at the war's outset. Most had assumed that the organized public presence of Confederate women would be only temporary, just as Confederate men's service at the front was assumed to be temporary. In the war's aftermath, however, it quickly became apparent that nothing could ever entirely re-turn ex-Confederate women to the inward-looking world of antebellum domestic relations. What the war had so publicly torn asunder, the do-mestic bond between soldiers and their female relations, had now left their women, at least in relation to their lost men, permanently frozen at public attention. This permanent public rendering of domestic life was, of course, most intense in the case of those families whose men died in the conflict, who were lost forever to their women in a direct personal way. But the loss was experienced by ex-Confederate women more generally whose men had been literally dismembered, losing arms or legs to the cause, or had suffered only a more figurative personal loss in the abolition of slavery, the decline in their wealth or their earning power.

Indeed, the plight of poor women and children, forced upon the re-sources of the town for their daily support, simply highlighted the most extreme and painfully exposed instance of the nearly universal problem that memorial activity was designed to address: the erosion of the power of white men to "protect" their women as they had in the past. As their men, and more generally their men's "protective" power, slipped ever further away, the women emerged with ever greater clarity and commitment onto the public stage. While women who found themselves stripped of adult male relations by the war continued to depend upon the public arena for economic support, elite women continued to be drawn into public organizational activity to provide for the Confederate Dead on the same basis established during the war.

The persistence of the most intensely "public" of domestic bonds forged by the experience of war, the relationship between Confederate women and those men who died in the local city hospitals, provided the root for the continued existence of women's organized endeavors in the town. With the close of the war and the return of men to their families, the structural needs met by wayside homes and ladies' aid societies tended to retreat into the privatized location of the household. However, for the soldiers who had died, especially those who had died in the city's hospitals far from their families and had been buried anonymously in the city cemetery, there could never be any coming home. During the war, the Ladies' Hospital and Relief Association had tended to the burial of these men as an extension of their activities in nursing the wounded and organizing critical supplies. In the war's immediate aftermath, the association continued to care for the graves of those men who had no female relations living in the town to do so.

Despite the frequent urgings of the local press to form a memorial association to take up this task among others, the Ladies' Hospital and Relief Association persisted in the work until the spring of 1868 when they finally reformed themselves into the Ladies' Memorial Association. It was not until it appeared to these women to be both possible and desirable to consolidate all the dead, both the town's own and those outsiders who had died in city hospitals, into a Confederate section in the city graveyard that they moved to form a new, more broadly based organization of women in the town. The first act of the newly reformed organization was to acquire a separate section of the city cemetery where the graves of all the war dead could be consolidated. They then commissioned a uniform headstone for each grave. The formation of the first and for at least a decade to follow the most popular postwar organization among white women in the town paralleled the move toward an increased standardization of the individual men lost in the war. They were transformed in the process from individual men lost to their families into an abstraction, the "Confederate Dead."[46]

If it had just been a question of each family's own war dead, the mourning for their passing and the tending of their graves could perhaps have retreated into the more privatized framework of each woman's particular family. Even the Ladies' Hospital and Relief Association found its original root in the domestic roles of its members. The women most active in the organization were the wives of doctors in the town. As the war had placed additional labor upon their husbands, they had responded by forming an auxiliary organization to assist them.[47] Of course the large number of men all lost to the same cause created a kind of collective and therefore extra-familial or "public" bond among their surviving kinfolk, but this bond, in itself, might not have been sufficient to necessitate the continued existence of a formally constituted autonomous organization among ex-Confederate women. At least not in the war's immediate aftermath. Only the anonymity associated with those men who died in the city's hospitals necessitated a continued public interface for women's domestic labor and thus compelled the continuation of the Ladies' Hospital and Relief Association after the war's end.

What was apparently behind the formation of the Ladies' Memorial Association was the fusion of the needs of these anonymous Confederate Dead with the continued crisis experienced by the living ex-Confederate men. It was the postwar economic and political decline of those men who remained to them that provided the necessary additional formative organizational factor, the necessity of valorizing their loss, alongside the greater loss of those actually killed in the war. So it was that under the expanded organizational rubric of the Ladies' Memorial Association, Augusta's elite women moved beyond the standardization of the graveyard, beyond the creation of the "Confederate Dead," to the public commemoration of their sacrifice and by extension that of the living as well. They took up the responsibility of making the ever more elaborate arrangements for Confederate Memorial Day activities in the town. While the decoration of the graves of the Confederate Dead remained an important aspect of the day's events, the ceremonies also took on a more public face as speakers were added in ceremonies held in the town's main square. The Ladies' Memorial Association selected these speakers with care, particularly as they quickly discovered that they were an important element in attracting large crowds. The organization increasingly looked to these crowds in order to promote their most ambitious effort to commemorate the wartime contributions of all ex-Confederates, the construction of a Confederate Monument.[48]

The construction of such a monument was part of the initial basis for the transformation of the Ladies' Hospital and Relief Association into the Ladies' Memorial Association. The original plan was to have it built within the walls of the city cemetery, as the focal point of the newly formed Confederate section of the graveyard. The names of all the town's Confederate Dead were to be listed on it. However, by the time the cornerstone of the monument was actually laid eight years later, both the location and the structure of the monument had been transformed. Instead of gracing the more secluded location in the city cemetery, the monument was actually placed on Broad Street, the town's main business thoroughfare. The original plan to inscribe the names of the individual dead was also dropped. In 1873 the officers of the association decided that this idea would "lessen the dignity of its mission and mar the beauty of its appearance." Instead, they determined that one figure, representing the common soldier, should be placed at the highest point of the monument.[49]

As the actual dead receded ever further into the background of the cemetery, the Confederate Monument and the Ladies' Memorial Association took an ever more prominent position on the center stage downtown. The creation of a more generalized and anonymous domestic bond, initially reflected both in the standardization of the Confederate graves and in the formation of a permanent postwar organization of women to carry it out, proceeded apace. The fusion of these women's expanded institutionalized role with the valorization of ex-Confederate men potentially put the women at cross-purposes. If their continued subordination was critical to the postwar reconstruction of ex-Confederate men, were they not, in taking a leading role in the public recognition of the Confederate Dead, acting to undercut their larger efforts to reaffirm the proper place of those men who remained to them? Despite the fact that the organization was initially called for by such men themselves in the local press, weren't ex-Confederate women violating their properly subordinate status by literally getting out of their place?

The task at hand for the members of the Ladies' Memorial Association was to somehow reconstruct their men without reconstructing themselves in the process, or at least without appearing to do so. During the war, this contradiction appeared to be no contradiction since the intrusion of domesticity into the public sphere was assumed to be temporary, a phenomenon that would retreat, along with the ladies themselves, into a properly privatized and subordinate place after hostilities ended. However, in the war's aftermath, it became apparent that the possibility of this structural retreat of ex-Confederate women (i.e., the return to simple male "protection" as they had previously known it) was not to be. At the same time, the very decline of their men that made this retreat impossible intensified the need to at least maintain the illusion that privatization continued to prevail on the old terms.

Insofar as they were able to do so, the Ladies' Memorial Association worked hard to maintain the conventional forms of public gender subordination, even as they eroded its underlying substance. They gave over the most conventionally "male" aspects of public organizational activities—public speech making, managing of the financial affairs connected with the construction of the monument, and negotiations with the various building contractors—to prominent men. They asserted their commitment to male representation in the public arena forthrightly, and perhaps somewhat defensively, in the local press. "Southern women," they wrote, "frankly acknowledge their dependence on Southern men, and waiving 'women's rights' and parliamentary usages, they claim the privilege of having their public announcements made by gentlemen." According to the Ladies' Memorial Association, this behavior was only to be expected because, as they concluded, "Southern ladies naturally shrink from contact with the outside world."[50]

Here they depicted the meaning of their public endeavors for the Confederate Dead in the most gender-conservative frame possible. Theirs was a defensive movement, a response to the incursions that war had made into the domestic arena. The war had essentially turned domestic life inside out. The Ladies' Memorial Association continued to be active in a public world now rendered structurally domestic as a result. This constituted no assertion of women's individual rights, of their autonomy or equality with reference to men. Quite the contrary, it was a celebration of their continued attachment to domesticity—albeit domesticity which unforeseen circumstances had compelled to assume a public face. It was, after all, domestic loss that had not only created distance and anonymity in particular domestic relations during the war but undermined the postwar political and economic position of men. Mothering, as a result, had acquired a public, anonymous dimension. This increased anonymity was not, however, tantamount to the acquisition of autonomy or independence for women as individuals. As the Ladies' Memorial Association expressed it, their organization was not committed to "women's rights." It was instead based on a politics of domestic loss. Ex-Confederate women could therefore form permanent public organizations while continuing to eschew the independent social status normally understood to undergird such organizational efforts on the part of men.[51]

As a result of this public institutionalization of the domestic position of white women, a kind of limbo space was created, neither public nor private, neither autonomous nor dependent. During the war itself, the wayside homes represented this sort of "limbo space," as Confederate women took up the task of running public homes in response to the unmet domestic needs of the wounded, hungry, and sick soldiers returning from the front. In the postwar era, those men that Confederate women cared for in the wayside homes all over the South, not just in Augusta, were transformed into men who returned home still wounded, if not literally in body, then certainly in spirit, not to mention in economic and political power. While the Ladies' Memorial Association formed itself into an organization intent upon the continued "rescue" of these men insofar as practicable, they simultaneously dedicated themselves to providing support for the widows and orphans that wartime loss had created. So it was that in 1868, many of the same women who came together to form the Ladies' Memorial Association also joined together to create another domestic "limbo space" in the town, the Widows' Home.

While the wayside home was necessitated by the public life of the soldier, the Widows' Home was necessitated by the persistent public claims of their widows and offspring and the inability of the town fathers to substitute collectively through municipal relief efforts for the wartime loss of the men. Hence in the postwar era, ex-Confederate women found themselves thrust into continued action as public mothers not only for the ex-Confederate men who had been killed in battle but for the ex-Confederate women whom their loss had displaced. As was noted in the minutes of the Widows' Home, it was created to serve as a "home for the homeless," a home which in its creation had "two mothers." One of these "mothers" was Maria McKinne, who had been the president of the county's wayside home during the war. She herself was "robbed by the war of many treasures, not the least was a home." She was therefore, according to the minutes of the Widows' Home, moved to found the home not only as a sort of mirror of her wartime labors to aid the hungry and wounded soldier but out of her own personal wartime experience as well. As the Widow's Home minutes concluded, "her experience and the impulse of charitable spirit" led her "to give to others what she felt the loss of most." [52]

Thus one result of the wartime domestic loss was to render the domestic bond between men and women forever public. However, it also created the basis for the development of a public bond among women as well, but this bond was limited to white women. While black women also developed organizational networks after the war to care for the needs of the black community, these "domestic" organizations of black and white women remained almost entirely segregated in the postwar South, regardless of how much they might actually resemble each other in their activities for their respective races. We can see how this racial segregation found its roots in the Confederate experience of defeat. For what began with support of the cause of white men in the war was transformed by the postwar domestic loss itself into the support of impoverished white widows and orphans. Public bonding between white women emerged only in a backhanded way out of the necessity of taking care of one other and of those women less fortunate than themselves who had lost all recourse to protection from men.

In explaining the necessity for the establishment of a Widows' Home, the ladies pointed to their continued duty both to the widows and orphans of the Confederate Dead and to their own female relations. "In addition to the sacred duty to the 'Confederate Dead' . . . having been so devoted to them in life, feeding the hungry by the wayside, nursing the sick and wounded . . . we must feel it a particular charge devolving upon us to finish the work begun by such noble women." [53] Thus, in an addendum to the new constitution of the Ladies' Memorial Association in 1873, the members decided that in "consideration of the devotion" of their first vice president and president to the soldiers, both during the war and in its aftermath, they too should be recognized by a tablet on the Confederate Monument. In addition, every decoration day, a double wreath would be placed on the monument in their memory. [54]

The development of the Widows' Home and that of the Ladies' Memorial Association were as interrelated in their history as they were in their membership. Initially, the ladies were able to standardize the graveyard and to find some form of shelter for the most needy of widows in 1868, but their efforts to make their mark on the physical shape of the town—on the one hand, through the construction of a Confederate Monument, on the other hand through the acquisition of a substantial structure for the Widows' Home—were limited by the depressed economic conditions of the late 1860s. It was not until 1871 that any effort was made at all to collect funds for the Confederate monument, "in consequence," as the Ladies' Memorial Association minutes explained, "of the extreme depression of the people generally soon after the war." By April 1872, however, they had solicited $221.65. In the same year the Widows' Home was also able to acquire a sizable residence.[55]

In 1873, the Ladies' Memorial Association was reconstituted, probably as a consequence of the deaths of the original president and vice president, but also in order to reflect an intensified commitment to the erection of the monument accompanying the town's improved economic prospects. In the new constitution the members committed themselves not only to observe Memorial Day on April 26, but to redouble their efforts toward the erection of a suitable monument, to be built in the Augusta city cemetery, to the "memory of the noble men who laid down their lives in defense of constitutional liberty." The funds were raised through the vice presidents, who were elected from all the city's white religious organizations (including not only the various protestant denominations but the Catholic church and the Jewish synagogue as well) and who were responsible for appointing committees from their own congregations to solicit contributions. Along with utilizing the organizational structure of the white churches, the Ladies' Memorial Association also appealed to the county's Confederate veterans to "unite with us in paying tribute to their fallen comrades." Perhaps in an effort to encourage more widespread financial participation, official membership in the organization was offered to anyone who contributed any amount, no matter how small.[56]

As of 1876, their membership list included close to a thousand citizens, and they claimed this list to be highly incomplete. They were particularly successful in organizing the public school girls, and close to four hundred of the members were listed under the entry, "school girls to put wreaths on the graves of the Confederate Dead." Although the first 136 "girls" were indeed girls, some 71 boys' names also appeared on this list. Among adults, the gender ratio of members was roughly equal, with some 211 male names listed. The list of men read like a who's who of the town's prominent white citizens, including the mayor and the governor, as well as prominent doctors, lawyers, merchants, bankers, and factory presidents. Even the city council and the police department were officially listed as members.[57]

The organization continued to meet biannually after it was reconstituted in 1873, largely to assess progress in soliciting funds. Local gentlemen gave rousing and laudatory speeches at these meetings, while the ladies declined to speak on their own behalf in public. The gentlemen also managed the finances and negotiated with the contractors for the ladies. Despite this apparent deference on the part of these women to the gendered prerogatives of their men, they persisted in their role as protective agents of other women. Along with their success in acquiring a larger building for the town's destitute widows in 1872, they also worked to raise funds for a memorial home for the widow and child of Stonewall Jackson. In 1875 they broke off their fund-raising activities for the Confederate Monument and appointed appropriate committees in each ward of the city to solicit funds for the Stonewall Jackson Memorial Home. Through these efforts they were enabled to send $312 as a contribution in October of 1875.[58]

This sum was collected not only through intensified solicitations but also through a whirlwind of social events, reminiscent of the ladies' earlier wartime fund-raising efforts. By 1876 the Ladies' Memorial Association had succeeded in raising close to the amount necessary to erect the monument. By 1876, however, the depressed state of the national economy began to take its toll on Augusta, and in 1877 the Ladies' Memorial Association determined to cease soliciting funds and to rely instead upon the interest on the principle they already had in order to achieve the final amount required.[59] Finally, on June 25, 1878, a special meeting was called in order to discuss the possible epitaphs to be inscribed upon the monument. Two were eventually chosen, one by C. A. Evans and the other by Charles Colcock Jones.[60]

At some point between 1873 and 1875, the organization decided to relocate the monument from the city cemetery, the site projected in the constitution of 1873, to a location on Broad Street, one of the town's main thoroughfares. It was this change in location that elicited the final difficulty in the effort, shortly before the monument itself was to be erected in the spring of 1878. Headed by M. A. Stovall, a former Confederate general and one of the town's leading cotton factors, a group of the town's prominent male citizens published a petition in the local press in April 1878. In this petition Stovall argued that the monument should be located in a less public site, perhaps in a park. "The undersigned," Stovall wrote, "have counselled with and consulted many of our citizens upon the subject, and believe that a large majority would prefer that location to the present one in the middle of a dusty, business thoroughfare, where no shrubbery or grass could be made to grow and thrive, and which is also too public to be a resort for the ladies."[61]

Gertrude Thomas, then an officer of the Ladies' Memorial Association, responded to this petition with a statement of her own, published on May 1, 1878. She contended that to "most of us" the location of the monument was "but a second consideration" in the face of the "realization of a long deferred wish" that they were finally about to attain, to pay "homage to the memory of those men who in our cause had suffered and died." She pointed out that during the war itself she had written of what she then supposed would be the war's outcome. When the Confederate soldiers returned, she had written, "war torn, scar covered veterans return, wearied and halt, arms in slings," they would receive their reward in the "exultant shouts of a grateful people." The war, however, did not end in victory, as she had hoped. There were no "exultant shouts" for its returning soldiers. For this reason, because the war ended in Confederate defeat, the civilian population of the South owed a special debt to the Confederate soldiers. For this reason, the monument should be located where it was, in the most public location possible. A location such that thousands would now recognize the sacrifice of the Confederate soldier and pay him his due and even visitors from outside the region would be moved to pay homage. Upon viewing the monument, according to Thomas, "they will exclaim, 'The South was defeated, but what a glorious fight she made.'"[62]

Perhaps, Thomas suggested, in a pointed reference to those men who signed the petition, "leading" men were now too ashamed to place a Confederate monument in such a public location. "We," she wrote, referring to the women of the Ladies' Memorial Association, "are not ashamed of those men who gave their lives for us; nor of the cause for which they died." Fortunately, this monument was not in the first instance dedicated to "leading" men but was rather a monument dedicated to the memory of the common soldier, the man "who," as Thomas wrote, "when country called, did his duty and was not ashamed of it." While elite white men had dominated the political and economic arena in the antebellum South and may actually have instigated the conflict to defend their power, according the Thomas, the common soldier only fought out of his sense of duty to his country and to his family. He, after all, had limited political power or immediate economic interests to defend.[63]

According to this feminized rewriting of history, both groups fought in the first instance from their domestic location. In Thomas' retelling of the story, then, the common soldier was as pure and noble in his sacrifice to his country and his home as were Confederate women. Moreover, in the postwar context of 1878, she invoked this common domestic sacrifice of lower-class men and Confederate women to shame these elite men, whose self-aggrandizing motives initiating the war had been questionable and who now seemed inclined to relegate the memory of their botched efforts to the shade. If Confederate women had been excluded from the initial decision to fight, at least the politics of war memorialization should be conducted on their terms. Thomas ended by defending the association's right to choose where the monument should be placed. As she concluded in her response to the last-minute effort to block the public location of the monument, "Bear with us, oh men of the South; aid us in caring for our dead, it is woman's place to linger around the tomb; help us to cherish the memory of those men 'who won renown and for a noble cause have nobly died.' " The outcome of this alliance between the Confederate Dead and organized elite women was to force male critics, like M. A. Stovall and his fellow petitioners, to acquiesce in the expanded public space and social power not only of the Confederate Dead, defined now as the common soldier, but of domestic relations in general, as a central organizing principle of public life, and the decision-making authority of the women who were its agents.[64]

On October 31, 1878, the Confederate Monument was finally unveiled. A procession similar to that organized for the laying of the cornerstone three years earlier was once again formed, led by the Richmond Hussars, with the Ladies' Memorial Association again last but certainly not least. On this occasion, however, the expanded significance of the Ladies' Memorial Association in the public organizational structure of the town was reflected in the fact that not only did the officers of the association participate in the march, but they were followed by the committees of the association and finally the "ladies generally." Unlike in the dedication ceremonies, the officers did not seat themselves on the more secluded verandah of Emily Tubman's house, but were instead arrayed publicly on the open platform along with the disabled Confederate officers, dignitaries from the various civic organizations represented in the procession, the orators of the day, the governor, congressmen, ex-mayors and city council members, and specially invited guests, not the least of whom was the widow of Stonewall Jackson, whose husband's statue was on the monument to be unveiled.

According to the speaker of the day, Charles Colcock Jones, it was in "woman's heart" that the "gallant deeds" of the Confederate Dead were "enshrined forever," while the "cares and anxieties of life" were such as to "almost blot such recollections from men's minds."[65] More critically for the survivors' understanding of the meaning of the war itself, according to Jones it was the "self-abnegation" of Confederate women that had "nerved so many arms" for combat in the first place. The war itself was now depicted as a question of "duty" on the part of Confederate men, inspired in the first instance by their domestic attachments. As Jones explained, the monument was only the "logical sequence" of the "love, sympathy, self-denial, encouragement and devotion which, exhibited by mother, wife, sister, daughter during the progress of the revolution, had, in manly breasts, inspired hopes the most exalted, stimulated patriotism the purest, and prompted action the most heroic."[66]

In the war's aftermath, when the entire region was "filled with mourning," it was this domestic relationship that had persisted, "brave" in the face of the defeat of the Confederacy. "Hope had fled," Jones asserted, "and expectation perished. Sorrow, penury, disappointment and ashes were the common heritage; and, in the general gloom that encompassed all, there shone not a single star of substantial promise." None, that is, except the continued dedication of the "loyal women of our own Southland." These women's continued allegiance had resulted in this concrete manifestation of their dedication to the "cause" of their men's honor, the Confederate Monument they were gathered to dedicate that day.[67]

It was fitting, according to Jones, that Robert E. Lee should occupy such a lofty location on the monument, for he was symbolic in his "noble person" of the "culmination of our patriarchal civilization." But the highest honor, Jones concluded, was rightly reserved for the "manly form of the private soldier" in recognition of the "devotion, the patriotism, the self-denial, the privations, the labors and the triumphs of the private soldiers of the Confederacy." Here, at the highest point of the Confederate Monument itself, the meaning of antebellum "patriarchal" notions of manhood were joined to and ultimately superceded by the highest form of "self denial," in the "manly" form of the Confederate soldier.[68]

Although the ladies made no public statement from the platform at the dedication ceremonies, they published the following day a pronouncement in the local press articulating the role they envisioned for the monument in the moral economy of the town. They expressed the hope that the prominently located monument would at least briefly arrest the attention of the town's busy populace, as they hurried past it in their "feverish race for gain, when the hard driven bargain and the false weight and the deceitful balances are changing men's hearts and consciences into the world's hard coin, even here within the shadow of its purity." The women hoped that the citizenry would pause before the monument and recall the lasting "golden" lesson of the conflict, that "men love their fellow men" and that they would feel their own "selfishness" rebuked. They expressed the desire that the story of the war that the citizens saw depicted before them, "that story of lives laid down that other men might live," would give the living "fresh faith and courage to redeem their own." Finally they wrapped the memorial in Christian rhetoric and analogy, expressing the hope that when men saw this monument "pointing ever to the sky," that "their hearts be lifted higherward, and their stained and sinful lives be led to Him— who gave His own most precious life for them and us—Thine only Son, our Lord."[69]

In this postwar memorial version of sectional conflict and war, the Confederate soldier went to war out of his domestic obligation as a responsible and dutiful son, brother, or husband. He did not enter the fray to advance his economic interests or to assert his political prerogatives as a free man. Instead, he went to war to meet his responsibility to defend his domestic dependents. He was seen as standing in defense of his own home ground, attempting to protect the innocent and vulnerable Southland against the violating tred of the aggressive, marauding, generally uncouth and unwashed Yankee. In this postwar retelling of the story, the Confederacy itself reemerged as the embodiment of the now-defeated position of the postwar white male, reduced to a position of defensive vulnerability by military defeat and the loss of his right to hold property in black slaves.

So in the form of the Memorial tradition, the postwar reconstruction of southern white men came to rewrite the very cause of the war itself. When the crowds gathered in Augusta to honor the Confederate Dead, their presence was therefore as much, if not more, a matter of honoring themselves and marking their own postwar transformation as it was a matter of honoring the fallen. After all, the Confederate Dead may or may not have participated in the war out of a sense of domestic duty, but the postwar survivor most certainly participated in a war for the daily survival of himself and his family. It validated the postwar experience of southern white men while also serving to rescue the besmirched honor of the Confederate Dead who, from the location of the more limited postbellum "place" of their survivors, had critically overstepped themselves in their drive for an independent slaveholding Confederacy.

So it was that as the actual memory of the dead receded with every passing year, the intensity of the Confederate Memorial activities came to loom ever larger. The crowd of ten thousand who gathered in 1875 in order to lay the cornerstone of the Confederate Monument was the largest in the history of the town. The crowd that gathered there three years later for its dedication doubled that record.[70] Although this reconstruction focused in the first instance on the restoration of the reputation of defeated Confederate men, it was never merely a question of restoring the old antebellum order of things. The motives of the Confederate Dead were redefined to reflect the expanded significance of the domestic arena in the experience of all the postwar Confederate survivors. They reflected both the domestication and privatization of male gender roles as well as the expanded public presence of their women. This was symbolized most concretely, perhaps, in the closing scene at the dedication. The official ceremonies completed, Confederate veterans in the audience converged upon the main platform and, filing by the widow of Stonewall Jackson, they respectfully shook her hand.[71]

Let us see to it, my Comrades, that we are not misinterpreted by our sons. A proper conception and a due observance of the principles and conduct of those who, in the past, illustrated the integrity, the virtues and the valor of the Old South, will best insure the manliness, the honor and the courage of the future.

—Charles Colcock Jones Jr., 1887

7

The Divided Mind as a Gendered Mind

THE CONFEDERATE SURVIVORS ASSOCIATION AND THE NEW SOUTH

The year 1878 was pivotal in the history of the postwar social transformation of Augusta. The construction and dedication of the Confederate Memorial in the fall of that year marked the culmination of ten years of organized effort on the part of the ladies of the town to preserve the memory of their wartime domestic loss through the public commemoration of the Confederate Dead. Perhaps the greatest achievement of the Ladies' Memorial Association was to be found not in the construction of this monument to the memory of the dead, but rather in the way this work of memorializing the dead also served to reconstruct the living. By understanding Confederate men's participation in the war as grounded in the first instance in their commitment to the defense of their homes and their women and children, the memorial movement served to validate the role that those men still living in the town and county had played in the conflict, despite their military defeat to the North and the loss of the right to slave ownership.

The success of this work of reconstructing the living came to structural fruition when on April 30, 1878, in the aftermath of the Ladies' Memorial Day celebration, a few prominent citizens of Augusta met to form a Confederate Survivors Association. While the Cavalry Association had been formed in the year immediately following the war, this new organization brought together Confederate veterans of all ranks and forms of service in the town and county. Its formation indicated that ex-Confederate men now intended to take up the task of honoring their own fallen dead and caring for their own needy comrades. The Ladies' Memorial Association, and in later years the United Daughters of the Confederacy, would continue to decorate the graves on Memorial Day, but they would no longer lead the memorial movement as a whole.[1]

Within a year of its formation, the Confederate Survivors Association claimed 243 members. Although this number constituted a substantial membership, especially for an organization scarcely a year old, it still represented only a fraction of the possible total.[2] At the first annual meeting in 1879, the president of the association, Charles Colcock Jones Jr., predicted that the membership would continue to expand. At the same time, with mingled pride and regret, he pointed to the ultimately finite character of the association's membership. Only those men who had actually served in the Confederate war effort could claim the status of survivors. Regardless of the organization's current popularity, it must inevitably begin to dwindle in size. Indeed, the annual meetings of the organization frequently began with a reading of the names of those members who had died in the previous year. As the president explained in his annual speech of 1887, this "heavy mortality" was not the result of the "flight of time only." It was also the consequence of the "burthensome losses, weighty disappointments, mental and physical afflictions" that Confederate veterans experienced in the postwar years.[3]

Left without a nation to support them, Confederate veterans initially could only look to their own immediate families and their larger kin networks to supply the material aid and social recognition that they otherwise lacked. As the years passed, however, and as the physical and emotional traumas of the war were compounded by the difficulties created by a sagging postwar economy and by the aging process itself, the condition of some veterans reached a critical state. According to the president of the Survivors Association, it was the increasing number of veterans dying premature deaths, some even ending their days without the resources to provide a decent burial, that had led to the formation of the association in 1878. Uniting as one "brethren," the association dedicated itself to promoting a "closer union and a more pronounced fellowship" among those men who had served as officers and common soldiers in the Confederate war effort. Like the members of one family, the supporters of the association committed themselves to care for each other in "seasons of sickness and distress" and to provide a decent burial for those unable to afford one.[4]

Of course, not all the men in Augusta and the surrounding county who joined together to form the association in 1878 were physically disabled or economically destitute. Certainly for Charles Colcock Jones, the president of the association and a prosperous lawyer in the city, the attraction of the organization lay not so much in the economic assistance it could afford him, but rather in the amelioration of a social and psychological wound that the war had inflicted upon him. Jones could never accept the loss of personal and political power that military defeat by the North and the emancipation of the slaves brought to men of his class and his race. For him, the economic destitution of some of the veterans signified not so much the class diversity of the veterans as the depths of their common social loss in the context of postwar defeat. If they had won the war, their victory would have assured all of them a public validation of their role in the conflict, regardless of their class position. As it was, they all found themselves confronting a future that was, as Jones put it, "disfigured by the skeletons of dead hopes and crushed expectations."[5]

Of course, organizational efforts to recognize the wartime sacrifices of Confederate veterans and to provide appropriate burial space for the Confederate Dead were already under way thanks to the work of the Ladies' Memorial Association. In the spring of 1878, when the Confederate Survivors Association was first formed, the Ladies' Memorial Association was itself at a turning point in its work. The Confederate Monument, which had provided the focus of their organizing efforts for the previous ten years, was on the verge of completion. In the establishment of this monument the association had not only ensured that the Confederate Dead would remain a vital presence in the collective public life of the town, they had also rendered permanently public their domestic relationship to their men, made temporarily public during the war. Thus when the Confederate Survivors Association formed itself into one "brethren," it quickly occupied this space originally opened by the public commemoration of domestic loss by the Ladies' Memorial Association. The Confederate Survivors Association could now look to the memorial movement to offer them an alternative source of public validation, as well as the private solace that they so craved and needed in the face of their political and military defeat.[6]

The ladies, having forged this public domestic space through their very presence in it, could now relinquish leadership to the Confederate Survivors Association, which embodied the highest manifestation of their own handiwork, their reconstructed men. While the monument served to mark ex-Confederate women's domestic loss and to construct that loss as a worthy and honorable one, the Confederate Survivors Association revealed that this strategy had proven successful after all. The Confederate veterans may have lost their political independence after being defeated by the North. The scope of their power as household heads may have been truncated through the emancipation of the slaves which ensued. Nevertheless, they had now at least gained a new "public" family in the memorial movement. Domestically empowered by their women to take up their own defense, they could once again organize as they had in the war to publicly express their solidarity as one "brethren."

From the outset, the Confederate Survivors Association set out to demonstrate that it would indeed take up the task of remembrance where the Ladies' Memorial Association had left off. As the women completed their task of erecting the Confederate Monument to commemorate the Confederate Dead, the survivors of the war took up the task of their own self-reconstruction. Indeed, the very emergence of the organization itself was accompanied by a transfer of power, as the Confederate Survivors

Association almost immediately moved to supplant the Ladies' Memorial Association as the leading organization in the city's memorial movement. Seizing the initiative at the first quarterly meeting of the association in August 1878, the members took it upon themselves to graciously encourage the Ladies' Memorial Association to remain organized, even though their task of erecting the Confederate Monument was at that point almost complete, and adopted a resolution inviting the Ladies' Memorial Association to join *them* in preserving the Confederate Monument and in carrying out Memorial Day activities. At their second quarterly meeting in October 1878, they went one step further in structurally subordinating the Ladies' Memorial Association when they extended to them the status of honorary members of the Confederate Survivors Association.[7]

It still remained the appropriate task of the women to decorate the graves of the Confederate Dead, as it had been their place to mark their loss through the establishment of a Confederate Monument. And in the fall of 1878, the Confederate Survivors Association took a supporting role in the final unveiling ceremonies for the monument. However, having finally put the Confederate Dead to rest, the Confederate Survivors now emerged to claim what they perceived to be their rightful place as the Confederacy's heroes. In the future, their president asserted, "paying suitable tributes to those who gave their lives in defense of home, country, right and liberty" belonged in the first instance to those who had stood in battle alongside them as comrades rather than to their women, as mothers, wives, or sisters, who could only passively consecrate this loss.[8]

This claim to the primacy of male fraternity within the larger memorial "family" was not, however, tantamount to a simple return to the military bonding these men had experienced during the war, when fraternity had been directly associated with the establishment of the Confederacy and the defense of their political and economic prerogatives in the slaveholders' republic. In their move to reassert control over the memorialization of the war, the men of the Confederate Survivors Association had to incorporate the domestic transformation of their wartime experience that the Ladies' Memorial Association had promoted in the decade after the war. It was, after all, in this public domestic space carved out by the Ladies' Memorial Association that their wartime behavior could be recognized as honorable. The Confederate Survivors Association reflected this in its initial date of formation in May 1878, following the Memorial Day Activities, and in the scheduling of its annual meeting on Confederate Memorial Day every year following. The Confederate Survivors president acknowledged this when he prioritized the defense of "home" before the assertion of "country, right and liberty." The preservation of slavery did not even appear on the list.[9]

Thus the Confederate Survivors Association took up the direction of the memorial movement, but within the domestic framework of reinterpretation that the Ladies' Memorial Association had initially set up. Indeed, the development of the Confederate Survivors Association followed the same pattern taken by the Ladies' Memorial Association a decade earlier. Initially both organizations focused on the needs of the dead and the dying among them. Just as during the war the ladies' hospital aid societies had found their basis for public association in the demands posed by nursing wounded soldiers, the Confederate Survivors Association focused their energies upon the social and economic support of the veterans of the war. As in the case of the immediate postwar efforts of the Ladies' Memorial Association to set off a separate burial ground for the Confederate Dead, the first request of the Confederate Survivors to the city council in 1878 was for a separate burial in the city cemetery. While the ladies proceeded to decorate the graves of the Confederate Dead, the Confederate Survivors Association also had their own burial rituals. They routinely provided a detail at the funeral of each member, with the maimed veterans providing the color guard. At times the entire association turned out, accompanied by a "wartorn, tattered and smoke grimed stand of Confederate colors."[10]

No one was actually buried in the Confederate Survivors lot in the city cemetery until January 20, 1881, when William Wright, a forty-nine-year-old carpenter and a thirty-year resident of Augusta, was interred. A single man, he had died of consumption in the hospital. Apparently, he had no family besides the veterans. Sick for three months before he died, he was probably dependent upon the support of the Confederate Survivors Association for his burial. In the next decade, three more men were also buried in the CSA plot, men with similar descriptions. All in their late forties or fifties, skilled workers or small businessmen, three of them were single or widowed. The epitaph of one of them, Joseph Smith, indicates the centrality of their military experience in their life, it read only, "Joseph Smith. Cobb's Legion. CSA."[11]

Through their association, Confederate veterans tried to ensure that at least among their own ranks these men would be accorded the kind of homage and respect that they would have received from the nation had they been victorious in the war. While the four men who were buried in the first decade of the organization indicate that a real need existed among some veterans residing in the city for a "decent" burial, the small number of such cases indicates the psychological role that the organization must have played for the majority of the members, who never personally found themselves threatened with the possibility of a pauper's grave.[12]

While both the Ladies' Memorial Association and the Confederate Survivors Association found their initial organizational basis in providing for the wounded, the aged, and the deceased among Civil War soldiers, they looked to the next generation of the memorial family to carry on this work. They realized that children were critical to their effort. From the outset, the Ladies' Memorial Association had recruited large numbers of children from the public schools to assist them in decorating the graves of the Confederate Dead on Confederate Memorial Day. While some of these children were boys, the overwhelming majority were girls, undoubtedly following the lead of their mothers, sisters, or other adult female relations who already belonged to the organization. The organization of ex-Confederate men in the Confederate Survivors Association also created the possibility for organizing a new generation of boys for the commemorative movement. In his annual speech of 1891, Charles Colcock Jones called for the organization of these young men. The success of the Confederate Survivors Association in replicating itself in the younger generation was evidenced by the recruitment of younger members and in the eventual formation of the Sons of the Confederate Veterans. The Daughters of the Confederacy, founded in 1891, stood in similar relationship to the Ladies' Memorial Association.[13]

With the formation of these second-generation memorial organizations it became apparent that even after those who actually experienced the war had died, their account of the war would be perpetuated through the continued activity of their sons and daughters. When ex-Confederate women in the town had formed the Ladies' Memorial Association in the immediate aftermath of the war, and even when the veterans formed the Confederate Survivors Association a decade later, they had no assurance that the movement would outlive their own generation. Thus, after having secured an appropriate burial for the dead, the Ladies' Memorial Association turned their organizational efforts toward the construction of the

Confederate Monument. The monument was critical in their eyes because it was one way to guarantee that their version of the story would outlast them and even their own families. They hoped that through the creation of such a public marker they could insure the respect and recognition that they felt was due to the Confederate soldiers.

The Confederate Survivors Association again followed a similar pattern of development. Once they had secured a separate burial ground for Confederate veterans, they committed the organization to providing every veteran, however destitute, with a decent burial there. Then they too turned their energies toward the establishment of Confederate monuments in the town. In June 1878, they took up the defense of what remained of the Confederate Powderworks. During the war, this establishment had been the largest producer of munitions in the Confederacy. After the war, the buildings of the manufactory were destroyed by occupying Union troops, and by the spring of 1878, when the Confederate Survivors Association was formed, only the massive chimney of the works remained. This chimney stood along the banks of the canal as a lone witness to the central role Augusta had played as a major supplier of war materiel for the Confederacy. But in 1878 even this last remnant of Augusta's Confederate past was threatened by plans for the construction of the first new postwar textile mill, the Enterprise Factory, on the site. Mill developers planned to incorporate the Powderworks chimney into the very structure of the new mill to provide a smokestack for the works. As this plan became public, however, a campaign was organized to defend the chimney, and the Confederate war effort that it represented, in the face of this challenge posed by the rush to embrace a New South.[14]

The mill construction was first seen as a threat to this relic of the Confederacy by Gertrude Thomas, at that time an officer in the Ladies' Memorial Association. In May 1878, she wrote a letter to the *Augusta Chronicle and Sentinel* urging that the millowners be prevented from going forward with their plans. "Save us," she wrote, "from this humiliation." The new textile mill, she argued, should never be allowed to subsume physically the chimney of the Confederate Powderworks, any more than the new order could be allowed to simply blot out the old. The chimney, she suggested, should remain as it was, an autonomous structure in front of the proposed new mill. An iron railing should be put around it to set it off forever from the everyday traffic that the mill would surely generate, and a marble tablet should be placed on the chimney, with the dedication, "To the Memory of the Southern Dead." [15]

As in the case of the Confederate Monument, Thomas claimed that her intent in urging the preservation of the chimney was not to intensify sectional conflict or to revive the cause of Confederate independence. She only hoped that the chimney could be preserved to help assure that, whatever new social and economic priorities the town developed, "the memory of that sacred time, hallowed by the tears of our women, and the bravery of our men," would never be entirely effaced. This appeal by Thomas reflected the central concerns of the Ladies' Memorial Association, to insure that the Confederate Dead would not be forgotten and that their own domestic sacrifice in the loss of these men would be publicly marked at the same time. [16]

Much as the formation of the Confederate Survivors Association indicated that Civil War veterans could now take up the task of their own reconstruction, the shift in the struggle over Confederate Monuments, from the marking of the Confederate Dead to the fate of the Powderworks chimney, indicated a parallel move among women. While the Ladies' Memorial Association had focused on validating their own domestic loss, the Confederate Survivors Association was committed, as Jones put it, to the "conservation of our identity." The chimney thus represented more than a struggle over the preservation of a piece of the Confederate legacy, for the Confederate Survivors it represented a struggle over their very understanding of themselves. [17]

Thus when Thomas wrote her letter to the local press, appealing to several male associations in the town to "save us from this humiliation," the Confederate Survivors Association promptly responded to her appeal. They petitioned the city council in June for some kind of redress. In response the Canal Committee of the city council agreed that the chimney should indeed remain as it was, an autonomous structure in the landscape of the town, and conferred the responsibility for the upkeep and protection of the monument on the Confederate Survivors Association. But while the city council granted the request of the Confederate Survivors Association to preserve the separate status of the Powderworks Chimney, they did so with one reservation. The chimney was to be transformed into a Confederate monument and granted a permanent place in the public life of the town, but only so long as no conflict arose between whatever was required to preserve the monument and the needs of the manufactory. The monument, they instructed the Confederate Survivors Association, was not to "interfere" with the normal functioning of the new mill.[18]

In President Jones's speech to the Confederate Survivors Association at its next annual meeting in 1879, however, he conveyed a very different understanding of the agreement that had been reached. He assured the membership that as a result of their petition to the city council, the chimney would not be "in any manner rendered subservient to the purposes of manufacture." In the years that followed, however, Jones's annual addresses indicated a deepening understanding that the textile development of the postwar era, in stark contrast to the initial construction of the Augusta Factory in the antebellum era, would not serve to reinforce the old agrarian, commercial order, but would gradually undermine it and replace it with a new, industrial social order.[19]

Indeed, the year 1878 was a pivotal year not only in the gender structure of Augusta's memorial movement but also in the economic development of the town, with construction at the first new postwar textile mill, the Enterprise Factory. Ever since the close of the war, when the city council had pointed to the desirability of building a new textile mill in order to provide employment for those white women and children who were left without husbands and fathers by war, mill boosters had been agitating for industrial development as an answer to the town's social and economic woes. The Augusta Factory, the one antebellum textile mill in the town, was able to engage in a substantial expansion in the 1870s, but despite the prosperous condition of the mill and the ready availability of white female and child labor, the city was not able to afford the costs of constructing a canal that would make possible the increase in waterpower necessary for a second factory. At the same time, they were unable to raise sufficient local or northern capital to defray capital costs. Finally, in 1872, the expansion of the canal commenced, and by 1878 sufficient capital had been raised to begin the construction of the first postwar mill. Thereafter many other new cotton mills would be constructed, transforming Augusta into the leading textile manufactory in the South by 1890. With eleven major mills, an aggregate capital of over $4.5 million, and a textile workforce of more than twenty-five hundred, local mill boosters could with some legitimacy refer to the city as the "Lowell of the New South."[20]

In his annual address to the Confederate Survivors Association in 1881,

Jones noted that in its very physical size the new mill construction was coming to overshadow the old Powerworks Chimney. He pointed out that "but for its towering altitude and robust proportions, its identity would be imperiled by the massive structures clustering about it." By 1881, the Enterprise had been joined along the banks of the canal by several even larger new mills, the King and the Sibley mills. In Jones's view, the increase in urban population that these mills facilitated loomed as a threat to the Confederate legacy. "No longer removed from the ebb and flow of the tide of life, [the chimney] will year by year confront the increasing multitudes that will visit and abide in our city." In 1882, however, Jones still hoped that Augusta would be able to avoid a complete transition to an industrial social order. He pointed to the fact that even while gripped with massive industrial development, the town remained a "peaceful, law-abiding community," not so large that "personal responsibility of individual membership was dissolved in general anomie or to create huge fortunes." By his annual address of 1889, however, Jones had lost all hope that this personal interface, which he identified as one of the key characteristics of Augusta's antebellum social order, would survive the onslaught of postwar industrial development. "I call you to witness," he urged one gathering of the Confederate Survivors Association, "that this adoration of wealth—this bending the knee to the Golden Calf—this worship of mortals gifted with the Midas touch, savors of a sordid and debasing fetishism at variance with the spirit of true religion and emasculatory of tokens of robust manhood. I call you to witness that 'Mammon is the largest slave-holder in the world.' "[21]

In Jones's view the old patriarchal, slaveholding household economy had provided the basis for a "robust manhood," constructed out of the direct interface between the white male head of household and subordinate members, both white and black. As the industrial development of the town progressed, however, it undercut this direct and personal manifestation of "robust manhood" and replaced it instead with a more impersonal market relationship based on wage labor. As Jones put it, in replacing the patriarchal, slaveholding household head with the coupon clipping capitalist, "Mammon" had been made the "largest slaveholder in the world." For Jones, then, the ultimate fate of the Confederate Powderworks, to be lost in the town's burgeoning industrial and urban growth, reflected not only this decline of an agrarian-based commercial economic order, but also the destruction of a particular construction of white manhood, which he had fought the war to defend.[22]

For Charles Colcock Jones, the Confederate memorial movement increasingly came to represent a last-ditch defense against the emergence of a full-blown industrial social order in the city and the southern region more generally. Other observers, however, understood the memorial movement to be part of a larger process of gender-based accommodation to the social and economic changes that the war and its aftermath presented to white southern men and women. This, at least, was the position taken by Wilbur Fiske Tillett, a professor at Vanderbilt University. An avid advocate of New South philosophy, Tillett published two articles in the *Century Magazine*, "White Man of the South" and "Southern Womanhood as Affected by the War," both of which discussed the relationship between the abolition of slavery, the expansion of the free-labor system, and the emergence of new gender roles among white southerners in the postwar South.[23]

According to Tillett, although most observers assumed that what was new about the New South was the altered status of the freedpeople, the postwar transformation of white men was equally as revolutionary. For as much as the abolition of slavery served to free the ex-slave, so too did it serve to emancipate the white man. Both white and black southerners had been held in the "thrall" of "degraded" attitudes toward labor created by slavery. It was therefore not only the black man and woman who were freed when slavery was abolished, labor itself was emancipated to a newly respectable status in the southern social order. For white men this meant liberation from a "bondage to leisure" that had been the consequence of the "contempt of labor" slavery had generated. The white man of the South was thus transformed into a "new man." No longer a "dependent idler" or a "gentleman of leisure," the southern white man was now rendered an "independent, self-reliant worker."[24]

Clearly the understanding that both Tillett and Jones had concerning what constituted a desirable form of manhood was directly related to their vision of what constituted a desirable larger social and economic order making this form of manhood possible in the first place. While Tillett could point to irreversible changes in the larger social and economic order to reinforce his argument, he nonetheless recognized that the emergence of a "new man" to match this new social and economic order was neither a simple nor a painless outcome of the war. Here, according to Tillett, was where the memorial movement, and the changes in white gender roles that it reflected, stepped in to play a pivotal role. As he put it, it took the white South over ten years of "wearing the black garb of mourning" and "sorrow over the lost cause" before white southern men were able to adapt to the "new condition of life and labor." According to Tillett, the New South could only really begin after this period of deepest mourning was completed. It was manifested structurally in the development of manufactures of various kinds, particularly in the boom in textile mill construction in the 1880s.[25]

The construction of these mills, according to Tillett, constituted the physical reflection of a new consciousness among white men of the South. Much as the Confederate Survivors Association envisioned the Powderworks Chimney to constitute the physical representation of their antebellum "identity" as free white men, so Tillet argued that the mills constituted the embodiment of newly reconstructed white men, as "earnest, progressive, public spirited working men." The war, and white reconstruction in its aftermath, had taught white men the necessity of thinking "less concerning himself and more concerning the common good than ever before." In his companion essay concerning new women in the New South, Tillett made a parallel argument for changes that the war wrought in white female gender roles. As white men had become more subordinated to the needs of their families and the white community as a whole, white women had become more independent and forthright. As ex-Confederate men turned their energies to the question of daily support of their households through their own labor, ex-Confederate women had increasingly looked to the larger public issues that affected white women and their families. Thus, according to Tillett, as middle-class white men became mill boosters, middle-class white women organized domestic reform movements like the Women's Christian Temperance Union. They worked to promote expanded educational opportunities for their daughters so that they might avoid the experiences of their own mothers, who too often found themselves without the personal resources for self-protection during the war and particularly in its aftermath.[26]

Tillett's vision was overly optimistic on a number of counts. While the break with slave labor and the move toward an industrial order clearly entailed both the loss of an old form of white male dominance and the demise of the household as the core economic unit of the southern social order, it is not at all clear that even ten years of mourning were sufficient to render white southerners happy participants in their new role as "workers" in the industrial social order. Nor is it clear that ten years of mourning were sufficient to make them even acquiesce in the new status of the freedpeople or increased autonomy among white women. Indeed, it is obvious that when Tillett discussed the emergence of a "new man" more concerned with the "common good," he meant a "common good" grounded in the interests of the white family and more generally in the white public. After all, the textile mills created a new form of labor for "whites only." Indeed, Tillett could not even bring himself to recognize that the real break with the antebellum social order that the textile mills effected was not only the expanded wage employment of white men, but perhaps more tellingly in the increased employment of white women, particularly the employment of married white women.[27]

Although Tillett applauded the decline of "helplessness" as an ideal for white women, the antithesis of this helplessness for him was not wage labor among white women. What Tillett envisioned was an expanded domestic presence for white women within the public realm, a presence that found its postwar genesis in the activities of the Ladies' Memorial Association and was grounded most strongly among the upper- and middle-class women in the town. As he noted, "so far as this movement may have any tendency to take woman out of her true place in the home, to give her man's work to do and to develop masculine qualities in her, it finds no sympathy in the South."[28]

For both ex-Confederate men and women, then, the memorial organizations allowed for a kind of fusion between the old self and the new. In the case of domestically organized women, they could continue in the work of "reconstructing" their men at the same time they pioneered the further development of an ever expanding public domesticity, in the schoolroom, in the childcare centers for working women, even to the organized effort to curb men's drinking in the WCTU. From this perspective, it was indeed the very persistence of a backward-looking memorial movement that made a forward-looking New South possible. Thus, rather than being entirely replaced by the individualistic values of a new social order grounded in free labor, as Tillett envisioned, the memorial organizations represented and sustained an expanded Confederate community alongside the move to a "New South."

Although on some level members of the Confederate Survivors Association realized that the basis for a "robust" manhood had indeed been lost with the war, the emancipation of the slaves, and the growth of the new urban, industrial order, they were still not prepared, or perhaps not even able, to part with the old on the level of their own identity. The very formation of the Confederate Survivors Association itself reflected their need to create some public space where they could continue, if only in memorialization, to persist as they had in the past, or as they imagined they had in the past. Thus after duly noting those members who had passed away since the preceeding meeting, the annual meetings of the Confederate Survivors provided its members with the opportunity to remember collectively critical moments in their wartime experiences. The topics of annual talks varied, but in general they focused on creating a history of the war that celebrated the manly conduct of the Confederate veteran. This identity-validating history was based on a selective remembering of wartime events, a remembering that forgot the very real breaches of white men's roles as protectors of their women and children that the war had revealed, as well as the active subordination of the black community. What it remembered were the moments of manly valor evidenced by the veterans against their foes and the depth of support for their cause expressed by all household dependents, both white and black.

Take by way of illustration the annual Confederate Survivors Association address of 1884, entitled, "General Sherman's March from Atlanta to the Coast." When Sherman's troops had actually threatened to attack Augusta in the fall of 1864, after already having burnt much of Atlanta to the ground, the failure of at least some of the city's white men to volunteer in defense of the city had led to sarcastic letters to the paper suggesting that if no "real" men remained to the city, perhaps white women and slaves should be armed to fight. Precisely because Sherman's March provided this moment when white women and children were rendered most vulnerable and when white men appeared to be most lacking in "robust manhood," it emerged as a critical event in the retelling of the history of the war.[29]

In the Confederate Survivors' reconstruction of this event some twenty years later, the responsibility for violating manly codes of behavior was attributed not to white southern men's failure to properly "protect" these white women and children, but rather to the utter lack of a "robust manhood" among the Yankees. According to this Confederate Survivors Association remembering, it was the Yankees who refused to acknowledge that every man's *first* responsibility was to protect *all* dependent white women and children. In attacking Confederate women and children in the march through Georgia and South Carolina in the fall of 1864, they had demonstrated that they were not real men. In this postwar remembering of the event the tables were turned, and rather than offering a clear example of the limits of Confederate men's ability (or willingness) to protect their dependents, the responsibility for violating manly codes was attributed to the northern troops instead. Confederate men's very failure to successfully defend their homes now fueled their refusal to accept the legitimacy of their defeat at the hands of foes such as Sherman and his men.

After violating what appeared in the postwar southern context to be the first principle of manhood, the protection of "defenseless" white women and children, the Yankees were depicted as going yet one step further in their violation of "manly" tenets. According to this history of Sherman's March, it was the Yankee soldiers who actually "compelled" slaves on the plantations to assist them in "transporting the booty" they took from "unprotected women, fatherless children and decrepit old men." Not satisfied to simply attack white women and children and strip their households bare, the Yankees were charged with forcing the slave members of plantation households to make war on their white owners as well. Here the Yankees were charged with pitting one form of white male dependency, slavery, against another, the patriarchal dependence of white women and children, in order literally to destroy the white manhood of the southern Confederacy by rending the household structure out of which it was constructed in two.[30]

In a revealing contrast, the president of the Survivors Association told the story of a Confederate officer, Major Early, who, finding himself with a similar opportunity to attack northern civilians, declined to do so. Having successfully occupied a Pennsylvania town, this Confederate officer refused to order it burnt to the ground. He explained his forebearance to the citizens of this town by noting that while burning the town "would have been fully vindicated as an act of just retaliation for the unparalleled acts of brutality perpetrated by your own army on our own soil . . . we do not war on women and children." [31]

Even given similar opportunities, the president of the Confederate Survivors Association claimed, southern soldiers had declined to engage in behavior similar to that of their northern foes. Here white southern men were presented as refusing to employ tactics that, while they might have gained them military victories in the short run, would have cost them the basis for fighting the war in the first place. They were clearly caught in a bind, a bind that the war had forced upon them, to choose between their independence and autonomy in relation to other men and their commitment to protect and defend their loyal dependents. While we might see this heightened commitment to their domestic responsibilities as simply a convenient rationale for their defeat at the hands of northern white men, in 1884 speakers for the Confederate Survivors Association presented it as the most "manly" choice, which in no way indicated that they lacked valor as warriors or men. Indeed, white southern men were at the same time portrayed as being so deeply imbued with manly fortitude that even young boys and old men took up arms against the invading Yankees and fought to the bitter end.

This at least was the conclusion to be drawn from the topic of the 1883 annual address, "The Defense of Fort McAllister." It was there, in December of 1864, that a small garrison of one hundred and fifty Confederates, "chiefly old men and youths," attempted to fight off a much larger contingent of nine regiments of infantry from Sherman's army. Indeed, even the Union commander was alleged to have noted the militance of this small and beleaguered force. "We fought the garrison through the Fort to their bombproofs," he recalled in later years, "from which they still fought, and only succumbed as each man was individually overpowered." "At great cost," President Jones asserted in this address to the Confederate Survivors Association, "was the manhood of Georgia thus demonstrated." [32]

Military courage in confronting the northern invaders, diligence in the defense of their own women and children, and respect for an honorable code of behavior even in relation to the women and children of the enemy—these were stock pieces in the Confederate Survivors' celebration of the Confederate past. Wartime disaffection among the civilian population, whether white women or black slaves, was notably absent in these histories. Much as with the displacement of responsibility for the failure to protect onto Sherman and his troops, the departure of the slaves from the surrounding plantations and their flood into Augusta, which had so un-nerved the white population in the last year of the war, was now converted into a critical moment in the defense of the sanctity and the stability of the relationship between master and slave. As Jones explained it in his annual address of 1889, it was precisely at this moment of greatest "peril and alarm" that the slaves redoubled their efforts, "ministered kindly to the needs of unprotected women and children, [and] performed all the customary services with the same cheerfulness and alacrity as when sur-rounded by the usual controlling agencies." "Nothing," Jones concluded in this speech, "attests more surely the attachment then entertained by the servant for his master and family." In this history of the war, white women also never wavered, and in the postwar period they continued to manifest their adherence to this understanding of their men's "brave deeds wrought in the name of truth and freedom" through the erection of monuments to honor the Confederate Dead.[33]

What we find here is the reconstruction of a white male "view from nowhere," built out of a selective remembering of the past that was em-powered through the continued adherence of white women to the "cause" of their men. This is not to suggest that these stories were not true, but rather that there were competing stories that they wrote over, stories of independence and autonomy on the part of those who continued to remain nondominant in the southern social order. The closer such subordinate groups came to achieving actual equality and independence, the more crucial it became to rewrite these stories, and the more central became the whole process of retelling to the establishment and expansion of the Con-federate Memorial tradition. On an individual level, these stories offered a way of resisting the new order and thereby "conserving" old "identities." At the same time, they offered a way of mediating the inevitable need to change by reconstructing a past that was appropriate to requirements of the present. What persisted was a white male identity that could survive even amid the new social realities, in which slaves were emancipated and white men were no longer able to "protect" their own women and children as they had in the past. In part the responsibility for this predicament was blamed on the Yankees. After all, they were the ones who attacked de-fenseless southern women, who forced the disaffection of their slaves. In these stories, Confederate men emerge as valiant even in defeat. Only the overpowering numbers and economic resources of the Yankees brought an undeserved victory. The heroic Confederates fought literally to the last boy and debilitated old man in hand-to-hand combat.

History emerges here as the residue of that which could not be transformed out of individual identities. It offered a way to continue to practice a social reality in a new social context in which critical aspects of the social construction of white manhood had been abolished. With the formation of the Sons and Daughters of the Confederacy, and eventually even the Children of the Confederacy, this "reality" could be passed on to a whole new generation who never directly experienced it but who with the rewriting of history could embrace it as "fact." As Charles Colcock Jones urged the Confederate Survivors Association in the annual meeting of 1887, "Let us see to it, my Comrades, that we are not misinterpreted by our sons. A proper conception and a due observance of the principles and conduct of those who, in the past, illustrated the integrity, the virtues and the valor of the Old South, will best ensure the manliness, the honor and the courage of the future."[34]

Nonetheless, in the case of both the Ladies' Memorial Association and the Confederate Survivors Association, such intentions simply to preserve the "facts" ironically contributed to the very changes they were supposed to suppress. In the case of the Ladies' Memorial Association, the very fact that white southern women became the centerpiece of their men's continued "honor" served to transform the basis for that honor in a newly domestic fashion while it increased these women's public power. In the case of the Confederate Survivors Association, the very effort to "conserve their identity" was actually part of a larger process of accommodation and transformation of white male gender roles to the rise of industrial capitalism with its free-labor work ethic and the corresponding alterations in the social relations of the New South.

In his classic work, *The Origins of the New South*, C. Vann Woodward pointed out what appeared to be a contradiction in the postwar attitudes of defeated white southerners, who at one and the same time turned their energies to promoting the development of such "Lowells of the New South" as late-nineteenth-century Augusta while simultaneously continuing to embrace the "myths of the Old South," as enshrined in the Confederate Memorial tradition. Woodward described this active promotion of an urban, industrial New South alongside the growing memorialization of the

Old as the "divided mind" of the South. He described the basis for the creation of this "divided mind" as lying in a "social revolution the most unrecorded and undepicted, in proportion to its magnitude that ever was," which followed upon the Confederacy's defeat. Given the scope and the depth of their loss, Woodward concluded, it was not hard to understand why the "starved spirit" of white southerners turned to the Confederate Memorial tradition. The "things of the heroic age, the four epic years," he wrote, rapidly came to serve as a "definite soothing salve." What appeared puzzling to Woodward about this intense attachment to the Confederate Memorial tradition, however, was the way in which those southerners who were most committed to the New Order, to the development of an urban, industrial South, were also frequently the most militant supporters of the Confederate Memorial tradition and the old, slaveholding, plantation society that it apparently sanctified. Indeed, Woodward concluded, "the deeper the involvements in commitments to the New Order, the louder the protests to the Old," and this with "no apparent sense of inconsistency, certainly none of duplicity."[35]

What Woodward termed the "divided mind" of the New South finds structural confirmation in the pattern of Augusta's postwar development. As we have seen, the Confederate Memorial tradition took root early in the town. Not only was the Ladies' Memorial Association one of the largest and most active in the region, the organization of the Confederate Survivors Association in 1878 was one of the earliest such organizations among Confederate veterans. These organizations flourished side by side with the emergence of an intense mill boosterism and a concentration of textile mills that dominated the postwar southern textile industry throughout the 1880s. These movements do appear to be antithetical to each other, if we regard the Confederate Memorial movement as an expression of the persistence of values rooted initially in an agrarian, slaveholding Old South, as opposed to those of an urban, industrial New South, presumably promoted by the mill movement. If, however, we shift our angle of vision from the white male class perspective from which Woodward (along with his subjects) perceived the situation and consider instead the relations of race and gender out of which the "divided mind" of these men was built, it becomes possible to understand how the memorialization of the Old South Confederacy can be reconciled with mill boosterism and a commitment to the New. What both movements shared was a continued commitment to the perpetuation of white race and male gender domination, as it could be perpetuated in the face of white men's postwar loss of political and economic power.

In the case of both the Confederate Memorial movement and the construction of the textile mills in Augusta, the role of white male heads of households as "protectors" of their dependents was continued out of the Old Order. Indeed, as we have seen already in the case of the Ladies' Memorial Association's vision of domestic defense as Confederate men's first motivation in the war, they made the gendered face of that role primary. From this perspective, the construction of the mills now offered the white male citizenry the opportunity to further manifest the depth of their commitment to the continued paternalistic "protection" of white women and children. As the Confederate Memorial movement had rendered forever public the loss of the Confederate Dead, so the expansion of the mills would allow them to continue to act on their heightened perception of their responsibilities as social fathers to Confederate widows and orphans. By creating the means whereby these women could find a substitute means of economic support, the construction of the mills created the possibility of carrying out in actual practice the domestic ideological commitments asserted by the Confederate Memorial movement.

As much as the Confederate Memorial movement and the construction of the mills continued and expanded the Confederate vision of white men as protectors of all white women, so too did both movements share a commitment to the perpetuation of white racial domination. Through the denial of the defense of slavery as a motive in secession and war, the Confederate Memorial movement not only laid the groundwork for intensifying the extent to which ex-Confederate men's sense of themselves was defined in relation to their women, it simultaneously created the basis for their denial of the newly freed status of the former slaves. By excluding the role of slavery in motivating secession, as well as by writing out the desires and activities of black Americans from the outcome of the war, the Confederate Memorial tradition contributed to the continued resistance of white southerners to the more egalitarian social order promised by emancipation. By offering better-paying mill work to white women and children only, the construction of the textile mills translated the continued denial of black rights into economic reality. Not only could mill construction reinforce the exclusionary racial vision of ex-Confederates in the town, it had the added advantage of maintaining the political domination of white men by increasing white rural migration to the town. By underwriting a white majority, it would, as one mill booster argued in support of the canal enlargement in 1872, "preserve us from radical rule."[36]

Of course this sorting out of the household dependents of the Old Order into the social categories of "loyal" white women and children, still presumably worthy of white male "protection," and the "disloyal" freed black population, now no longer a part of this white paternalistic vision, actually mirrored the real structural changes that had occurred during the war. It would be a mistake to think, however, that because they were confronted with these changes, the white male citizenry of Augusta could simply transform themselves to fit them, even for the sake of continued rule. Both the Confederate Memorial movement and the drive for new mill construction in the town in and of themselves indicate a process of working out a new form of white racial and male gender domination that was fraught with conflict and ambiguity, even for elite white men.

So it was that in 1891 Joseph Cumming gave the speech commemorating the one-hundredth anniversary of the establishment of the city of Augusta. Cumming spoke with a keen awareness of his own family legacy and a deep sense of the way Augusta's history had been entwined with his own. His grandparents were among the early white settlers in the region, and his grandfather, Thomas Cumming, was the town's first intendant. Along with his three brothers, Joseph Cumming himself had served loyally in the Confederate army, despite the concern of their mother, Julia Cumming, that all four of her sons were simultaneously risking death at the front. In the case of her youngest son, Julian, who died in a northern prison, this fear had sadly proven warranted. Her husband, Henry Harford Cumming, one of the leading antebellum promoters of textile development, had also played a critical role in Augusta's growth and in the war effort. Joseph Cumming recounted how Henry had stepped forward to greet Jefferson Davis after the president had been taken prisoner, and had later become so demoralized by the experience of defeat that he took his own life in the following year. Perhaps burdened by guilt along with overpowering memories, Joseph himself had returned from the war, where he had served as a captain, and proceeded to build up a successful law practice in the ensuing decades, a career he pursued alongside his central role in the Confederate Memorial movement.

Both because and in spite of all this history, in the face of everything that had changed since Augusta was founded as a small Indian trading power at the fall line of the Savannah, and everything that had not changed, Joseph Cumming delivered the speech celebrating the centennial year of Augusta's municipal history. In this speech he compared the one hundred year history of his city to the seven ages of man. Like any man, Augusta had experienced seven historical phases as it traveled a trajectory from youth to old age. Its "Golden Age," according to Cumming, occurred in the antebellum period, when Augusta was the central trading point for the cotton-producing slave plantations and farms in a two-hundred-mile radius. Farsighted men like his father had held on to this commercial dominance, even in competition with new urban centers, through the development of Augusta's antebellum textile industry. Through the construction of a canal on the Savannah River, civic-minded members of the city council insured the continued viability of Augusta's economic existence as a handmaiden to the cotton-producing, slave plantation economy of the region.[37]

As a result a new age emerged, what Cumming named the "Age of Manufactures." Although mill construction marked the advent of this new age in Augusta's history, according to Cumming it constituted no true break with the previous "Golden Age" but rather the extension of the town's early promise into less auspicious times. The "War Age" that followed was also envisioned as a further extension of the idealized old order. Indeed, it was during the "War Age" that Augusta's citizens experienced their "highest as well as intensest life," as they rose to the northern challenge to defend the social order that had created the basis for the "Golden Age." The result was a period in Augusta's history when "the sordid, the selfish, the commercial in us was subdued by our higher nature."[38]

In his history of the war, Cumming chose to forget the manner in which the wartime development of the city did not in fact serve to develop or even to maintain the regional cotton-producing, slave plantation economy of the "Golden Age." He chose to forget the charges launched against Augusta's merchants for hoarding and speculating in response to wartime market opportunities. He chose to forget the failure of some white men to rise to the military defense of their city. Perhaps most critically, he chose to forget the independent activity and active dissent of white women and the African-American community in Augusta during the war.

In accounting for the history of the city in terms of the seven ages of man, Cumming clearly did not mean to refer to "man" in the generic sense of all mankind. For him the experience of white men, especially elite white men, was synonymous with the history of the city itself. Thus his centennial history presented a picture of the city that was limited by his own social location as much as it was driven by it. In this regard it was no accident that the Civil War experience was both the most pivotal and most problematic moment in this account. On the one hand, Cumming could not but fail to recognize the ways in which the war had transformed Augusta's class, race, and gender order even as he failed to acknowledge the agency of nonelite white male groups. Indeed, it is in the course of his own self-presentation that he registers the way that these transformations had altered the way white manhood was constructed both in Augusta and in his account. Where others might have recognized the acquisition of autonomy and independence by members of the social order who had been previously "dependent," Cumming could only validate his own experience in the war and its aftermath in terms of the sacrifice white men made of themselves in order to preserve the old social order. In Cumming's history this transformation of white men from self-seeking to self-sacrificing thus became the critical "fact" about the war.

Indeed, it was this self-abnegating wartime experience that, according to Cumming, prepared "Augustans" for the postwar era, an era he named the "Iron Age," to contrast it to the antebellum "Golden Age." As he explained to his Centennial audience, Golden Ages were always characterized by "ease and plenty, love and peace, life blessed with good things acquired without effort and crowned with tranquil happiness." In the altered conditions of the postwar "Iron Age," however, "Augustans" found themselves "pressed with the hard conditions, the bitter struggles of life . . . in the past [life] was golden. Now it is iron in its hardness."[39]

Neither the destruction of slavery, the social and economic establishment of the freedpeople, nor the activity of white women and children as the primary labor force in the mills or in the newly established public school system figured in Cumming's discussion of the development of his postwar "Iron Age." Indeed, when forced to confront the question of the New South, Cumming vehemently denied its existence. In a speech delivered in 1893 before the New England Society of Charleston entitled "New Ideas, New Departures, New South," Cumming spent the entire time explaining why there actually could be no New South. "The subject assigned me is in effect, the 'New South.' I can only treat that subject as it presents itself to my mind. I could not deal with the subject by telling you what the New South is; for to my vision no New South is revealed."[40]

In this speech Cumming explained that it was the position of white men, especially slaveowning white men, that made the antebellum social order particularly "southern." "Slavery," he asserted, "made white men of the South absolute lords and masters of millions of men." It was this experience of mastery, the way that it empowered at least some white men to see the world as an extension and reflection of themselves, that marked the true southerner. According to Cumming, this concentration of power in the hands of white men created the best possible social order, a "Golden Age," because it brought out the best in white men. As he explained in his speech, the "term that most characterizes the representative southerner, in his sentiments, his conduct . . . is chivalry. [The South] was high minded. It was generous. It forebore to its own advantage." Precisely because white men had so much power in the antebellum South, they were put in a position to develop the ability to "forebear," to use their power in a "chivalrous" manner.[41]

The war and the white "reconstruction" that followed, while creating a crisis for this white male chivalry, also provided an opportunity to reconstitute it in an even purer, more sanctified form. In Cumming's account it was the war and the defeat and loss of slaveholding that emerged from it that transformed this manly "forebearance" into the task of subduing the "selfish" in their natures. By the time that Cumming delivered the annual Confederate Memorial Day speech in 1895, the conflict begun by the pursuit of power and self-interest had become an event motivated more by "sentiment" than any other war in all of recorded history. Southern men had, after all, been animated by a "true love" of their prerogatives, willing even to die for them. "We went to war not for conquest," Cumming asserted to his Memorial Day audience, "not for glory, not to escape oppression. But a proud and high spirited people flew to arms to defend what they considered their sacred right, from high-handed and presumptuous interference, albeit the right itself was little better than an abstraction."[42]

Northern men, by contrast, had been fired by self-interested, mercenary motives. In the long run they had been unmanned by their honorless pursuit of material gain. The result, Cumming asserted, was that southern men had in fact proven who were the "real" men. While "industrial might" may have given the North victory in battle, southern white men's dedication to their "honor" had given them the greater, moral victory. Assuming, that is, that the war had nothing to do with white southern men's relationship to northern men, nothing to do with their relationship to their slaves, now freed. Assuming that white men's "honor" stood or fell with their manliness as they now much more narrowly defined it, in terms of their role as "protectors" of their own white women and children. Assuming all this, remembering all this, as Cumming and his Memorial Day audience certainly did, then southern white "manliness" did, indeed, have the victory.

Notes

Introduction Masculinity in Crisis: Civil War History
as a "View from Somewhere"

1. *The Collected Works of Abraham Lincoln* (Washington, 1959), 2:461; Charles
   A. Beard and Mary R. Beard, *The Rise of American Civilization* (New York,
   1927), 2:53–54.
2. For surveys of this literature see David Donald, "American Historians and
   the Causes of the Civil War," *South Atlantic Quarterly* 59 (Summer 1960):
   340–61; Eric Foner, "The Causes of the American Civil War: Recent Inter-
   pretations and New Directions," *Civil War History* 20 (Sept. 1974): 197–214;
   and James McPherson, *Abraham Lincoln and the Second American Revolution* (New York, 1991), 3–22.
3. For a discussion of the literature on gender as a social construction, see Joan
   Wallach Scott, *Gender and the Politics of History* (New York, 1988), 28–50.
4. As cited by Jim Cullen, "'I's a Man Now': Gender and African American
   Men," in *Divided Houses: Gender and the Civil War*, ed. Catherine Clinton
   and Nina Silber (New York, 1992), 91. See also James McPherson, *The
   Negro's Civil War: How Americans Felt and Acted during the War for Union*
   (Urbana, 1965); Joseph Glathaar, *Forged in Battle: The Civil War Alliance*

between *Black Soldiers and White Officers* (New York, 1991); David Blight, *Frederick Douglass' Civil War: Keeping Faith in Jubilee* (Baton Rouge, 1989), 148–74; Dudley Cornish, *The Sable Arm: Negro Troops in the Union Army, 1861–1865* (New York, 1966).

5. David Roediger, *Toward the Abolition of Whiteness* (London and New York, 1994).

6. Susan Bordo, "Feminism, Postmodernism, and Gender-Scepticism," in *Feminism/Postmodernism*, ed. Linda J. Nicholson (New York, 1990), 133–156. While Thomas Nagel first coined the term "view from nowhere" in his book *The View from Nowhere* (New York, 1986), it is Susan Bordo who has placed it in its larger social context.

7. Bell Wiley, *Confederate Women* (Westport, Conn., 1975); and H. E. Sterx, *Partners in Rebellion: Alabama in the Civil War* (Cranbury, N.J., 1970). More recent works that emphasize the loyalty of Confederate women include George C. Rable, *Civil Wars: Women and the Crisis of Southern Nationalism* (Urbana, 1989); Jean E. Friedman, *The Enclosed Garden: Women and Community in the Evangelical South, 1830–1900* (Chapel Hill, 1985); and Jean Bethke Elshtain, *Women and War* (New York, 1987), 94–102.

8. Drew Faust, "Altars of Sacrifice: Confederate Women and the Narratives of War," *Journal of American History* 76 (March 1990): 1200–1228. Many historians have discussed Confederate women taking up directive roles; see for instance Anne Firor Scott, *The Southern Lady: From Pedestal to Politics, 1830–1930* (Chicago, 1970), 81–102; and more recently, Joan Cashin, "'Since the War Broke Out': The Marriage of Kate and William McClure" in Clinton and Silber, *Divided Houses*, 200–212; and Drew Faust, *Southern Stories: Slaveholders in Peace and War* (Columbia, Mo., 1992), 174–192.

9. Victoria Bynum, *Unruly Women: The Politics of Social and Sexual Control in the Old South* (Chapel Hill, 1992), 130–50.

10. Many historians have discussed the ambiguous meaning of slave loyalty in these terms. See for example Eugene Genovese, *Roll, Jordan, Roll: The World the Slaves Made* (New York, 1974); Paul Escott, *Slavery Remembered: A Record of Twentieth-Century Slave Narratives* (Chapel Hill, 1979). For a discussion of the material deprivation Confederate women faced during the war, see Mary Elizabeth Massey, *Ersatz in the Confederacy* (Columbia, S.C., 1952); Bell Wiley, *Plain Folk of the Confederacy* (Baton Rouge, 1943), 36–67; for poor women more generally, Bynum, *Unruly Women*, 111–29.

11. Booker T. Washington, *Up from Slavery* (1900; rpt. New York, 1965), 9.

12. Perhaps no works better articulate this elite white southern "view from nowhere" than Bertram Wyatt-Brown, *Southern Honor: Ethics and Behavior*

in the Old South (New York, 1982); and Catherine Clinton, "Southern Dishonor," in *In Joy and in Sorrow: Women, Family and Marriage in the Victorian South,* ed. Carol Bleser (New York, 1991), 52–68.

13. Nina Silber, *The Romance of Reunion* (Chapel Hill, 1994).

14. Eric Foner, *Free Soil, Free Labor, Free Men: The Ideology of the Republican Party before the Civil War* (New York, 1970), 40–72.

15. For a further discussion of this point, see Lacy K. Ford Jr., *Origins of Southern Radicalism: The South Carolina Upcountry, 1800–1860* (New York, 1988); and J. William Harris, *Plain Folk and Gentry in a Slave Society: White Liberty and Black Slavery in Augusta's Hinterlands* (Middletown, Conn., 1985), 15–40.

16. Eric Foner, *Free Soil, Free Labor, Free Men,* 30–39. On the spectrum of gender politics among abolitionists, see Aileen Kraditor, *Means and Ends in American Abolitionism: Garrison and His Critics on Strategy and Tactics, 1834–1850* (New York, 1969); Jean Fagan Yellin, *Women and Sisters: The Antislavery Feminists in American Culture* (New Haven, 1989); and Wendy Hamand Venet, *Neither Ballots nor Bullets: Women Abolitionists and the Civil War* (Charlottesville, 1991).

17. Michael P. Johnson, *Toward a Patriarchal Republic* (Baton Rouge, 1977).

Chapter 1. Independent Men and Dependent Women: Augusta and the Outbreak of War

1. Take for instance the pattern of intermarriage in the Thomas Cumming family, one of the oldest, most prominent, and established families in the town. Thomas and Ann Cumming migrated to Augusta in 1787–88. He became the first mayor of the town in 1798, having established himself as a successful merchant. His son, Henry Cumming, became a prominent lawyer in the town and an active promoter of industrial development. He married Julia Bryan, from a planter family in Hancock County, Georgia. Their daughter, Emily Cumming, married back into the planter class when she married Henry Hammond, a member of a prominent planter family in South Carolina. Through this pattern of intermarriage the Henry Hammonds acquired stock in the Augusta Factory, while the Henry Cummings expanded their holdings in slaves. Cumming Family Papers, Richmond County Historical Collection, Augusta College, Augusta, Georgia; and Hammond, Bryan, Cumming Papers. For a further discussion of the two families, see *The Hammonds of Redcliff,* ed. Carol Bleser (Oxford and New York, 1981); and *Secret and Sacred: The Diaries of James Henry Hammond, A Southern Slaveholder,* ed.

Carol Bleser (Oxford, 1988); Drew Faust, *James Henry Hammond and the Old South: A Design for Mastery* (Baton Rouge, 1982); and Steven M. Stowe, *Intimacy and Power in the Old South* (Baltimore, 1987), 106–21.

2. Florence Fleming Corley, *Confederate City: Augusta, Georgia, 1860–1865* (Columbia, S.C., 1960), discusses Augusta's position as a manufacturing center of the state. The intimate relationship between dominance of cotton production in the region and the particular pattern of development of Augusta's industries has been discussed at some length. See Richard W. Griffen, "The Augusta (Georgia) Manufacturing Company in Peace, War and Reconstruction," *Business History Review* 32 (1958): 60–73; and "The Origins of the Industrial Revolution in Georgia: Cotton Textiles, 1810–1865," *Georgia Historical Quarterly* 42 (1958): 355–75; Gavin Wright, "Cheap Labor and Southern Textiles before 1880," *Journal of Economic History* 39 (1979): 655–80; and John Richard Detreville, "The Little New South: Origins of Industry in Georgia's Fall Line Cities, 1840–1865," (Ph.D. diss., University of North Carolina, 1986).

3. Take for instance the Sibley brothers, Amory, Royal, and Josiah, who emigrated to Augusta in the 1820s from Uxbridge, Massachusetts, where their father was a small farmer. They established themselves as merchants in the town and by the time of the Civil War their cotton factoring firm of Sibley and Sons was one of the most prominent and respected in the town. Charles Colcock Jones Jr. and Salem Dutcher, *Memorial History of Augusta, Georgia* (1890; 3d ed. Spartanburg, S.C., 1980), 26–29.

4. Henry and Julia Cumming were put in particular difficulty by the act of secession. Their son, Joseph Cumming, had recently married Katherine Hubbel of New York, and their family therefore spanned the sections. Katherine Hubbel Cumming described her own feelings upon secession. "That was a sad day, and I shed tears of real sorrow and felt for the first time that I was an alien—in a different country. O! How fortunate that the future was veiled, or then and there I would have wished to lie down & die, rather than endure what was before me the next four years." Katherine H. Cumming, *A Northern Daughter and a Southern Wife: Civil War Reminiscences and Letters of Katherine H. Cumming*, ed. Kirk Wood (Augusta, 1976), 3. Her mother wrote to her in consolation that at least her own father-in-law, Henry Cumming, was himself anguished over the act. "The manner in which Col. Cumming views the state of things is great comfort to me, proving that, although, true to his southern instincts, he deems Secession a necessity and advisable, he is not heartless enough to rejoice over it, but like all both North and South who have heart and soul worthy [of] man who is made in God's

image, he mourns and is sad at this most heartrending state of our nation."
Ibid., 27. Julia Cumming could only write to her daughter Emily Cumming
Hammond, "I have a double trouble in Joe's going (to the front) for I do not
see how Katherine can possibly get along without him, and there is now not
a word said about her going to her parents." Julia Bryan Cumming to Emily
Cumming Hammond, August 8, 1861, Hammond, Bryan, and Cumming
Papers.

5. Joseph Jones to Charles Colcock and Mary Jones, June 6, 1861, Joseph
Jones Papers, Special Collections, Hill Memorial Library, Tulane University, New Orleans. An extensive selection of the family's papers have been
published. See *The Children of Pride: A True Story of Georgia and the Civil
War*, ed. Robert Manson Meyers, 2d rev. ed. (New Haven, 1972).

6. Corley, *Confederate City*, 14–15. According to Jones and Dutcher, *Memorial History of Augusta*, 179–80, over two thousand soldiers were eventually
raised. Out of that number, 292 died.

7. *Augusta Chronicle and Sentinel*, May 29, 1862.

8. For a further discussion of the particular fusion of white male liberty and
black slavery in the Augusta region, see J. William Harris, *Plain Folk and
Gentry in a Slave Society: White Liberty and Black Slavery in Augusta's
Hinterlands* (Middletown, Conn., 1985). On the centrality of the household
to the antebellum southern social order, see Elizabeth Fox-Genovese, "Antebellum Southern Households: A New Perspective on a Familiar Question,"
Review 7 (Fall 1983): 215–53; and *Within the Plantation Household: Black
and White Women of the Old South* (Chapel Hill, 1988), 37–99; and in the
particular context of the secession crisis, see Stephanie McCurry, "The Politics of Yeoman Households in South Carolina," in *Divided Houses: Gender
and the Civil War*, ed. Catherine Clinton and Nina Silber (New York, 1992),
22–42; and LeeAnn Whites, "The Civil War as a Crisis in Gender," in ibid.,
3–21.

9. For a discussion of the common interests of white farmers and planters in
Augusta's hinterlands, see Lacy K. Ford Jr., *Origins of Southern Radicalism: The South Carolina Upcountry, 1800–1860* (New York, 1988); Harris,
Plain Folk and Gentry in a Slave Society, 3; and Orville Vernon Burton, *In
My Father's House Are Many Mansions* (Chapel Hill, 1985).

10. *Augusta Chronicle and Sentinel*, April 18, 1861.

11. For a further discussion of the connections between abolitionism and feminism in the North, see Wendy Hamand Venet, *Neither Ballots nor Bullets:
Women Abolitionists and the Civil War* (Charlottesville, 1991); Blanche Glassman Hersh, *The Slavery of Sex: Feminist-Abolitionists in America* (Urbana,

1978); and Jean Fagan Yellin, *Women and Sisters: The Antislavery Feminists in American Culture* (New Haven, 1989).

12. On slave subversion during the war, see Winthrop Jordan, *Tumult and Silence at Second Creek* (Baton Rouge, 1993); Wayne Durrill, *War of Another Kind: A Southern Community in the Great Rebellion* (New York, 1990); Ira Berlin, Barbara J. Fields, Steven F. Miller, Joseph P. Reidy, Leslie S. Rowland, *Free At Last* (New York, 1992); and Clarence L. Mohr, *On the Threshold of Freedom: Masters and Slaves in Civil War Georgia* (Athens, Ga., 1985).

13. Among the most notable texts applauding Southern white women for their apparent single-minded identification with their men's cause in the struggle for southern independence are Reverend J. L. Underwood, *The Women of the Confederacy* (New York, 1906); Matthew Page Andrews, *The Women of the South in Wartimes* (Baltimore, 1920); and Francis Butler Simkins and James Welch Patton, *The Women of the Confederacy* (Richmond and New York, 1936). More recently scholars have been less likely to actively applaud, but many still see women's participation in the war effort as a fairly straightforward affirmation on their part of their subordinated gender position. See H. E. Sterkx, *Partners in Rebellion: Alabama in the Civil War* (Cranbury, N.J., 1970); George C. Rable, *Civil Wars: Women and the Crisis of Southern Nationalism* (Urbana, 1989); "'Missing in Action': Women of the Confederacy," in Clinton and Silber, *Divided Houses*, 134–46; Jean Bethe Elshtain, *Women and War* (New York, 1987), 94–101.

14. Simkins and Welch, *Women of the Confederacy*, 9–10.

15. Joseph Jones to Caroline Davis Jones, October 8, 1861, Joseph Jones Papers. For a further discussion of the role of elite white planter women, see Anne Firor Scott, *The Southern Lady: From Pedestal to Politics, 1830–1930* (Chicago, 1970); Catherine Clinton, *The Plantation Mistress: Woman's World in the Old South* (New York, 1982); and Fox-Genovese, *Within the Plantation Household*. What we know about antebellum white urban and rural women more generally tends to bear out a general pattern of subordination based on gender. See Victoria Bynum, *Unruly Women: The Politics of Social and Sexual Control in the Old South* (Chapel Hill, 1992); Jean E. Friedman, *The Enclosed Garden: Women and Community in the Evangelical South, 1830–1900* (Chapel Hill, 1985); and Suzanne Lebsock, *The Free Women of Petersburg: Status and Culture in a Southern Town, 1784–1860* (New York, 1984).

16. Joseph Jones to Caroline Davis Jones, February 12, 1859, Joseph Jones Papers.

17. Joseph Jones to Caroline Davis Jones, February 27, 1859, Joseph Jones Papers.
18. Caroline Davis Jones to Joseph Jones, November 12, 1861, Joseph Jones Papers.
19. *Augusta Chronicle and Sentinel*, April 25, 1861.
20. Ibid.
21. Ibid.
22. These statistics were compiled from the 1860 Augusta manuscript census and based on all white women, aged fifteen and over, who listed themselves as gainfully employed, for a total of 554 women.
23. For a further discussion of the role of race in structuring women's employment options, see Claudia Goldin, "Female Labor Force Participation: The Origin of Black and White Differences, 1870 and 1880," *Journal of Economic History* 37 (March 1977): 87–108.
24. For examples of works that argue for the clear primacy of race and class identification, see Jacqueline Jones, *Labor of Sorrow, Labor of Love* (New York, 1985); and Fox-Genovese, *Within the Plantation Household*. For those that point to the basis for some common identification, see Clinton, *Plantation Mistress*, and Scott, *Southern Lady*. For works that take a middle ground, see Deborah Gray White, *Ar'n't I a Woman* (New York, 1985); and Bynum, *Unruly Women*.
25. Susan Cornwall, Journal, January 31, 1861, Southern Historical Collection, University of North Carolina, Chapel Hill.
26. Ibid.
27. Ella Gertrude Clanton Thomas, Journal, January 2, 1858, Special Collections, Perkins Library, Duke University, Durham, North Carolina. For a further discussion of Ella Gertrude Clanton Thomas, see Virginia Burr, "A Woman Made to Suffer and Be Strong: Ella Gertrude Clanton Thomas, 1834–1907," in *In Joy and in Sorrow: Women, Family, and Marriage in the Victorian South*, ed. Carol Bleser (New York, 1991), 215–32; Nell Irvin Painter, "The Journal of Ella Gertrude Clanton Thomas: An Educated White Woman in the Eras of Slavery, War and Reconstruction," in Ella Gertrude Clanton Thomas, *The Secret Eye: The Journal of Ella Gertrude Clanton Thomas, 1848–1889*, ed. Virginia Ingraham Burr (Chapel Hill, 1990), 1–67; and Mary Elizabeth Massey, "The Making of a Feminist," *Journal of Southern History* 39 (February 1973): 3–22.
28. Thomas, Journal, January 2, 1858. Many historians have noted the connection between planter women's concern over their men's power to sexually exploit slave women and their opposition to the institution of slavery. See

for example Scott, *Southern Lady*, 53–57; Gerda Lerner, *The Grimké Sisters from South Carolina: Pioneers for Women's Rights and Abolition* (New York, 1967), 30–38; Clinton, *Plantation Mistress*, 180–98. More recently Nell Painter has argued that this power of the slaveholding man to sexually abuse his slave women created a critical basis for tension and competition between southern white and black women. See Nell Painter, "Of *Lily*, Linda Brent, and Freud: A Non-Exceptionalist Approach to Race, Class and Gender in the Slave South," *Georgia Historical Quarterly* 76 (Summer 1992): 241–59.

29. Thomas, Journal, January 2, 1858. While the sexual exploitation of slave women was tolerated, the prospect that was clearly intolerable was that white men might legitimize their relations with black women and place them in a position equal to that of white women. James Henry Hammond's long suffering wife, Catherine Hammond, finally fled to Augusta in response to his affairs with two of his slaves, Louisa and Sally, but Nell Painter has argued that Gertrude Thomas, despite her claims to a sexually faithful husband, actually tolerated a longstanding relationship between her husband and one of their slave women. See *Secret and Sacred*, 231–232, and Thomas, *The Secret Eye*, 55–67. Catherine Clinton has dubbed this behavior on the part of slaveowning men "Southern Dishonor," and there is a considerable literature to document the "acceptability" of hidden sexual relations and the virtual impossibility of legitimizing those relations, even if planter men themselves desired to do so. See Catherine Clinton, " 'Southern Dishonor': Flesh, Blood and Bondage" in Bleser, *In Joy and in Sorrow*, 52–68; and "Caught in the Web of the Big House: Women and Slavery," in *The Web of Southern Social Relations: Women, Family and Education*, ed. Walter J. Fraser Jr. and Jon L. Wakelyn (Athens, Ga., 1985), 19–34; Adele Logan Alexander, *Ambiguous Lives: Free Women of Color in Rural Georgia, 1789–1879* (Fayetteville, Ark., 1991); Kent Anderson Leslie, "Amanda America Dickson: An Elite Mulatto Lady in Nineteenth-Century Georgia," in Virginia Bernhard, Betty Brandon, Elizabeth Fox-Genovese, and Theda Perdue, eds., *Southern Women: Histories and Identities* (Columbia, Mo., 1992), 71–86.

30. Thomas, Journal, August 18, 1856.

31. Ibid.

32. Ibid., January 1, 1858; April 12, 1856.

33. Cornwall, Journal, March 7, 1857.

34. Ibid., March 18, 1857.

35. Ibid., March 7, 1857; Thomas, Journal, January 1, 1859.

36. Cornwall, Journal, March 11, 1857.

37. Thomas, Journal, July 15, 1861.

38. Ibid., November 10, 1861.

39. Ibid., July 16, 1861.

40. Cumming, *Northern Daughter and Southern Wife*, 4.

41. Goode Bryan to Julia Bryan Cumming, August 8, 1861, Hammond, Bryan, and Cumming Papers.

42. Julia Bryan Cumming to Emily Cumming Hammond, August 23, 1861, Hammond, Bryan, and Cumming Papers.

43. Julia Bryan Cumming to Emily Cumming Hammond, May 24, 1861; Julian Cumming to Emily Cumming Hammond, September 10, 1861, Hammond, Bryan, and Cumming Papers.

44. Julia to Emily, August 23, 1861; Emily Cumming Hammond to Harry Hammond, January 1862, Hammond, Bryan, and Cumming Papers; Thomas, Journal, October 12, 1861.

45. Catherine Barnes Rowland, Diary, February 28, 1864, Georgia State Archives, Atlanta. Caroline Davis Jones recorded a similarly intense attachment to place upon her husband's departure. "I . . . sit alone in these dear rooms where every book & article of furniture is so associated with him that in being there alone I feel surrounded with his presence and can scarcely believe that if I raise my eyes I shall not see him." Caroline Davis Jones to Joseph Jones, n.d., 1861; March 2, 1864; August 28, 1864, Joseph Jones Papers.

46. Caroline Davis Jones to Joseph Jones, April 27, 1864. Caroline Davis Jones provides a counterexample of a woman who remained in her own home throughout the war. Even here, however, her correspondence with her husband makes it clear that she seriously contemplated a move. Her husband urged her not to move despite the "loneliness" it would entail because she would "be enjoying the perfect independence which has been secured for you entirely and solely by your husband's personal exertions and means." Joseph Jones to Caroline Davis Jones, October 11, 1861, Joseph Jones Papers. For a further discussion of familial regrouping during the war see Mary Elizabeth Massey, *Refugee Life in the Confederacy* (Baton Rouge, 1964).

47. Thomas, Journal, July 16, 1861; Rowland, Diary, February 7, 1864; Joseph Jones to Caroline Davis Jones, October 11, 1861, Joseph Jones Papers.

48. Rowland, Diary, February 1, 1864. Jane Turner Censer, in her study of North Carolina antebellum planter families, suggests an infant and child mortality rate for these families of 230 out of 1,000. According to Censer's research, at least one child in four did not reach his or her fifth birthday. See Jane Turner Censer, *North Carolina Planters and Their Children, 1800–1860* (Baton Rouge, 1984), 28.

49. Rowland, Diary, February 1, 1864. In a more general study of motherhood in

the antebellum South, Sally G. McMillen draws a similar conclusion about the primary responsibility of the mother in infant and child nursing and the frequently hopeless task that it presented them. See Sally G. McMillen, *Motherhood in the Old South: Pregnancy and Childbirth and Infant Rearing* (Baton Rouge, 1989), 135–64. The war itself actually increased the possibility of infant and child mortality, as the army created a veritable breeding ground for epidemic disease. James M. McPherson estimates that 50,000 southern civilian casualties should be added to the known 260,000 Confederate soldier deaths; *Battle Cry of Freedom* (New York, 1988), 619. Caroline Davis Jones was in fact unable to visit her husband when he was stationed in Liberty County because of the outbreak of a measles epidemic in the area. Joseph Jones described the plight of one family where the father had brought the disease home with him from his service in the army at Port Royal. "Whilst he [the father] was lying dangerously ill his poor wife who was nursing a young infant of two months and who was the mother of six girls, was also taken & died after two days sickness. She was sitting up in her chair nursing the infant, when her sick husband noticed that she breathed strangely & appeared unable to sit in the chair. He rose and attempted to place her on the bed, but life was gone. The young physician who was sent for to attend the distressed family refused to go because he was afraid of the measles. Hearing of their destitute condition I rode on horseback to see them. . . . I found one of the girls very ill with pneumonia. This is the disease which is so often fatal in the measles." Joseph Jones to Caroline Davis Jones, December 18, 1861, Joseph Jones Papers.

50. Rowland, Diary, February 1, 1864; Thomas, Journal, January 1, 1856. For a further discussion of the consolation women took from their religion in the face of infant and child loss, see McMillan, *Motherhood in the Old South*, 165–88. For further discussion of the place of religion in antebellum southern women's lives, see Friedman, *The Enclosed Garden*, 1–20, 37–53; and Donald G. Mathews, *Religion in the Old South* (Chicago, 1977), 101–24.

51. Thomas, Journal, January 1, 1856. Upon her second pregnancy she wrote, "And at the same time there is such a oneness of feeling, such a mutual interest in everything between Mr. T and myself . . . in this consists the charm of married life . . . and then what a new tie, what a strong cord of love to bind two hearts together is the birth of a child"; Journal, February 20, 1857. Both Censer and McMillen point out that although men and women were both deeply affected by the loss of their children, they expressed their grief differently, women being more likely to sink into depression or to openly display grief. For instance, Isaac T. Avery, a North Carolina planter, took a

similar position in a letter discussing the loss of his child. "She was turned of nine months old, and had never been sick an hour in her life, had been the heartiest child. . . . I feel this dispensation as a parent and endeavor to bear it as a man, but to a Mother, to have a promising child at that interesting age where it is just beginning to discover the first gleams of intelligence[,] the loss is almost insupportable." Cited in Censer, *North Carolina Planters and Their Children*, 30.

52. Thomas, Journal, January 5, 1856.
53. Rowland, Diary, July 4, 1865.
54. Julia Bryan Cumming to Emily Cumming Hammond, May 24, 1861, Hammond, Bryan, and Cumming Papers.
55. Caroline Davis Jones to Joseph Jones, November 12, 1861, Joseph Jones Papers.
56. Thomas, Journal, July 15, 1861.
57. *Augusta Chronicle and Sentinel*, September 22, 1862; Myers, *Children of Pride*, 1516.
58. *Augusta Chronicle and Sentinel*, May 7, 1861.
59. Ibid., June 2, 1861; January 9, 1863. Lydia Cullen Sizer, "Acting Her Part: Narratives of Union Women Spies," in Clinton and Silber, *Divided Houses*, 114–33.

Chapter 2. Fighting Men and Loving Women: The Mobilization of the Homefront

1. On the ways in which the demands of fighting the war served to transform the southern economy, see Mary Elizabeth Massey, *Ersatz in The Confederacy* (Columbia, S.C., 1952); Charles W. Ramsdell, *Behind the Lines in the Southern Confederacy* (Baton Rouge, 1944), 42–82; Emory M. Thomas, *The Confederate Nation, 1861–1865* (New York, 1979), and *The Confederacy as a Revolutionary Experience* (Englewood Cliffs, N.J., 1971). For Augusta in particular, see Edward J. Cashin, *The Story of Augusta* (Augusta, 1980), 111–42; Florence Fleming Corley, *Confederate City: Augusta, Georgia, 1860–1865* (Columbia, S.C., 1960); and Mary A. DeCredico, *Patriotism for Profit: Georgia's Urban Entrepreneurs and the Confederate War Effort* (Chapel Hill, 1990).
2. *Augusta Chronicle and Sentinel*, June 7, 1861.
3. Ibid., August 10, 1861. Mounting sectional hostility and finally secession brought an accompanying recognition of the inappropriateness of southern economic dependence upon the North not only in the local Augusta papers

but in widely read agricultural journals as well. See also *Augusta Chronicle and Sentinel*, January 3, 1860; February 19, 1860; September 7, 1860; March 6, 1860; and C. W. Howard, "Things Worthy of Attention," *Southern Cultivator* 19 (1861): 201–3, 233–35; "The Future of Confederate States," *Southern Cultivator* 19 (1861): 137; "Southern Patronage to Southern Imports and Domestic Industry," *Southern Planter* 31 (1861); 58–63. Serious efforts to shift from cotton to subsistence crops only occured, however, in the spring of 1862 as the blockade became increasingly effective. Massey, *Ersatz in the Confederacy*, 38–42; and Thomas, *The Confederate Nation*, 199–200.

4. On the history of economic development in Augusta, see Charles C. Jones Jr. and Salem Dutcher, *Memorial History of Augusta, Georgia* (New York, 1890), 428–30; Corley, *Confederate City*, 4–11. For discussion of various factors involved in the origin the textile mill in particular, see Richard W. Griffen, "The Augusta (Georgia) Manufacturing Company in Peace, War, and Reconstruction," *Business History Review* 32 (1958): 60–73; and "The Origins of the Industrial Revolution in Georgia: Cotton Textiles, 1810–1865," *Georgia Historical Review* 42 (1958); Charles Colcock Jones Jr., "Pioneering Manufacturing in Richmond County," *Textile History Review*, July 1964, 69–83; Gavin Wright, "Cheap Labor and Southern Textiles before 1880," *Journal of Economic History* 39 (1979): 655–80; and most recently, John Richard Detreville, "The Little New South: Origins of Industry in Georgia's Fall Line Cities, 1840–1865," (Ph.D. diss., University of North Carolina, 1986). Corley points to the opposition of "merchants and old families" to the construction of the canal; *Confederate City*, 8. According to J. William Harris, it was the hegemony of Republican ideology "with its archaic ideals of individual, rather than community, independence" that undergirded the aversion to industrialization among yeomen and slaveholders alike in Augusta's hinterlands; *Plain Folk and Gentry in a Slave Society: White Liberty and Black Slavery in Augusta's Hinterlands* (Middletown, Conn., 1985), 33. Richard Griffen argues that this aversion to factory labor was "more pronounced in regions where cotton cultivation was most prominent" because the "small farmer was actuated by the hope of someday elevating himself to the rank of the planter aristocracy"; "Poor White Laborers in Southern Cotton Factories," *South Carolina Historical Magazine* 61 (1960): 29.

5. Detreville discusses the relationship between declining cotton prices and increasing rates of poor, especially female poor; "The Little New South," 65–68. Richard Griffen concludes that the Augusta Mill "came as a great blessing to such persons who could find no employment in the city, especially to women and children for whose labor there was little demand. Almost

overnight they were transformed from burdens on the public to producers of wealth and useful citizens"; "The Augusta Manufacturing Company," 62. Griffen also concludes that although poor white men were hesitant to enter the mills, "they had no objection to their wives and children doing so"; "Poor White Laborers," 30. This appears to have been the case in nearby Graniteville as well where, in order to acquire sufficient female and child labor in the 1840s, William Gregg was forced to develop a policy of giving land to the male heads of household. See Broadus Mitchell, *William Gregg, Factory Master of the Old South* (Chapel Hill, 1928), 56–57. Alice Kessler-Harris discusses the gender dynamics in rural New England in similar terms, *Out to Work: A History of Wage Earning Women* (Oxford, 1982), 17–23.

6. Jones and Dutcher, *Memorial History of Augusta*, 2:26–29.

7. *Augusta Chronicle and Sentinel*, April 14, 1862.

8. Ibid.

9. Ibid., March 11, 1862; April 14, 1862.

10. James Roark, *Masters without Slaves: Southern Planters in the Civil War and Reconstruction* (New York, 1977), 35–45.

11. Jones and Dutcher, *Memorial History of Augusta*, 428–30. According to Jones and Dutcher, Augusta was "one of the most important posts during the civil struggle." Even before the expansion of manufacturing that the war brought, it was the center of manufacturing capital in the state. It was for this reason that Edwin Stanton, Lincoln's war secretary, was "horrified" that General Sherman marched to the sea instead of taking the town. "So long as Augusta remained intact, the army in Northern Virginia, under General Lee, was furnished with ammunition and materials from the government workshops, and the Southern armies were enabled to hold their ground, and it was believed that had Sherman made Augusta the base of his operations instead of Atlanta, the Civil War would have come to an end at least a year before it did." *Memorial History of Augusta*, 185.

12. Griffen, "The Augusta Manufacturing Company," 68. In passing the Exemption Act of 1862, the Confederate Congress recognized the essential relation of the textile industry to the cause. They also endeavored to use the industry's dependence on this exemption of skilled workers from the draft to hold down prices. Factories were required by the legislation to charge no more than 75 percent profit on their goods.

13. Griffen, "Poor White Laborers," 39; "The Augusta Manufacturing Company," 68–70; and Mary A. DeCredico, *Patriotism for Profit: Georgia's Urban Entrepreneurs and the Confederate War Effort* (Chapel Hill, 1990), 49–59. Both authors discuss the critical gap between demand for textiles and

the ability of the company to produce them. The government responded with legislation allocating virtually the entire production of the mill to the military and the poor, as well as with efforts to compensate for the gap, for instance by distributing cotton yarns, cards, or spinning wheels so that women might make their own cloth. For a further discussion of these efforts see *Augusta Chronicle and Sentinel*, May 19, 1863; May 29, 1863; and April 21, 1864.

14. For a further discussion of Confederate women's contributions to the war effort, see Mary Elizabeth Massey, *Bonnet Brigades* (New York, 1966); George Rable, *Civil Wars: Women and the Crisis of Southern Nationalism* (Urbana, 1989). Francis Butler Simkins and James Welch Patton, *The Women of the Confederacy* (Richmond and New York, 1936); Anne Firor Scott, *The Southern Lady: From Pedestal to Politics, 1830–1930* (Chicago, 1970), 58–77; H. E. Sterkx, *Partners in Rebellion: Alabama in the Civil War* (Cranbury, N.J., 1970); and Bell I. Wiley, *Confederate Women* (Westport, Conn., 1975).

15. For a further discussion of how other wars have served to transform women's labor, see Mary Beth Norton, *Liberty's Daughters: The Revolutionary Experience of American Women, 1750–1800* (Boston, 1980), 195–227; and D'Ann Campbell, *Women at War with America: Private Lives in a Patriotic Era* (Cambridge, Mass., 1984), 65–100.

16. Jones and Dutcher, *Memorial History of Augusta*, 179–80.

17. Catherine Barnes Rowland, Diary, January 11, 1864, Georgia State Archives, Atlanta.

18. From the outset of the war the Augusta City Council found it necessary to contribute two hundred dollars to each of the companies from the county as they were called up to the front so that they might have the necessary resources to "complete their outfit" Augusta City Council Minutes, April 26, 1861, Richmond County Municipal Building, Augusta. The economic state of many of the enlistees was also indicated by the necessity, immediately after their departure, for the city authorities to appoint a committee to "solicit and receive subscriptions for [needy soldiers'] families." Augusta City Council Minutes, April 11, 1861.

19. Although this choice confronted Confederate men first in the case of their women, they would quickly be faced with the same issue around the labor of their slaves, as the Confederacy began impressing slaves to work in ever greater numbers, removing them entirely from the control of their white owners. See Clarence L. Mohr, *On the Threshold of Freedom: Masters and Slaves in Civil War Georgia* (Athens, Ga., 1985). Owners would also lose control over their slaves as northern armies invaded and slaves took the op-

portunity to escape behind Union lines or when fleeing owners were unable to move them with them. Residents of Augusta were spared the threat of invasion until the last year of the war, so they did not experience the loss of their slave property as early as did other areas more exposed to invasion. See Barbara Jeanne Fields, *Slavery and Freedom on the Middle Ground: Maryland during the Nineteenth Century* (New Haven, 1985), 91–130; Wayne Durrill, *War of Another Kind: A Southern Community in the Great Rebellion* (New York, 1990), 68–90, 145–66; Michael Fellman, *Inside War: The Guerilla Conflict in Missouri during the Civil War* (New York, 1989), 65–80; Ira Berlin, Barbara J. Fields, Thavolia Glymph, Joseph Reidy, and Leslie Rowland, eds., *Freedom: A Documentary History of Emancipation, 1861–1867*, series 2, vol. 1, *The Destruction of Slavery* (Cambridge and New York, 1985).

20. *Augusta Chronicle and Sentinel*, June 7, 1861.
21. Ibid.
22. Ibid.
23. Ibid., June 18, 1861. For a discussion of antebellum southern women's voluntary organizations, see Suzanne Lebsock, *The Free Women of Petersburg: Status and Culture in a Southern Town, 1784–1860* (New York, 1984), 195–236. More recently, Anne Scott has suggested that southern women's voluntary organizations were basically similar in form and content to those found in the North. See Anne Scott, *Natural Allies: Women's Associations in American History*, (Chicago, 1991), 19–20. Jean Friedman and Elizabeth Fox-Genovese have both argued, however, that the development of such organizations was limited in the antebellum South by the relatively slow growth of urban areas. See Jean E. Friedman, *The Enclosed Garden: The Politics of Social and Sexual Control in the Old South* (Chapel Hill, 1985), 2–20; and Elizabeth Fox-Genovese, *Within the Plantation Household: Black and White Women of the Old South* (Chapel Hill, 1988), 70–82. As a result, the expansion of Confederate women's voluntary organization during the war was massive when compared with the antebellum organizational structure, and southern women's organizations in the postbellum era would be distinctively marked by this pattern of development in a continuing intense attachment to the support and defense of their men. This is manifested by the Ladies' Memorial Association and the United Daughters of the Confederacy, discussed in chapter 6 of this book. Northern women's organizations, in stark contrast, developed their larger political attachments in the context of antebellum social reform movements, aligning themselves with other non-dominant groups in society, with labor, and perhaps most critically with

the abolitionist movement. What emerged out of this pattern of development was a politics of autonomy and independence for women in their own right. For further discussion, see Barbara Berg, *The Remembered Gate: Origins of American Feminism* (New York, 1978); Nancy F. Cott, *The Bonds of Womanhood: 'Woman's Sphere' in New England, 1780–1835,* (New Haven, 1977); Ellen DuBois, *Feminism and Suffrage: The Emergence of an Independent Women's Movement in America, 1848–1869* (Ithaca, N.Y., 1978); Keith Melder, *The Beginnings of Sisterhood: The American Women's Rights Movement, 1800–1850* (New York, 1977); Mary Ryan, "The Power of Women's Networks: A Case Study of Female Moral Reform in Antebellum America," *Feminist Studies* 5 (Spring 1979): 66–86. Although a women's suffrage movement did eventually emerge in the postwar South, it was always limited by the association of the suffrage cause with race progressivism and by the persistence of the organized Confederate memorial tradition. See Marjorie Spruill Wheeler, *New Women of the New South* (New York, 1993).

24. For a further discussion of the association between poverty and autonomy for white women in the antebellum South, see Victoria E. Bynum, *Unruly Women: The Politics of Social and Sexual Control in the Old South* (Chapel Hill, 1992), 33–58; Lebsock, *Free Women of Petersburg*, 146–89.

25. Rowland, Diary, March 1, 1864.

26. Annie Branch, *A Sketch of the Ladies Foreign Missionary Society* (n.p., 1904).

27. Ibid.

28. I am indebted to Grattan Whitehead Rowland Sr., Atlanta, Georgia, for this genealogical information. This generational continuity was not unique to the Whiteheads. Similar lines can be drawn in the Sibley family, who were also members of the First Presbyterian Church. Mrs. Josiah Sibley, roughly Catherine's mother's contemporary, was also active in antebellum church organizations, especially in the Foreign Missionary Society, but also in the sewing circle. Her grandaughter Anna Safford became a foreign missionary herself, and in 1888 a home was established for female missionaries in Soochow, China, named after Mrs. Josiah Sibley. Mrs. Sibley's daughter-in-law, Mrs. William Sibley, was active in the local sewing circle, was a directress of the Ladies' Aid Society during the war, and later became the state president of the WCTU in the 1880s. Mary D. Irvine and Alice L. Eastwood, *Pioneer Women of the Presbyterian Church* (Richmond, 1923), 148–49.

29. *Augusta Chronicle and Sentinel*, June 7, 1861.

30. Ibid.

31. In some cases the intensity of this bond prompted Confederate women to

give more than they could afford, stripping their own households. Simkins and Patton, *Women of the Confederacy*, 27; According to Massey, this was one of the major reasons why the domestic population suffered from serious shortages; see *Ersatz in the Confederacy*, 31.

32. *Augusta Chronicle and Sentinel*, June 18, 1861; Addison Burnside to Miss May, July, 1862, Addison M. Burnside Letters, 1862–1863, Georgia State Archives, Atlanta.

33. *Augusta Daily Constitutionalist*, August 13, 1861.

34. *Augusta Chronicle and Sentinel*, July 31, 1861.

35. Ibid., August 5, 1861; September 8, 1861.

36. Ibid., June 1861.

37. Ibid., August 12, 1862. See also August 14, 18, 26, 28; and September 5, 1862.

38. Ibid., June 2, 1861; September 7, 1861.

39. Ibid., July 14, 1862.

40. Rowland, Diary, January 28, 1864; February 23, 1864.

41. Ibid., February 4, 1864. This experience stood Catherine Rowland in good stead, as in the postwar period she became one of the leading figures in Augusta's women's voluntary organizations, serving variously as president of the King's Daughters and of the Ladies' Memorial Association; vice president of the Widows Home and the United Daughters of the Confederacy; and as a member of the executive committee of the Women's Exchange.

42. *Augusta Chronicle and Sentinel*, March 12, 1862.

43. Ibid., April 1, 1862. R. H. May, the town's mayor, had no similar gender compunctions when he recommended to the city council that they vote to contribute the twenty thousand dollars. "I recommend that your subscription be liberal as under no circumstances in which it is probable we be placed can a portion of our means be devoted to a purpose better calculated to advance our interest and contribute to our success. Individual contributions have poured in without stint, and it is not for the City Council of Augusta to hang back when so excellent an opportunity for doing service is afforded." Augusta City Council Minutes, March 31, 1862.

44. *Augusta Chronicle and Sentinel*, May 7, 1862.

45. Many historians have suggested the critical role of civilian disaffection in the collapse of the Confederacy. See Bell Wiley, *Plain Folk of the Confederacy* (Baton Rouge, 1943); Ella Lonn, *Desertion in the Confederacy* (New York, 1928); Ramsdell, *Behind the Lines in the Southern Confederacy*. Drew Faust has more recently given a gendered interpretation to this analysis, suggesting that by the midpoint in the war, Confederate women were growing

increasingly disaffected by their men's failure to protect and provide. See Drew Faust, "Altars of Sacrifice: Confederate Women and the Narratives of War," *Journal of American History* 76 (March 1990): 1200–28. Other historians suggest that the men themselves experienced a gender role crisis and, unable to accept their own inability to provide and protect, deserted in record numbers. See Bynum, *Unruly Women*, 111–30; and Donna Rebecca Dondes Krug, "The Folks Back Home: The Confederate Homefront during the Civil War" (Ph.D. diss., University of California, Irvine, 1990).

46. *Augusta Chronicle and Sentinel*, August 8, 1862.
47. Ibid., June 12, 1862.
48. Ibid.

Chapter 3. Benevolent Men and Destitute Women: The Domestication of the Market

1. Augusta City Council Minutes, April 11, 1861, Richmond County Municipal Building, Augusta. Despite the critical role that the families of the common soldiers played both in providing fighting men in the first place and in holding down the homefront, surprisingly few studies have considered their role in the war at any length. See Victoria Bynum, *Unruly Women: The Politics of Social and Sexual Control in the Old South* (Chapel Hill, 1992), 111–50; Mary Elizabeth Massey, *Bonnet Brigades* (New York, 1966), 197–219; Francis Butler Simkins and James Welch Patton, *The Women of the Confederacy* (Richmond and New York, 1936), 111–28; Bell Wiley, *Plain Folk of the Confederacy* (Baton Rouge, 1943), 36–69.

2. Augusta City Council Minutes, May 3, 1861.

3. The mayor was the city official who dealt with the needs of the poor, and in recognition of the manner in which his work load had increased with the war his salary was doubled in January of 1862. Augusta City Council Minutes, January 30, 1862.

4. *Augusta Chronicle and Sentinel*, October 23, 1861. For a discussion of the ways in which inflation and extortion created a crisis for the entire Confederacy, see Drew Faust, *The Creation of Confederate Nationalism: Ideology and Identity in the Civil War South* (Baton Rouge, 1988), 39–57; and for the particular case of Georgia, see Peter Wallenstein, *From Slave South to New South: Public Policy In Nineteenth-Century Georgia* (Chapel Hill, 1987), 99–120.

5. *Augusta Chronicle and Sentinel*, July 3, 1862. Even those most inclined to dismiss charges of extortion and speculation on the part of the town's mer-

chants were forced to recognize that at least some of the merchants were guilty as charged. See also Ibid., October 3, 1861.

6. Ibid., May 11, 1861.
7. Ibid., July 3, 1862.
8. Ibid., April 3, 1862.
9. Ibid., May 1, 1861.
10. The possibilities for a voluntary solution to the problem presented by needy soldiers' families did not get off to a good start. The city council, having created a committee to oversee the collection of funds, went downstairs to a meeting that was being held by the "citizens" to see if a corresponding private committee could be formed. The council member returned to report that "there was no prospect of organizing the meeting downstairs." Augusta City Council Minutes, April 11, 1861. As of the fall of 1862, the council records indicated that $41,000 had been given to soldiers' families, only $5,000 of that total from private contributions. The council also recorded a total of $6,000 given to the poor by the city, along with an unspecified amount given by private individuals. Augusta City Council Minutes, October 30, 1862.
11. Catherine Barnes Rowland, Diary, November 11, 1863; December 1, 1863, Georgia State Archives, Atlanta.
12. Ibid., January 2, 1865.
13. Ibid., April 26, 1864; January 2, 1865.
14. For a further discussion of the particular significance of women's consumption and the war effort, see Faust, *Creation of Confederate Nationalism*, 51–57.
15. Ella Gertrude Clanton Thomas, Journal, December 27, 1864, Special Collection, Perkins Library, Duke University, Durham, North Carolina.
16. Ibid.
17. *Augusta Chronicle and Sentinel*, April 12, 1862. Two days later another letter offered to "send gratis a wagon and team for the use of all those who avail themselves of the offer"; ibid., April 14, 1862.
18. Ibid., April 16, 1862.
19. Ibid., April 17, 1862. Thomas signs herself "A Friend" in this article, but she discusses the article in her journal.
20. As Thomas recorded in her journal, "Out of all our old house servants not one remains except Patsy and a little boy Frank. . . . After it [breakfast] was over I assisted her [Patsy] in wiping the breakfast dishes a thing I can never remember to have done more than once or twice in my life." Thomas, Journal, May 29, 1865.
21. *Augusta Chronicle and Sentinel*, February 15, 1862; November 2, 1861. The

seriousness with which the city council regarded drinking among the "common sort" as a threat to social order can be seen in their decision to close down the saloons once the town, which was a hospital center, was inundated with wounded soldiers. Augusta City Council Minutes, April 15, 1862.

22. Augusta City Council Minutes, October 30, 1862.

23. Ibid.

24. Mayor Robert H. May to Governor Joseph E. Brown, December 31, 1863, Incoming Executive Correspondence, Georgia State Archives, Atlanta.

25. *Augusta Chronicle and Sentinel*, October 28, 1863; October 29, 1863. For a discussion of the shifting fortunes of the elite, the general rise of urban areas, and the industrialists and bureaucrats in the Confederacy as a whole, see Emory M. Thomas, *The Confederacy As a Revolutionary Experience* (Englewood Cliffs, N. J., 1971), 100–118.

26. *Augusta Chronicle and Sentinel*, November 3, 1863.

27. Augusta City Council Minutes, October 2, 1863.

28. *Augusta Chronicle and Sentinel*, May 19, 1863.

29. Augusta City Council Minutes, October 7, 1864; October 6, 1865.

30. *Augusta Chronicle and Sentinel*, June 12, 1862.

31. Statistics compiled from the 1860 manuscript census for Augusta, Georgia.

32. Thomas, Journal, March 30, 1856. Thomas described a similar situation of yet a third seamstress that she employed. "In the last seven years her husband has not paid one cent toward supporting her. Last year she obtained a divorce from him." Journal, April 27, 1856.

33. Caroline Davis Jones to Mary Jones, November 19, 1863, Joseph Jones Papers, Special Collections, Hill Memorial Library, Tulane University. See also November 18, 1863; December 19, 1861; March 11, 1863; November 19, 1863; December 18, 1861.

34. Caroline Davis Jones to Mary Jones, November 19, 1863; Caroline Davis Jones to her parents, September 14, 1861, Joseph Jones Papers.

35. *Augusta Chronicle and Sentinel*, November 21, 1861.

36. Ibid., November 27, 1862. Although this writer supported the government taking over the responsibility of clothing the troops, he was critical of the extended powers of the state government to take over private property. "The army must be clothed at any cost, and private rights must yield to public necessity, but the State authorities should hesitate long before they infringe the sacred rights of property." Here the writer was particularly concerned about the private status of the state's factories. "It is contrary to all experience to suppose that the State Government can work the shoe and cotton factories as well as private companies or individuals, the supply must diminish and prices of articles increase under its administration."

37. Ibid., February 14, 1863.

38. Rowland, Diary, March 24, 1864.

39. *Augusta Chronicle and Sentinel*, July 31, 1863.

40. Ibid., May 29, 1863. See also May 19, 1863.

41. Ibid., August 18, 1863.

42. Ibid., March 30, 1862.

43. Ibid., April 14, 1864.

44. Ibid.

45. For more on women's role as nurses in the war, see Massey, *Bonnet Brigades*, 43–60; George Rable, *Civil Wars: Women and the Crisis of Southern Nationalism* (Urbana, 1989), 121–28; H. E. Sterkx, *Partners in Rebellion: Alabama in the Civil War* (Cranbury, N. J., 1970); and Kristie Ross, "Refined Women as Union Nurses," in *Divided Houses: Gender and the Civil War*, ed. Catherine Clinton and Nina Silber (New York, 1992), 97–113.

46. *Augusta Chronicle and Sentinel*, September 17, 1862.

47. Rowland, Diary, December 14, 1865.

48. Ibid., July 6, 1864.

49. *Augusta Chronicle and Sentinel*, July 1, 1863. One man, J. B. Crum, wrote to the local newspaper, expressing his gratitude for the efforts of the ladies in a similar vein. "Will you be so kind as to tender to the ladies my thanks for their kindness to my brother while he suffered in their midst. Language cannot paint my feelings of gratitude toward those who so faithfully and attentively watched over my brother while fighting his last enemy. . . . Oh how my broken heart and wounded spirit were revived when I heard of the kind treatment my brother received from these kind ladies. God bless them. We shall meet in Heaven." *Augusta Chronicle and Sentinel*, September 13, 1862.

50. Thomas, Journal, July 28, 1864.

51. Ibid.

52. Rowland, Journal, June 16, 1864. "I heard today of the death of Jim Hull & am truly sorry to hear it as he is an old friend of mine. . . . Poor Georgia! How deeply do I sympathize with her & her two little fatherless children. I met her just about six weeks ago, on the cars & then she was so bright & happy, she is a young widow"; February 9, 1864.

53. Thomas, Journal, April 17, 1862.

54. Ibid., June 2, 1862.

55. Ibid., March 29, 1865.

56. Susan Cornwall, Journal, August 22, 1865, Southern Historical Collection, University of North Carolina, Chapel Hill.

57. Thomas, Journal, April 26, 1862. Her fears were not at all misplaced, as

indicated by her husband's account for the local newspaper of the fate of his cavalry company, the Richmond Hussars, after only one engagement on September 8, 1862. "Most of the twenty-one Hussars that went into the fight had their clothing pierced by balls or sabres." Members of his own family were particularly hard hit. "My brother Jack, severely wounded in the head. . . . My brother, Pinckney, badly wounded; the ball passing through the fleshy part of the arm and entering the side. . . . My brother-in-law, James L. Clanton, badly, in the left shoulder. . . ." *Augusta Chronicle and Sentinel*, November 23, 1862.

58. Thomas, Journal, September, 1862.

Chapter 4. Defeated Men and Vulnerable Women: The Collapse of the Confederacy

1. J. R. Simms to his wife, July 9, 1864, Charles Colcock Jones, Jr. Papers, Perkins Library, Duke University. For a further discussion of the extent of destruction, see Joseph T. Glathaar, *The March to the Sea and Beyond: Sherman's Troops in the Savannah and Carolinas Campaigns* (New York, 1985), 66–81, 134–155. *"War is Hell!": William T. Sherman's Personal Narrative of His March through Georgia*, ed. Mills Lane (Savannah, 1974); Richard Wheeler, *Sherman's March* (New York, 1978).

2. For a discussion of women's experience in particular see, Matthew Page Andrews, *The Women of the South in Wartimes* (Baltimore, 1920), 303–35. Katherine M. Jones, *When Sherman Came: Southern Women and the Great March* (Indianapolis, 1964); Reverend J. L. Underwood, *The Women of the Confederacy* (New York, 1906).

3. Charles Rowland to his wife, Catherine Barnes Rowland, May 21, 1864, Charles Rowland Letters, Richmond County Historical Society Collection, Augusta College, Augusta, Georgia. For a further discussion of Sherman's March as a crisis in protection, see Jane E. Schultz, "Mute Fury: Southern Women's Diaries of Sherman's March to the Sea, 1864–1865," in Helen M. Cooper, Adrienne Auslander Munich, Susan Merrill Squier, eds., *Arms and the Woman: War, Gender and Literary Representation* (Chapel Hill, 1989), 58–79; and on war and protection more generally, Judith Stiehm, "The Protected, The Protector, The Defender," *Women's Studies International Forum* 5 (1982), 367–76.

4. For a further discussion of the impact of Sherman's March on slavery, see Clarence L. Mohr, *On The Threshold of Freedom: Masters and Slaves in Civil War Georgia* (Athens, Ga., 1986); and Ira Berlin, Barbara J. Fields, Thavolia

Glymph, Joseph Reidy, and Leslie Rowland, eds., *Freedom: A Documentary History of Emancipation, 1861–1867,* series 2, vol. 1, *The Destruction of Slavery* (Cambridge and New York, 1985), 9–10.

5. *Augusta Chronicle and Sentinel,* August 21, 1864. In a letter to the Augusta citizenry appealing for aid to the refugees, the mayor wrote, "The population has doubled in the last few months as a result of the influx of refugees."

6. Augusta City Council Minutes, November 6, 1863, Richmond County Municipal Building, Augusta.

7. Catherine Barnes Rowland, Diary, August 20, 1864, Georgia State Archives, Atlanta.

8. See Mary Elizabeth Massey, *Refugee Life in the Confederacy* (Baton Rouge, 1964) for a further discussion of the composition of the refugee population.

9. Augusta City Council Minutes, October 6, 1865. As early as December of 1863, the mayor claimed that eight hundred families were supported by the association, but the numbers clearly rose dramatically in the last year of the war. See R. H. May to Joseph E. Brown, December 31, 1863, Executive Office Correspondence, Georgia State Archives, Atlanta; *Augusta Chronicle and Sentinel,* April 26, 1865; *Augusta Daily Constitutionalist,* April 26, 1865.

10. Augusta City Council Minutes, October 7, 1864.

11. Eliza M. Smith to her daughters, February 2, 1864, in *Mason Smith Family Letters, 1860–1868,* ed. Daniel Huger, Alice R. Huger, and Arney Childs (Columbia, S. C., 1950), 80.

12. The Smith family fortune was swept away by the war. In early 1866 Eliza Smith and her daughters were able to return to Charleston, where they shared the home of Mrs. Robert Smith. Mrs. Smith kept a day school for girls for some years after the war and in 1869 she was able to purchase a separate dwelling for her family in Charleston. Arney Childs, "Introduction," *Smith Family Letters,* xxi.

13. Eliza M. Smith to her daughters, February 16, 1864.

14. Ella Gertrude Clanton Thomas, Journal, September 22, 1864, Special Collections, Perkins Library, Duke University, Durham, North Carolina.

15. Ibid., September 17, 1864.

16. Rowland, Diary, November 26, 1864.

17. Ibid., August 24, 1864; October 12, 1864.

18. Ibid., July 28, 1864; Emily Izard to Eliza Smith, July 21, 1864, *Smith Family Letters,* 116. Emily Izard was the wife of Allen Izard, who was listed in the 1867 Pugh City Directory for Augusta, Georgia, as a planter residing in the city on Broad Street, one of the main streets.

19. Augusta City Council Minutes, October 7, 1864.

20. James Verdery to his sister, November 27, 1864, James Paul Verdery Papers, Special Collections, Perkins Library, Duke University, Durham, North Carolina. See also F. M. Stovall to Adelle Verdery, February 26, 1865, Verdery Papers. This collection consists primarily of the correspondence of two sons of a prominent planter family who had a residence in Augusta. The sons both served in the Confederate Army and wrote home of their experiences. James clerked in Augusta after the war and by 1872 was listed as a lawyer in the firm of Verdery and Verdery in *Haddock's Augusta Georgia Directory and General Advertizer* (Augusta, Ga., 1872), 178.

21. Rowland, Diary, September 9, 1864.

22. Mrs. Emily Izard to her mother, Mrs. Daniel E. Huger, November 23 or 24, 1864, Smith and Wells Family Papers, South Caroliniana Library, University of South Carolina, Columbia; Catherine Rowland, Journal, November 17, 1864; November 26, 1864.

23. Rowland, Diary, December 9, 1864.

24. Thomas, Journal, November 27, 1864; December 12, 1864.

25. Ibid.

26. Rowland, Diary, December 16, 1864.

27. Ibid., Journal, January 3, 1865.

28. *Augusta Chronicle and Sentinel*, February 20, 1864.

29. Rowland, Diary, January 3, 1865; Howell Cobb to his wife, January 19, 1865, Cobb-Erwin-Lamar Collection, Special Collections, University of Georgia, Athens.

30. Augusta City Council Minutes, October 7, 1864. Governor Joseph Brown made a strikingly similar appeal for the defense of Atlanta in the *Augusta Daily Constitutionalist*, July 15, 1864.

31. Augusta City Council Minutes, February 21, 1865; *Augusta Daily Constitutionalist*, April 12, 1865. See also February 16, 18, 21; March 11; April 7, 1865.

32. James Verdery to his sister, January 22, 1865, Verdery Papers.

33. *Augusta Daily Constitutionalist*, February 7, 1865.

34. Emily Middleton Izard to Eliza Middleton Smith, July 21, 1864, *Smith Family Letters*, 116.

35. *Augusta Daily Constitutionalist*, January 27, 1865.

36. Ibid.

37. Ibid.

38. Thomas, Journal, December 12, 1864; Rowland, Journal, February 23, 1865. Numerous appeals for aid for the women and children who were burnt out of Columbia and who continued to suffer in Atlanta appeared in the local

press; *Augusta Chronicle and Sentinel*, May 28, 1864; February 28, April 2, 1865.

39. Eliza M. Smith to her daughters, February 16, 1864, *Smith Family Letters*, 83. Men of the local elite also sometimes expressed similar sentiments about contact with the common soldier. See Charles Rowland to Catherine Rowland, January 24, 1864, Charles Rowland Letters; and Alfred Cumming to Julia Bryan Cumming, October 20, 1861, Cumming Family Papers, Richmond County Historical Collection, Augusta College, Augusta, Ga.

40. Thomas, Journal, July 28, 1864.

41. Mrs. Irby Morgan, *How It Was: Four Years among the Rebels* (Nashville, 1892), 136, 137.

42. Kate Cumming to Julia Bryan Cumming, March 5, 1862. See also Joseph Cumming to Julia Bryan Cumming, July 19, 1861, Cumming Family Papers.

43. Augusta City Council Minutes, July 3, 1863; October 2, 1863; November 6, 1863.

44. Augusta City Council Minutes, April 15, 1862; Richmond County Grand Jury Presentments, April 22, 1864, Georgia State Archives, Atlanta; *Augusta Chronicle and Sentinel*, February 28, 1865.

45. Colonel William Browne to Major Norman W. Smith, August 17, 1864, Charles Colcock Jones, Jr. Papers; Richmond County Grand Jury Presentments, January 20, 1865.

46. James Verdery to his sister, January 22, 1864, Verdery Papers.

47. Augusta City Council Minutes, October 7, 1864; Morgan, *How It Was*, 110.

48. Richmond County Grand Jury Presentments, January 20, 1865; Rowland, Journal, January 31, 1865; February 7, 8, 16, 17, 1865. See also *Augusta Chronicle and Sentinel*, December 29, 1864; December 11, 1864; and February 28, 1865.

49. As Irby Morgan notes herself in her recollections, *How It Was*, 119.

50. See Mohr, *On the Threshold Of Freedom*, 120–89, for a further discussion of the uses of impressed slave labor in the war effort.

51. Mohr also attributes part of the expansion of the Georgia free black population to the increased tendency for masters to simply abandon their slaves in urban areas, as they could no longer profitably work them under wartime conditions. Mohr, *On the Threshold of Freedom*, 204–6.

52. Census of the City of Augusta, 1852, taken by Wm. H. Pritchard, Georgia State Archives, Atlanta. See also Whittington B. Johnson, "Free Blacks in Antebellum Augusta, Georgia: A Demographic and Economic Profile," *Richmond County History* 14 (Winter 1982): 10–21.

53. Because male slaves had greater opportunities to escape from the planta-

tions, probably most of those who arrived in Augusta as runaways were also male. Berlin et al., *Freedom: A Documentary History of Emancipation*, 1:12. Earlier in the city's history, the construction of the canal required a kind of labor that was similar to that of building fortifications. This earlier construction was carried out primarily by Irish immigrants. Slaveowners were loathe to use their valuable slaves in such a fashion.

54. Richmond County Grand Jury Presentments, June 21, 1861.

55. Ibid., June 21, 1861; December 20, 1862.

56. *Augusta Chronicle and Sentinel*, February 16, 1865.

57. Ibid., January 15, 1864. For a similar discussion of the black-white collusion during the war, see Victoria Bynum, *Unruly Women: The Politics of Social and Sexual Control in the Old South* (Chapel Hill, 1992), 111–29.

58. See *Augusta Chronicle and Sentinel*, August 5, 1864; December 11, 1864. See also August 21, 1864.

59. Joseph Jones to Caroline Davis Jones, Joseph Jones Papers, Special Collections, Hill Memorial Library, Tulane University, New Orleans, October 11, 1861.

60. Morgan, *How It Was*, 119.

61. Ibid., 119–20.

62. Ibid.; Emily Middleton Izard to her sister, Eliza Middleton Smith, June 20, 1865, Smith and Wells Family Papers.

63. Rowland, Diary, November 29, 1864.

64. Ibid.

65. Ibid., December 9, 1864; December 3, 1864; see also December 7, 1864.

66. Thomas, Journal, December 12, 1864. The return of the one slave, Albert, who had apparently left willingly with the Union troops was reassuring to Rowland. As she wrote in her journal, he had only left because the soldiers, "drew their guns, & told him if he dared to run they would shoot him, & then carried him off with the horses; he says he has been trying to get away ever since he was carried off but only effected his escape last Tuesday." Rowland, Journal, December 18, 1864.

67. *Augusta Daily Constitutionalist*, February 2, 1865. See also March 1, 1865; March 12, 1865.

68. Ibid., February 2, 1865.

69. Ibid., February 3, 1865; March 12, 1865.

70. Ibid., February 2, 1865.

71. Ibid., April 7, 1865.

72. Thomas, Journal, March 29, 1865.

73. Ibid., May 1, 1865. See also *Augusta Daily Constitutionalist*, May 2, 1865.

74. Thomas, Journal, May 1, 1865; May 7, 1865.
75. Morgan, *How It Was*, 145.
76. Ibid., 146.
77. Thomas, Journal, May 29, 1865.
78. Ibid., May 27, 1865.
79. Ibid., May 29, 1865.
80. Ibid., May 29, 1865.
81. Ibid., May, 1865; Mr. & Mrs. Izard to Mrs. Smith, June 24, 1865, *Smith Family Letters*, 219.
82. Thomas, Journal, May 29, 1865.
83. Ibid., June 1865.

Chapter 5. The Domestic Reconstruction of Southern White Men

1. That Davis purposely donned his wife's attire was as vehemently denied by the South as it was asserted by the North. For an overview of the incident, see Burke Davis, *The Long Surrender* (New York, 1985), 135–48; and for a discussion of the gender implications in particular, see Nina Silber, "Intemperate Men, Spiteful Women, and Jefferson Davis," *American Quarterly* 41, no. 4 (1989): 614–35. While some of the northern press went so far as to claim that Davis was caught in his wife's hoops, which was clearly untrue, even Varina Davis herself alluded to her efforts to disguise her husband by throwing her shawl over his head. She concluded in her memoir that she would have done more to "protect" him had she known what fate awaited him. Varina Howell Davis, *Jefferson Davis: A Memoir* (New York, 1890), 2:638–41.
2. Ella Gertrude Clanton Thomas, Journal, May 8, 1865, Special Collections, Perkins Library, Duke University, Durham, North Carolina.
3. Joseph Bryan Cumming, *A Sketch of the Descendents of David Cumming and Memoirs of the War between the States* (Augusta, Ga. 1925), 19–20. Probably the most famous suicide in response to the failure of the Confederacy was that of Edmund Ruffin. Many accounts of the state of the South in the immediate aftermath of the war note more generally the widespread depression among defeated white men of the region. See John T. Trowbridge, *The Desolate South: 1865–1866*, ed. Gordon Carroll (1866; rpt. New York, 1956); John Richard Dennett, *The South as It Is, 1865–1866*, ed. Henry M. Christman (1866; rpt. Athens, Ga., 1986); Whitelaw Reid, *After the War: A Tour of the Southern States, 1865–1866*, ed. C. Vann Woodward (New York, 1965).
4. For a further discussion of the way military defeat and emancipation posed a

fundamental challenge to white men's understanding of themselves, see Dan Carter, *When the War Was Over: The Failure of Self-Reconstruction in the South* (Baton Rouge, 1985); James Roark, *Masters without Slaves: Southern Planters in the Civil War and Reconstruction* (New York, 1977), 156–209; Suzanne Lebsock, *Free Women of Petersburg: Status and Culture in a Southern Town, 1784–1860* (New York, 1984), 237–49; and Gaines Foster, *Ghosts of the Confederacy: Defeat, the Lost Cause, and the Emergence of the New South* (New York, 1987), 22–35.

5. See Joel Williamson, *The Crucible of Race: Black-White Relations in the American South since Emancipation* (New York, 1985), for a discussion of the failure of postwar white efforts to replace the "organic" power that slavery had conferred upon them.

6. In general, historians who have argued for persistence in postwar white gender roles have focused on the experience of white women. See, for example, Jean E. Friedman, *The Enclosed Garden: Women and Community in the Evangelical South, 1830–1900* (Chapel Hill, 1985), 92–109; and George C. Rable, *Civil Wars: Women and the Crisis of Southern Nationalism* (Urbana, 1989), 265–88. Less attention has been paid to the impact of the war on male gender roles. For a discussion of change in white southern men's class and race position in the postwar South, see Ted Ownby, "The Defeated Generation at Work: White Farmers in the Deep South, 1865–1890," *Southern Studies* 23 (Winter 1984): 325–47; David Herbert Donald, "A Generation of Defeat," in *From the Old South to the New: Essays on the Transitional South*, ed. Walter J. Fraser Jr. and Winfred B. Moore Jr. (Westport, Conn., 1981), 3–20. Both Joel Williamson, *Crucible of Race*, and Jacquelyn Dowd Hall, *Revolt against Chivalry: Jessie Daniel Ames and the Women's Campaign Against Lynching* (New York, 1979) suggest that the decline of white men's race and class position heightened their need to continue to "protect" their women in the postwar South.

7. See Silber, "Intemperate Men, Spiteful Women, and Jefferson Davis," for a discussion of the response of the northern press.

8. See Lebsock, *Free Women of Petersburg*, 237–49, for a further elaboration of this point.

9. *Augusta Chronicle and Sentinel*, April 4, 1865.

10. Anne Firor Scott makes a case for the transformative effect of the war on elite white gender roles in *The Southern Lady: From Pedestal to Politics, 1830–1930* (Chicago, 1970), 105–33. Here Scott bases her assessment of the change in elite women's roles on the extent to which women were able to take up expanded public position, rather than upon the place that domestic

life itself assumed for these women, as well as for their men, in the postwar social order.

11. George Fitzhugh, *Sociology for the South, or the Failure of Free Society* (New York, 1966). "In truth, woman, like children, has but one right, and that is the right to protection. The right to protection involves the obligation to obey," 214.

12. *Augusta Daily Constitutionalist*, February 28, 1865.

13. Ibid., February 1, 1865.

14. Ibid., April 12, 1865.

15. Ibid., February 28, 1865.

16. Thomas, Journal, May 1, 1865.

17. Ibid.

18. Susan Cornwall, Journal, August 22, 1865, Southern Historical Collection, University of North Carolina, Chapel Hill.

19. Ibid.

20. Ibid.

21. Joseph Jones to Mary Jones, June 27, 1863, Joseph Jones Papers, Special Collections, Hill Memorial Library, Tulane University, New Orleans; Charles Rowland to Catherine Rowland, December 22, 1864, typescript, Charles Rowland Letters, Richmond County Historical Society Collection, Augusta College, Augusta, Georgia.

22. *Augusta Chronicle and Sentinel*, May 5, 1865.

23. Thomas, Journal, May 8, 1865; Cornwall, Journal, May 29, 1866.

24. Charles Rowland to Catherine Rowland, May 1, 1865; Charles Rowland to Catherine Rowland, April 25, 1865, Charles Rowland Letters. Gertrude Thomas also wrote of the pleasure she took in ordering her domestic life. "Doing all this with such a feeling of perfect satisfaction with only those who have lived in constant expectation of a raid can experience"; Journal, May 1, 1865.

25. *Augusta Daily Constitutionalist*, May 6, 1865. See also May 17, 1865; May 18, 1865; May 25, 1865; August 26, 1866.

26. Ibid., May 17, 1865.

27. Augusta City Council Minutes, October 6, 1865, Richmond County Municipal Building, Augusta.

28. *Augusta Daily Constitutionalist*, May 25, 1865; Mrs. Irby Morgan, *How It Was: Four Years among the Rebels* (Nashville, 1892), 52–53. For a further discussion of Robert E. Lee as *the* hero of the lost cause, see Thomas L. Connelly and Barbara L. Bellows, *God and General Longstreet: The Lost Cause and the Southern Mind* (Baton Rouge, 1982), 73–106.

29. *Augusta Daily Constitutionalist*, June 14, 1865; *Augusta Chronicle and Sentinel*, April 21, 1866.

30. Joseph Jones to Paul Eve, July 20, 1866, Joseph Jones Papers.

31. Daniel E. Huger to Bell Smith, July 24, 1865, Smith and Wells Papers, South Caroliniana Library, Columbia, South Carolina; James Verdery to his sister, August 3, 1865, James Paul Verdery Papers, Special Collections, Perkins Library, Duke University, Durham, North Carolina.

32. James Verdery to his sister, October 3, 1865, Verdery Papers.

33. Ibid., October 1, 1865; October 11, 1865.

34. *Augusta Chronicle and Sentinel*, September 27, 1866.

35. Margaret R. Higonnet and Patrice L.-R. Higonnet, "The Double Helix," in *Behind the Lines: Gender and the Two World Wars*, ed. Margaret Randolph Higonnet, Jane Jenson, Sonya Michel, Margaret Collins Weitz (New Haven, 1987), 31–47, have identified this weaving back and forth more generally for the phenomenon of world wars in the twentieth century. They have likened it to a "double helix," although they fail to consider that in the process of this weaving of public and private identification, the gendered bond itself might be transformed or transformative.

36. *Augusta Chronicle and Sentinel*, September 27, 1866.

37. Ibid. Ironically, given the overwhelmingly hostile response of white southerners to Harriet Beecher Stowe's antebellum novel *Uncle Tom's Cabin*, this argument for the domestic benefits of rationalizing the household through "labor saving devices" strongly resembles the position of Harriet and her sister, Catherine Beecher, in their book, *The American Woman's Home* (New York, 1869), published at almost the same time. Here we see the recipe for the properly bourgeois "separation of spheres," where the household was cleansed of relations of class and race and the labor of servants was replaced in large part by the more efficient labors of the housewife and her machines. Nevertheless, Ruth Schwartz Cowan has convincingly argued that this transformation, to the extent that it actually even occurred, did not reduce the amount of household labor for the housewife; see *More Work for Mother: The Ironies of Household Technology from the Open Hearth to the Microwave* (New York, 1983).

38. *Augusta Chronicle and Sentinel*, September 27, 1866.

39. Gerald F. Linderman, *Embattled Courage: The Experience of Combat in the American Civil War* (New York, 1987), 266–97, makes the case that the soldier's understanding of the meaning of the war changed in the context of the actual fighting of it. The civilian population's initial vision of war as an expression of manhood, however, having no such mitigating experience, remained constant.

40. *Augusta Chronicle and Sentinel*, May 31, 1865.

41. Joseph B. Cumming Jr., *Reminiscences of Joseph B. Cumming, Jr.* (Augusta, Ga., 1983), 9–10.

42. *Augusta Chronicle and Sentinel*, April 18, 1866.

43. Ibid., September 27, 1866.

44. Ibid., April 25, 1861. Indeed there was virtually no increase in the participation rate of white women in the town's wage labor force in 1870 as compared to 1860, according to the manuscript census. Even those women required to take up self-support because they were widowed or unable to find a husband in the aftermath of wartime casualties were both lauded for their efforts and encouraged to believe that eventually they too would find "protection." See *Augusta Chronicle and Sentinel*, "What Our Girls Can Do," September 30, 1866.

45. P. M. Nightingale to Charles Colcock Jones, August 1, 1870, Charles Colcock Jones, Jr., Papers, Perkins Library, Duke University.

46. On the issue of how marriages were renegotiated, see also Carol Bleser and Frederick M. Heath, "The Clays of Alabama: The Impact of the Civil War on a Southern Marriage, in *In Joy and in Sorrow: Women, Family and Marriage in the Victorian South*, ed. Carol Bleser (New York, 1991), 135–53; Elisabeth Muhlenfeld, *Mary Boykin Chesnut: A Biography* (Baton Rouge, 1981); Virginia Burr, "A Woman Made to Suffer and Be Strong; Ella Gertrude Clanton Thomas, 1834–1907," in Bleser, *In Joy and in Sorrow*, 230–32; and Joan Cashin, "Varina Howell Davis," in *Portraits of American Women*, ed. G. J. Barker-Benfield and Catherine Clinton (New York, 1991), 259–78. Victoria Bynum suggests the ways in which the state intervened in divorce cases to reinforce the diminished powers of men in the social order as a whole, see "Reshaping the Bonds of Womanhood: Divorce in Reconstruction North Carolina," in *Divided Houses: Gender and the Civil War*, ed. Catherine Clinton and Nina Silber (New York, 1992), 320–34.

47. Upon emancipation the Thomases owned ninety slaves and would have inherited more once her father's will was settled. As Gertrude Thomas wrote, "by the surrender of the Southern army slavery became a thing of the past and we were reduced from a state of affluence to comparative poverty." Personally, she was reduced to "utter beggary," as her entire dowry of $30,000 had been invested in slave property. Thomas, Journal, October 9, 1865. See also *The Secret Eye: The Journal of Ella Gertrude Clanton Thomas, 1848–1889*, ed. Virginia I. Burr (Chapel Hill, 1990).

48. Ibid., September 20, 1866; December 4, 1868.

49. Ibid., May 3, 1869.

50. Ibid., March 2, 1870; August 1, 1870.

51. Ibid., August 3, 1870; August 7, 1869.

52. Ibid., August 3, 1870.

53. Ibid., December 4, 1868.

54. Ibid.

55. Ibid., May 4, 1869.

56. Ibid., May 4, 1869; June 26, 1869.

57. Ibid., November 30, 1870. Mary Elizabeth Massey indentifies Gertrude Thomas's loss of confidence in her husband's ability to manage their affairs as the critical factor turning her toward feminism; "The Making of a Feminist," *Journal of Southern History* 39 (February 1973): 3–22. As early as June 19, 1869, Thomas recorded having criticized her husband's management and his reply that she "did not have confidence in his judgement, and I would have been better satisfied to have been sure I had acted right." But she concluded, "Most men dislike to admit that their wives own anything. It is all the masculine 'my' and 'my own.'" She became increasingly dissatisfied with her husband's failure to consult with her. The passage of the Married Women's Property Act in Georgia emerges in this context as something of a joke. As she wrote, "I laughingly told some gentleman that the bill . . . had been passed now that most of the women in Georgia had nothing to lose— like locking the stable door after the horse has been stolen." She soon became convinced that her husband's financial abilities were not what they might be. "I think a great deal of what we call bad luck is bad management." Journal, June 19, 1869; August 1, 1870.

58. Thomas described her own lapse of faith in her journal. "I alone know the effect the abolition of slavery has had on me. I did not know until then how intimately my faith in revolution and faith in the institution of slavery had been woven together—true I had seen the evil of the latter but if the *Bible* was right then slavery *must be*—slavery was done away with and my faith in Gods Holy Book was terribly shaken. For a time I doubted God." Journal, October 9, 1865. She went into a deep melancholia and miscarried the child she was carrying, almost dying herself. She finally recovered several months later, only, as she wrote, because "I . . . determined that I would regard my continued sickness as a chastening form of the Lord and submit without murmuring to his will." Her recovery was not an easy one and she clung to her newly recovered faith. "During the last few days I have been constantly repeating to myself that precious promise . . . 'as thy days demand so shall thy strength ever be.'" Journal, October 4, 1865.

59. Ibid., August 29, 1870.

60. Ibid., December 19, 1870.

61. Ibid., May 27, 1871.
62. Ibid.

Chapter 6. The Politics of Domestic Loss:
The Ladies' Memorial Association and the Confederate Dead

1. *Augusta Constitutionalist*, April 27, 1875. The headline of this article read "the largest procession ever seen in the town" and claimed that ten thousand were present to witness the laying of the cornerstone.
2. Ibid.
3. Ibid.
4. *Ceremonies in Augusta, Georgia, Laying the Cornerstone of the Confederate Monument with an Oration by Clement A. Evans*, 8, copy in the Rare Books Collection, University of Georgia, Athens.
5. Ibid., 11.
6. For a further discussion of the silence of the Confederate Memorial Tradition on slavery and race, see Charles Reagan Wilson, *Baptized in Blood: The Religion of the Lost Cause, 1865–1920* (Athens, Ga., 1980), 100–118, and Gaines M. Foster, *Ghosts of the Confederacy: Defeat, the Lost Cause and the Emergence of the New South* (New York, 1987), 60, 194. David Blight discusses Frederick Douglass's ultimately unsuccessful efforts to keep slavery at the center of the postwar understanding of the conflict, in *Frederick Douglass' Civil War: Keeping Faith in Jubilee* (Baton Rouge, 1989), 189–219. On the Black Codes, see W. E. B. Du Bois, *Black Reconstruction in America, 1860–1880* (New York, 1935), 167; Eric Foner, *Nothing but Freedom: Emancipation and Its Legacy* (Baton Rouge, 1985), 39–73; James Roark, *Masters without Slaves: Southern Planters in the Civil War and Reconstruction* (New York, 1977), 140; and Dan Carter, *When the War Was Over: The Failure of Self-Reconstruction in the South* (Baton Rouge, 1985), 178–84.
7. *Ceremonies in Augusta*, 11.
8. Ibid. According to Clement Evans, the city and county sent two companies of artillery, six of cavalry, and fourteen of infantry, besides Jackson's battalion. "The ranks of these companies were sadly thinned by the oft recurring battles, but they were from time to time filled up until scarcely any remained in the city or county but the aged, the disabled and the children"; *Ceremonies in Augusta*, 12. In their *Memorial History of Augusta*, Dutcher and Jones claim that out of a total white population of 10,000, over 2,000

men served in the course of the war. Of those 2,000, they claim 292 were killed or died. Charles C. Jones Jr. and Salem Dutcher, *Memorial History of Augusta, Georgia* (1890; 3d ed. Spartanburg, S.C., 1980), 180.

9. Mayor's Annual Message, October 7, 1864, Augusta City Council Minutes, Richmond County Municipal Building, Augusta, Georgia.

10. *Ceremonies in Augusta*, 12, 9.

11. Ibid., 9. Although the more elite Cavalry Association was formed in the year after the war, no general veterans' organization was formed until the Confederate Survivors Association was organized in 1878. Charles Colcock Jones, *Reports of the Annual Meetings of the Confederate Survivors Association of Augusta, Georgia* (Augusta, Ga., 1879–92). Although many historians of the Confederate memorial tradition have noted its initially female domination, they have seen little social or political significance in it. See Rollin Osterweis, *The Myth of the Lost Cause, 1865–1900* (Hamden, Conn., 1973); Foster, *Ghosts of the Confederacy*; E. Merton Coulter, "The Confederate Monument in Athens, Georgia," *Georgia Historical Review* 40 (September 1956): 230–47. Historians of women in the postbellum period have also given the organization scant attention.

12. See, for example, Ella Gertrude Clanton Thomas, Journal, April 17, 1862; July 28, 1864, Special Collections, Perkins Library, Duke University; Mrs. Irby Morgan, *How It Was: Four Years among the Rebels* (Nashville, 1892), 136–37; Kate Cumming to Julia Bryan Cumming, March 5, 1862, Cumming Family Papers, Richmond County Historical Collection, Augusta College, Augusta, Ga.

13. *Ceremonies in Augusta*, 12. Although historians have overlooked the role of gender in the formation of the memorial movement in the immediate postwar era, some have considered its role in sectional reunion in the late nineteenth century. See Paul H. Buck, *The Road to Reunion, 1865–1900* (Boston, 1937); and more recently, Nina Silber, *The Romance of Reunion* (Chapel Hill, 1993).

14. In her novel, *Macaria*, one of the most popular Civil War novels in the postwar era, J. Augusta Evans exudes this politics of domestic sacrifice. Drew Faust has underscored the significance of this position in Confederate women's initial commitment to the war. Drew Faust, "Altars of Sacrifice: Confederate Women's Narratives of War," *Journal of American History* 76 (March 1990): 1200–1228.

15. For a further discussion of the way that war and defeat transformed men's understanding of themselves, see Gerald F. Linderman, *Embattled Courage: The Experience of Combat in the American Civil War* (New York, 1987); and Wilson, *Baptized in Blood.*

16. *Ceremonies in Augusta*, 13–14.

17. Augusta City Council Minutes, October, 1865.

18. Ella Gertrude Clanton Thomas, *The Secret Eye: The Journal of Ella Gertrude Clanton Thomas, 1848–1889*, ed. Virginia Ingraham Burr (Chapel Hill, 1990), 278; entry for December 31, 1865.

19. James Verdery, Correspondence, January 17, 1866, James Paul Verdery Papers, Special Collections, Perkins Library, Duke University.

20. Grand Jury Presentments, January 1866, Georgia State Archives, Atlanta.

21. Ruth Currie-McDaniel, *Carpetbagger of Conscience: A Biography of John Emory Bryant* (Athens, Ga., 1987).

22. Augusta City Council Minutes, January 24, 1866; Mayor's Annual Message, ibid., October 6, 1865.

23. Augusta City Council Minutes, October, 1865. Prior to Federal occupation in May of 1865, the city had $350,000 invested in Confederate assets. With the collapse of all Confederate paper, they were forced to issue certificates of indebtedness that left them with a debt of $180,000 by the following October.

24. Mayor's Annual Message, Augusta City Council Minutes, October 6, 1865. At the immediate close of the war the Augusta Purveying Association continued to give out rations to five hundred families at a cost of $1,000 a month. The mayor held out hope that with the improvement in circulation of currency and expanded employment, they would soon be able to support themselves. However, this figure did not appear to decline in the following eight months, as charitable expenditures between May 1865 and January 1866 accounted for $18,818. It was not until 1868 that the level of expenditures on charity began to decline. By 1870 the figure was roughly half of 1866 level, standing at $9,904. Augusta City Council Minutes, April 23, 1866; April 14, 1868; March, 1870.

25. Augusta City Council Minutes, February 1, 1867.

26. Mayor's Annual Message, October 6, 1865, Augusta City Council Minutes.

27. See for example the City Council Minutes, October 1864 and October 1865.

28. City Council Minutes, October 1864; October 6, 1865; June 25, 1865.

29. *Augusta Chronicle and Sentinel*, September 26, 1866.

30. Ibid., October 4, 1866.

31. Ibid.

32. Ibid.

33. Although Gertrude Thomas supported her husband's initial enlistment, after a year of service her attitudes, and presumably his as well, had altered considerably. See September, 1862; October 21, 1864, in *The Secret Eye*, 209–10, 239–40.

34. *Augusta Chronicle and Sentinel*, October 4, 1866.

35. Joseph B. Cumming, *Personal Reminiscences of the War between the States* (Augusta, n.d.); Joseph B. Cumming Jr., *Memoirs of Joseph B. Cumming, Jr.* (Augusta, 1988).

36. Joseph B. Cumming, "Address by Major Joseph B. Cumming at the Unveiling of the Cenotaph On Greene Street, December 31, 1873," in Cumming, *Occasional Addresses* (Augusta, n.d.), 3. The monument was erected by the members of the Sunday school of the St. James Methodist Episcopal Church in memory of the twenty-three teachers and students who died in the conflict. The monument listed 292 names of county Confederate Dead and was erected at a cost of $5,400. Jones and Dutcher, *Memorial History of Augusta*, 181.

37. Cumming, "Address by Major Joseph B. Cumming," 4.

38. Indeed, it was Joseph Bryan Cumming who recorded the conversation between his father and Jefferson Davis as Davis was being taken prisoner through Augusta by Federal troops at the close of the war. *A Sketch of the Descendents of David Cumming* (Augusta, 1925), 19–20.

39. Cumming, "Address by Major Joseph B. Cumming," 5.

40. Joseph B. Cumming, "On the Occasion of Decorating Confederate Soldiers' Graves at the Augusta Cemetery, 1895," in *Occasional Addresses*.

41. *Augusta Chronicle and Sentinel*, March 29, 1866.

42. Ibid.

43. *A History of the Origins of Memorial Day* (Columbus, Ga., 1898), 6, 7.

44. Ibid., 25.

45. *Augusta Chronicle and Sentinel*, April 5, 1866.

46. The Confederate Dead were gathered in one section, consisting of 540 graves. The section was enclosed with a stone coping and a fountain placed at the center, at a cost of $3,530.20, Ladies' Memorial Association Minutes, April 22, 1872–May, 1924, Richmond County Historical Society Collection, Augusta College, Augusta, June 30, 1875. See also Jones and Dutcher, *Memorial History of Augusta*, 181–82.

47. Both the first president, Mrs. Dr. John Carter, and the first vice-president, Mrs. Dr. H. H. Steiner, of the Ladies' Memorial Association were wives of doctors who had been instrumental in the Ladies' Hospital Association. Jones and Dutcher, *Memorial History of Augusta*, 181.

48. The Ladies' Memorial Association determined in April of 1881 to discontinue the public speakers on Memorial Day, since the monument was completed. They found, however, that the attendance and contributions to grave decoration declined precipitously the following year, and they reinstated speakers in 1883. Ladies' Memorial Association Minutes, April 1883.

49. Ibid., June 24, 1878. See also the Constitution of the Ladies' Memorial Association, ibid., April 22, 1872.

50. *Augusta Chronicle and Sentinel*, April 2, 1873.

51. The initial emergence of permanent public organization not in the name of independence and autonomy but rather to shore up domestic life has been discussed at some length for the Northeast in the early nineteenth century. See Kathryn Kish Sklar, *Catherine Beecher: A Study in American Domesticity* (New Haven, 1973); Nancy F. Cott, *The Bonds of Womanhood: 'Woman's Sphere' in New England, 1780–1835* (New Haven, 1977); Mary Ryan, *Cradle of the Middle Class: The Family in Oneida County, New York, 1790–1865* (New York, 1980); and Ann Douglas, *The Feminization of American Culture* (New York, 1977). In the South this process of feminization was intensified by a more intense experience of domestic loss.

52. John Davidson, "Dedicatory Address of New Widows Home Residence," in Widows' Home Minutes, 1871–1900, now in the vault of the downtown office of Georgia Federal Bank, Augusta.

53. *Augusta Chronicle and Sentinel*, April 2, 1873; see also April 26, 1866.

54. Ladies' Memorial Association Minutes, April 5, 1873.

55. Ibid. While the lot for this structure was a gift from the Augusta City Council, and the largest single donation of $500 was contributed by Emily Tubman, the remainder of the total cost of $2,500 was contributed by donations from the public and by the membership of the organization, which stood at 258 members in 1874. *Augusta Chronicle and Sentinel*, January 17, 1874.

56. Ladies' Memorial Association Minutes, April 5, 1873.

57. Ibid.

58. Ladies' Memorial Association Minutes, October 18, 1875; April 20, 1876.

59. As of April 1877, they had raised $13,413 and needed a total of $14,490. At this point Charles Colcock Jones offered to help them petition the U.S. Congress for a remission of import duties on the marble and by June, as a consequence of this remission, they had sufficient funds. See Ladies' Memorial Association Minutes, April 1, 1877; April 11, 1878; June 24, 1878; November 7, 1878.

60. The two inscriptions read "No nation rose so white and fair, None fell so pure of crime"; and "Worthy To have lived and known Our Gratitude: / Worthy To be hallowed and held In tender remembrance. / Worthy The fadeless fame which Confederate soldiers Won. / Who gave themselves in life And death for us: / For the honor of Georgia, / For the rights of the States, / For the liberties of the people, / For the sentiments of the South, / For the principles of the Union, / As these were handed down to them, / By the fathers of our common country." Ladies' Memorial Association Minutes, June 24, 1878.

61. Newspaper Clipping, April 24, 1878, Ella Gertrude Clanton Thomas Scrapbook, in possession of Mrs. Gertrude Despeaux, Stone Mountain, Georgia.
62. Ibid., May 1, 1878.
63. Ibid.
64. Ibid. Thomas stated her conviction that ex-Confederate women should take a leading role in telling the story of the war even more forcefully in a letter she wrote to the *Augusta Chronicle and Constitutionalist* in the spring of 1880.

> Ah! Who is to distinguish between right and might? The man who, when approached, pleads policy? The poet who, when appealed to write a few words touched with divine inspiration, keeps silent? The man of business who is so absorbed in building his shattered fortune, that he has no time for aught besides? No. They all give liberally, 'tis true; to this let our beautiful monument give evidence, but it is the women of the South who will preserve the legends of war. It will be the mothers who will tell to the children.

> clipping, Thomas Scrapbook.

65. Charles Colcock Jones Jr., "Dedicatory Address," in *Ceremonies in Augusta*, 16. Jones was apparently selected to give the dedicatory address because his "reputation as a scholar, gentleman and soldier is without flaw." Ladies' Memorial Association Minutes, April 11, 1878. The son of Rev. Dr. Charles Colcock Jones, a prominent planter of Liberty County, Georgia, and the older brother of Joseph Jones, a physician in Augusta, C. C. Jones Jr. was himself trained as a lawyer. Much of the family's wartime correspondence has been published; see *The Children of Pride: A True Story of Georgia and the Civil War*, ed. Robert Manson Meyers, 2d, rev. ed. (New Haven, 1984). After the war, C. C. Jones went to New York and worked as a lawyer, returning to Augusta in the late 1870s. He immediately became active in the memorial movement in the town, helping the Ladies' Memorial Association to get tax-free status for the marble used in the monument and contributing one of the inscriptions on the monument as well as the dedicatory address. He was also one of the founding members of the Confederate Survivors Association in 1878. He and Salem Dutcher, also a member of the Confederate Survivors Association, wrote what is one of the most authoritative histories of Augusta, *Memorial History of Augusta, Georgia*.
66. Jones, "Dedicatory Address," 20.
67. Ibid.
68. Ibid., 25. See Thomas L. Connelly and Barbara L. Bellows, *God and General Longstreet: The Lost Cause and the Southern Mind* (Baton Rouge, 1982), 29–30; and Thomas L. Connelly, *The Marble Man: Robert E. Lee and His*

Image in American Society (Baton Rouge, 1977), for Lee's mediatory image in the memorial tradition.

69. *Augusta Chronicle and Constitutionalist*, November 1, 1878.
70. *Augusta Chronicle and Constitutionalist*, April 27, 1875; November 1, 1878.
71. Ibid., November 1, 1878.

Chapter 7. The Divided Mind as a Gendered Mind: The Confederate Survivors Association and the New South

1. Charles Colcock Jones Jr., *An Address Delivered before the Confederate Survivors Association* (Augusta, 1886), 8.
2. Charles Colcock Jones Jr., *An Address Delivered before the Confederate Survivors Association* (Augusta, 1879), 5. Jones claimed elsewhere that two thousand men served from the county, so this was not unreasonable on his part; Jones and Salem Dutcher, *Memorial History of Augusta, Georgia* (1890, 3d ed. Spartanburg, S.C., 1980), 179. By 1904, the organization still claimed 251 members, 188 of whom had served as privates or sergeants. Charles Edgeworth Jones, *Annual Report*, United Confederate Veterans, Georgia Division, CSA Camp no. 435, Richmond County Historical Society Collection, Augusta College.
3. Charles Colcock Jones Jr., *An Address Delivered before the Confederate Survivors Association* (Augusta, 1887), 5.
4. Charles Colcock Jones Jr., *An Address Delivered before the Confederate Survivors Association* (Augusta, 1879), 4.
5. Charles Colcock Jones Jr., *An Address Delivered before the Confederate Survivors Association* (Augusta, 1881), 4. See Jones's eulogy of James Clanton for a further discussion of the impact of social decline on the local elite. Jones, *An Address Delivered before the Confederate Survivors Association* (Augusta, 1892), 27–30.
6. On the ameliorative role that the Confederate Memorial Movement played, see Gerald F. Linderman, *Embattled Courage: The Experience of Combat in the American Civil War* (New York, 1987), 266–97; Foster, *Ghosts of the Confederacy*, 22–35; and Charles Reagan Wilson, *Baptized in Blood: The Religion of the Lost Cause, 1865–1920* (Athens, Ga., 1980), 1–17.
7. Jones, "An Address Delivered before the Confederate Survivors Association" (Augusta, 1879), 5.
8. Ibid.
9. On the mediatory role of gender in this postwar reconstruction of white men, see Nina Silber, *The Romance of Reunion* (Chapel Hill, 1993), 159–96.

10. Jones and Dutcher, *Memorial History of Augusta*, 298.

11. Sexton Records, Magnolia Cemetary, Augusta, Georgia. A total of twenty-nine men were eventually buried in this lot. Sixteen of them were single or widowed, eight were married. The last burial was in 1941. Most held working-class or lower-middle-class occupations: shoemaker, operative, machinist, carpenter, clerk, wood dealer.

12. For a further discussion of Jones's role in the Confederate Memorial Movement, see Gaines Foster, *Ghosts of the Confederacy: Defeat, The Lost Cause, and the Emergence of the New South* (New York, 1987), 82–90; Michael M. Cass, "Charles C. Jones and the 'Lost Cause'," *Georgia Historical Quarterly* 55 (Summer 1971): 222–33; and Charles Edgeworth Jones, "Colonel Charles C. Jones, Jr., LL.D., of Georgia: Historian, Biographer, and Archeologist," in *Literature: A Weekly Magazine* (New York), February 9, 1889, 265–77.

13. Jones called for the formation of these organizations in his annual address of 1891, and the Augusta United Daughters of the Confederacy was indeed formed in that year. See the Minutes of the Augusta Daughters of the Confederacy, Richmond County Historical Society Collection, Augusta College, Augusta, Georgia). Charles Jones's own son, Charles Edgeworth Jones, had become the historian of the Confederate Survivors Association by 1904.

14. Jones, "An Address Delivered before the Confederate Survivors Association" (Augusta, 1879), 5. For a further discussion of the Confederate Powderworks, see also Florence Fleming Corley, *Confederate City: Augusta, Georgia, 1860–1865* (Columbia, S.C., 1960); and Joseph B. Milgram and Norman R. Gerlieu, *George Washington Rains, Gunpowder Maker of the Confederacy* (Philadelphia, 1961).

15. Ella Gertrude Clanton Thomas, Scrapbooks, n.d., in the possession of Gertrude Despeaux, Stone Mountain, Georgia.

16. Ibid.

17. Jones, "An Address Delivered before the Confederate Survivors Association" (Augusta, 1881), 4.

18. Augusta City Council Records, June 2, 1879, Richmond County Municipal Building, Augusta.

19. Jones, "An Address Delivered before the Confederate Survivors Association" (Augusta, 1881), 8.

20. LeeAnn Whites, "Southern Ladies and Millhands: Augusta, Georgia, 1870–1890." (Ph.D. diss., University of California, Irvine, 1982), 191–92; and William Ludwick Whatley, "A History of Textile Development in Augusta, 1865–1883 (M.S. thesis, University of South Carolina, 1964), iii–iv.

21. Jones, "An Address Delivered before the Confederate Survivors Association"

(Augusta, 1881), 7; Jones, "An Address Delivered before the Confederate Survivors Association" (Augusta, 1889), 25.

22. Jones, "An Address Delivered before the Confederate Survivors Association" (Augusta, 1889), 25.

23. Wilbur Fisk Tillett, "The White Man of the New South," *Century Magazine*, 33 (1886–87): 769–76; and "Southern Womanhood as Affected by the War," *Century Magazine* 43 (1891–92): 9–16.

24. Tillett, "White Man of the New South," 769. For further examples of mill booster ideology, see Broadus Mitchell, *The Rise of the Cotton Mills in the South* (1921; rpt. New York, 1968); Daniel Augustus Tompkins, *Cotton Mill, Commercial Features* (Charlotte, N.C., 1899); Holland Thompson, *From Cotton Field to Cotton Mill* (New York, 1906).

25. Tillett, "White Man of the New South," 769.

26. Ibid., 770. The Sibleys and the Rowlands offer a good example of this pattern. William C. Sibley returned from the war to become first president of Langley Mills and eventually president of Sibley Mills, named after his father, Josiah Sibley, of the cotton factoring house. In the meantime his wife, who had served in the Ladies' Aid Society during the war, became the state president of the WCTU when it was founded in the state in 1881. While Charles Rowland returned from the war to continue his business as a cotton factor, he served as a member of the board of directors for the mills. His wife, Catherine Rowland, who worked for the Ladies' Aid Society during the war, went on to participate in the establishment of the Widows' Home, the Confederate Monument, eventually becoming president of the United Daughters of the Confederacy and the King's Daughters.

27. For a further discussion of changes in the postwar gender structure of the Augusta textile work force, see LeeAnn Whites, "The Degraffenried Controversy: Race, Class and Gender in the New South," *Journal of Southern History* 54, no. 3 (August 1988): 458–61; and "Southern Ladies and Mill-hands," 185–231.

28. Tillett, "Southern Womanhood as Affected by the War," 16.

29. Jones, "An Address Delivered before the Confederate Survivors Association" (Augusta, 1884), 13.

30. Ibid.

31. Ibid.

32. Jones, "An Address Delivered before the Confederate Survivors Association" (Augusta, 1883), 11.

33. Jones, "An Address Delivered before the Confederate Survivors Association" (Augusta, 1889), 29–32.

34. Jones, "An Address Delivered before the Confederate Survivors Association" (Augusta, 1887), 8.

35. C. Vann Woodward, *Origins of the New South: 1877–1913* (Baton Rouge, 1951), 157.

36. *Augusta Chronicle and Sentinel*, April 12, 1872.

37. Joseph B. Cumming, "Address of Major Joseph B. Cumming, On Occasion of Celebration of Municipal Centennial of the History of Augusta," in *Occasional Addresses* (Augusta, n.d.), 1–16.

38. Ibid., 13.

39. Ibid., 14.

40. Cumming, "New Ideas, New Departures, New South," address delivered to the New England Society of Charleston, South Carolina, December 22, 1893, in *Occasional Addresses*," 10.

41. Ibid., 5, 7.

42. Cumming, "True Lovers on the Occasion of Decorating Confederate Soldiers Graves at the Augusta Cemetery, Memorial Day, 1895," in *Occasional Addresses*, 3.

Index

Abolitionists, 18–19; southern women as, 25–27, 100, 231–32 (n. 28)

Adultery, 26–28

African Americans: in military service, 3, 8; communities of, 6, 116–17, 122, 191; labor of, 23, 219–20; as refugees, 97–98; response of, to emancipation, 127–31, 169–70, 174. *See also* Slaves

Albert (slave of Thomas), 250 (n. 66)

Anonymity: of Confederate Dead, 186–90

Armistice, terms of, 142

Atlanta, fall of, 96, 98, 100

Augusta: economy of, 15–16, 42–47, 171–74, 228 (n. 2), 259 (n. 23); refugees in, 96–100, 124; expectation of invasion of, 102–3, 106, 110, 213–14; as supplier of war materiel, 206, 220–24, 237 (n. 11). *See also* City council; May, Robert H.

Augusta Canal, 42–43, 173, 208–10, 236 (n. 4)

Augusta Factory, 42–43, 46, 80–81, 208

Augusta Ladies' Aid Society, 85

Augusta Manufacturing Company, 89–90

Augusta Purveying Association: origin of, 78–82; families' dependence on, 99–100, 172–73, 247 (n. 9), 259 (n. 24)

Authority of men, challenged, 61–63, 75–76, 154–55

Benevolent societies, 165

Blockade, Union, 44–45, 235–36 (n. 3)

Boss, John (slave of Thomas), 123
Bridwell, L. O., 85–86
Brown, Governor, 88
Bryan, Goode, 31–32
Burials: by women's organizations, 90–94, 186; by Confederate Survivors Association, 201, 204–5, 206, 264 (n. 11)
Bynum, Victoria, 5

Capitalists, 54. *See also* Merchants
Carolina, Sherman's march through, 110
Charity: work by elite women as, 50–52, 57–59; for soldiers' families, 64–70, 73–74, 77–78; jobs for poor women as, 81–83, 88, 89–90, 173–74, 236–37 (n. 5); need for, 172–74; money for, 175, 243 (n. 10). *See also* Augusta Purveying Association
Childbirth, as female gendered experience, 12
Children: increased importance of, 34–36, 153–55; work by, 43–44, 89–90, 155, 236–37 (n. 5); telling Confederate story to, 178–79, 217, 262 (n. 64); in memorial movement, 192, 205–6, 264 (n. 13)
Children of the Confederacy, 217
Chivalry, as vision of manhood, 223
Churches. *See* Religion
City council: support for soldiers' families by, 65, 77–78, 168–71, 243 (n. 10), 261 (n. 55); and soldiers, 102, 112–14, 238 (n. 18), 243–44 (n. 21); and economy, 107, 173–75; struggle to maintain social order by, 112–14, 119, 170–71, 243–44 (n. 21); and memorial movement, 207–8, 241 (n. 43)
Civil War: causes of, 1–2; as test of competing systems, 17–18, 135; reconceptualization of motives for, 165, 168, 176, 181, 195, 196–98, 199–200, 203–4, 209–10, 223–24; reconstructions of, 180, 213–16
Clanton, Turner, 74–76
Class divisions: among white women, 23–24, 70–73, 87, 93, 212; vs. gender identity, 72–77; effect of increased interface among, 100, 111–12, 249 (n. 39); and hostility and thefts, 114–15, 166, 264 (n. 11); among soldiers, 195, 200
Clayton, Mrs., 94
Cloth/clothing: shortages of, 45–46, 99–100, 237–38 (n. 13); as female gendered area, 91–92
Cobb, Howell, 106
Confederacy: women's support for, 11–12, 87–89, 104–6, 105–6, 230 (n. 13), 259–60 (n. 33); as a cause, 16, 140–41, 162–65, 180–81; government of, 84–89, 85–86, 125–26, 237–38 (nn. 12, 13); waning support for, 114, 241–42 (n. 45); fall of, 127. *See also* Defeat, military
Confederate Dead: women and, 160–68, 201–2; social mothering of, 166–68, 182–91; symbolism of, 176–81, 199–200; gathering of graves of, 186, 188, 260 (n. 46)
Confederate Monument, 167–68, 178, 202–3, 261–62 (nn. 59, 60); significance of, 160–65, 187–88,

193–98, 205–6; donations for, 191–92, 261 (n. 59)

Confederate monuments, 206, 207–8, 260 (n. 36)

Confederate Powderworks: chimney of, 206–8

Confederate Survivors Association: membership of, 178, 200–201, 202–9, 217, 218, 258 (n. 11), 262 (n. 65); reconstructions of war by, 213–16

Conspicuous consumption, among elite women, 70–71

Cooking: by women's organizations, 57–59, 90–94

Corn, 45

Cornwall, Susan, 24–25, 27–31, 139–40

Cotton: in Augusta's economy, 15–16, 43, 228 (n. 2); disposition of, 60–61, 107

Courage, 143, 215, 216

Crop failure, 175

Cultures, Civil War as test of, 17–18

Cumming, Henry Harford, 42–43, 137, 177, 228–29 (n. 4); and Jefferson Davis, 133, 260 (n. 38)

Cumming, Joseph B. Jr., 149, 177–80, 228–29 (n. 4); intertwines family history with Augusta's, 220–24

Cumming, Julia Bryan, 31–32, 228–29 (n. 4)

Cumming, Katherine, 31, 112

Cumming family, 227 (n. 1), 260 (n. 38)

Daughters of the Confederacy, 205, 217

Davis, Jefferson, 88–89; capture of, 132–33, 251 (n. 1); and Gertrude Thomas, 157–59, 257 (n. 63)

Debt, 151–54; of Augusta's government, 172–73, 259 (n. 23)

Defeat, military: and gender identity, 9–11, 136–38, 142; and effects on women, 99, 100, 105–6; preparing for, 106–8, 126–27; as domestic victory, 139, 141–42, 224; gender differences in responses to, 139, 148; responses to, 140–41, 161–62, 194; and loss of power for planter class, 169, 174, 201; and effects on Augusta economy, 171–72, 259 (n. 23); denial of, 214–15, 224

Dependence, women's: benefits of, 20, 71; acknowledgment of, 32, 74, 77; on men's identity, 100, 148–47

Desertions, increase in, 114, 241–42 (n. 45)

Disease and infant mortality rate, 34, 172, 234 (n. 49)

"Divided mind" of the South, 217–20, 265 (n. 26)

Domestic labor: restructuring of, 12, 48–62; increased significance of, 22–24, 53, 136–37; of elite women, 129–30, 144–45, 150–51, 254 (n. 37). See also Home manufacturing

Donations: for war materiel, 56–57, 59–60, 85, 241 (n. 43); to soldiers' families, 78, 243 (n. 10), 261 (n. 55); for wayside home for soldiers, 91; for Confederate Monument, 261 (n. 59). See also Charity

Early, Major, 214–15

Economic systems, competition of, 17–18, 208, 217–20

Economizing, as women's contribution, 22, 83–84, 150–51
Economy: effect on households, 41, 48–49, 100–101; of Augusta, 144, 208–10, 228 (n. 2); post-war, 171–72, 175, 191–92
Elite. *See* Merchants; Planter class
Ellis, Sergeant, 53–54
Emancipation, 125–31, 128, 210; effect on economy of, 172–74, 255 (n. 47)
Empowerment: of slaves, 26, 116–17, 124–25; of women, 47, 48–49, 56–59, 60, 154–56; class differences in women's, 66, 72; women's, through jobs, 81–83, 86–87, 89–90, 146–48; women's lack of, 100–101; of freedpeople, 130–31; of men, through subordination of dependents, 134–37, 149, 181, 188–90; of men by women, 167, 187, 202
Enlistments: women's response to, 19–21, 29–35, 39–40, 47–48, 102, 259–60 (n. 33)
Enterprise Factory and Powderworks chimney, 206–8
Evans, C. A., 161–64, 180, 193
Evans, J. E., 141
Eve, George, 26
Eve, Philoclea Edgeworth, 39

Fairs, as fundraisers, 56–57, 60
Familialization, of market relations, 68, 75
Families, 5, 33–34, 228–29 (n. 4); in women's organizations, 52, 240 (n. 28); support of soldiers', 87–88, 190–91, 219, 238 (n. 18), 243 (n.

10); men's recommitment to, 140–42, 143–46, 151–57, 165–66, 195; comfort of soldiers', 184–85
Faust, Drew, 4–5
Female kin networks, 12, 33–34
Feminists, 18–19, 256 (n. 57)
Finances: of planter class, 56–57, 98–100, 150–56, 240–41 (n. 31), 255 (n. 47); of Ladies' Memorial Association, 192–93
Fitzhugh, George, 137
Foner, Eric, 9–10
Food, 67, 103, 119–20
Fort McAllister, 215
Fraternal bonds, 165, 200–203
Freedmen's Bureau, 171
Freedom, 7, 17; and manhood, 36–38. *See also* "Free men"; Independence
Freedpeople. *See* African Americans
"Free lovers," 18–19
"Free markets," to provide for soldiers' families, 77–81
"Free men," 7; definitions of, 9–11, 16–21; and industries, 42–46, 90

Garner, James, 126
Gender, possession of, 4
Gender conventions, 2–3, 39–40
Gender differences: during infant loss, 35–36, 234–35 (n. 51); and defeat, 139, 148, 265 (n. 26)
Gendered experiences: of Confederate women, 12, 91–94, 138–39, 167; caring for dead as, 186, 191–92, 195
Gender hierarchy, white men's need for, 136
Gender identity: changes in men's,

8, 130–31, 216–17; vs. class divisions, 72–77, 87, 115, 166; and race, 130–31, 231–32 (nn. 28, 29)

Gender relations: and domestic labor, 12–13, 48–63, 145–46; in marriages, 19–21, 150–56; shifts in, 36–38, 134–35, 181–82; of women and idle men, 83, 109; and race relations, 124

Gender roles: and gender conventions, 2–3, 11–12, 40; women's support for, 4–5, 19, 28–29; masculinization of, 22–23, 135–37; attempts to preserve, 40, 217, 241–42 (n. 45); of Confederate men, 59–60, 64–67, 79, 109–10; feminization of, 135–36; domestic reconstruction of, 177–78, 184–85, 188–89; and changed image of labor, 210–12

Gender studies, 7–8

Gender transformations, 3

Georgia: secession of, 16; response to Sherman's advance, 96–97, 100–102, 108

Georgia Ladies' Gunboat Fund, 60

Gibson, William, 81

Grand Jury: attempts to maintain order by, 113, 117–19, 170–71; and economics, 118, 175

Graves, care of, 186–87, 200, 203

Gunboat fund, 59–60, 241 (n. 43)

Hack drivers, blacks as, 117, 119

Hammond, Catharine, 232 (n. 29)

Hammond, Emily Cumming, 32–33

Health, 151; effect of defeat on, 200–201, 256 (n. 58). *See also* Diseases

Henry (slave of Thomas), 104

Hierarchies, 50–51, 68, 74–76

Home manufacturing: as women's service, 22, 24, 44; inefficiency of, 48, 55–56; of uniforms, 85–86

Hospitals, 98, 112–13

Households: economics of, 21–22, 41, 86–87; woman-headed, 43–44, 57–58; restructuring of, 47, 146–47; blacks in their own, 122, 128, 131. *See also* Subordination

Hucksters, blacks as, 117, 119–20

Impressment of slaves, 121–22, 238–39 (n. 19)

Independence: women's, 20–21, 77, 124; increase in women's, 22, 211, 239–40 (n. 23); Augusta's economic, 42–47, 235–36 (n. 3); for poor women through jobs, 86–87, 89–90; men's pursuit of, 109, 135; for free blacks, 116–17; individual vs. societal, 125–26; loss of Confederate, 133–34, 139–40, 163

Industries, 10, 244 (n. 36); employment in, 12, 14; of Augusta, 15–16, 143, 228 (n. 2); opposition to, 42–44, 236 (n. 4); donations to "free markets" by, 80–81; increasing status of, 89–90; in "divided mind" of the South, 217–20. *See also* Textile industries

Infant loss: as female gendered experiences, 12, 34–37, 36–38, 233–35 (nn. 49, 50, 51)

Infant mortality, 34–36, 233–34 (nn. 48, 49)

Interests of men and dependents: similarity of, 20–21, 37–38; short-

Interests of men: (continued)
  term vs. long-term, 37–38; no
  longer alike, 61–62, 109, 135, 152
Izard, Emily Middleton, 99, 103, 109,
  122

Jackson, George, 127
Jackson, Stonewall, 193; widow of,
  196, 198
Jackson, William E., 80–81
Jobs: for poor women, 81–83, 89–
  90, 173–74, 236–37 (n. 5); for elite
  women, 100–101, 127, 155–56;
  for free blacks, 117, 120. See also
  Domestic labor; Labor
Joe (slave of Morgans), 115–16,
  121–22
Johnson, Michael, 11
Jones, Caroline Davis, 19–21, 37, 233
  (nn. 45, 46); finances of, 83–84,
  120–21
Jones, Charles Colcock Jr.: in memorial movement, 193, 196, 201, 217,
  261 (n. 59), 262 (n. 65); opposition of, to industrialization, 208,
  209–10
Jones, Joseph, 16, 140; marriage of,
  19–21; finances of, 83–84, 144

Labor: loss of men's, 65–67; changed
  image of, 143–44, 210–12; freedpeople's, 171; wages for women's,
  208, 212, 249–50 (n. 53), 255
  (n. 44). See also Domestic labor;
  Slaves
Labor systems: Civil War as test of,
  17–18
Ladies' aid societies, 85, 182, 185
Ladies' Aid Society, 92, 145–46

Ladies' Foreign Missionary Society, 51
Ladies' Hospital and Relief Association, 186–88
Ladies' Memorial Association, 161,
  168, 182–95, 217, 218, 260 (n.
  47); and Confederate Survivors,
  202–7
"Ladies of Augusta," 65–66
Ladies' Sewing Circle, 51
Ladies' Volunteer Association, 49–
  50, 52, 77
Leadership, of women's organizations,
  51–52, 240 (n. 28), 241 (n. 41),
  260 (n. 47)
Legislation: to force enlistment, 102;
  to regulate blacks, 119
Loss: of husbands, 33–34, 245 (n.
  52); of loved ones, 36–38, 139–
  40; economic, 65–67, 72–75; fear
  of, 92–95, 100, 105–6, 245–46
  (n. 57); domestic, 164, 190–91,
  199–200, 202
Loyalty: of Confederate women, 4–5,
  7, 19–20, 30–31; of slaves, 5–7,
  13, 121–23; in reconstructions of
  Confederate Survivors, 213

Manhood: and race, 3, 130–31; loss of
  traditional, 8–11, 133–37; threatened by women's status changes,
  13, 18, 59–60; in military service,
  32, 214–15; and freedom, 36–38;
  Southern definition of, 125–26,
  223; providing as element of, 133,
  137, 144, 150, 174–75; reconstruction of southern white, 137,
  140, 142–46, 163; under industrialization, 209–12. See also "Free
  men"

Market relationships, 78–80, 209–10
Marriage, 35–36, 232 (n. 29); and
employment of white women, 82–
83, 212; self-subordination of
women in, 149–50, 157
May, Robert H., 65, 114, 143, 164–
65, 242 (n. 3); and Augusta Purveying Association, 78–81, 98–99,
247 (n. 9), 259 (n. 24); on postwar
crisis, 169, 174
May, Mrs. Robert H., 49
McKinne, Anne, 52
McKinne, Maria Whitehead, 52,
190–91
Memorial Day, 164, 167–68, 202–
3, 260–61 (n. 48); symbolism
of, 176–81; history of, 182–83,
187–88
Memorial movement, 200–209, 262
(n. 64), 264 (n. 13); and industrialization, 210, 217–20. See also
Confederate Survivors Association
Men, 3; and lack of social location,
4, 7; reasons of, for fighting, 7,
16–18; identity of, 9–11; class divisions among, 115, 126, 127–28.
See also Gender roles; Manhood;
Subordination
Merchants, 49; price increases by,
65–71, 242–43 (n. 5); and "free
markets," 77–81
Migrations, to Augusta, 43. See also
Refugees, in Augusta
Military service: of blacks, 3, 124–
26; as gender convention, 39–40;
desertions from, 87–88, 95, 114,
241–42 (n. 45), 259–60 (n. 33)
Militia, local, 101–2, 127; using
impressed slaves, 116, 121–22
Morale of soldiers, 62, 114; after de-

feat, 143, 152, 155, 251 (n. 3), 256
(n. 58)
Morgan, Mrs. Irby, 112, 114, 115–16,
143
Mortality rates: of children, 34–36,
233–34 (nn. 48, 49)
Mother-daughter relationships, 58–59
Mothers: power for, through enlistment of sons, 38–39, 47, 62–63;
raising the South's redeemers, 159,
257 (n. 63); and infants, 234 (n.
49), 234–35 (n. 51). See also Social
mothering

Negro Soldier Bill (1865), 125–26
New South: creation of, 206–8, 211–
13; and traditional culture, 217–20,
222–23
Night patrols, of white men, 118–19
Nursing: by women's organizations,
57–59, 90–94, 111–12, 114, 245
(n. 49)

Obedience, and protection, 5, 253 (n.
11)
Occupation: learning to live under,
142, 148–49, 171, 175; Union
monuments during, 178–79
Origins of the New South, The (Woodward), 217–18
Outfitting troops. See War materiels

Paternalism. See Social fathering
"Patriarchal republic," 11
Patriarchy: charity and, 50–51, 73,
196–97
Patriotism: of women, 53, 60; gender
differences in, 61–62; and prices,
65–68, 74
Patrol Laws, 117–18

Sacrifices: acknowledgment of
women's, 53, 62–63, 139–40, 184,
207; women's, used to encourage
men, 105–6, 107; of soldiers,
108–9, 195; as female gendered experience, 167, 181; and memorial
movement, 167, 183; of elite white
men, 222
Saloons, closing of, 113, 243–44 (n.
21)
Schley, William, 42–43
Schley, Mrs. William, 50
Secession, 11, 16, 228–29 (n. 4);
effect of, on industrialization,
44–45
Sexual double standard, 26–27, 232
(n. 29)
Sexual relations: of white men and
slave women, 25–27, 231–32 (nn.
28, 29)
Sherman, William Tecumseh: advance
of, 96–97, 100, 102; and Augusta,
110, 213–14, 237 (n. 11). *See also*
Union troops
Sibley, Amory, 42–44
Sibley, Josiah, 69
Sibley, Mrs. William, 50
Sibley family, 228 (n. 3), 265 (n. 26)
Silber, Nina, 9
Simms, J. R., 96–97
"Slave power": northern fear of, 9–10,
18, 100
Slavery: as a cause, 17; defense of,
24–25, 30, 124–26, 256 (n. 58);
given up as lost, 163, 165, 180–81;
denial of, as motive, 204, 219–20
Slaves: loyalty of, 5–7, 120–23,
215–16; in household hierarchies,
24–31; labor of, 100, 120–21,
238–39 (n. 19); and Union troops,

101, 104, 214, 250 (n. 66); white
women's dependence on, 115–16,
120–22; impressed for work, 116–
17, 121–22; escaped, 116–18,
249–50 (n. 53); abandonment of,
249 (n. 51)
Smith, Eliza Mason, 99–100, 111
Smith, Emily, 247 (n. 12)
Social construction, manhood as, 3,
7–10, 216–17
Social fathering: of soldiers' families,
74–76, 78–82, 118, 168, 172–74,
214, 219; failure of, 168–71
Social location, 4–9
Social mothering, 51, 72; Ladies' Volunteer Association as, 52; wayside
homes as, 91–93; of Confederate
Dead, 166–68, 182–91
Social order: and industrialization, 47, 217–20; challenges to
Augusta's, 98, 99, 110–11, 117–
19, 243–44 (n. 21); resistance to
more egalitarian, 124–26, 169–71,
209–12, 219–20
Social reconstruction: postwar, 199–
200; of war, 216–18; of history of
Augusta, 220–24
Soldiers: social mothering of, 50, 53,
57–59, 166–67; support for families of, 64–70, 74–76, 78–81, 118,
172–74; jobs for families of, 81–
82, 84–90; fears of, for families,
87–88, 102; elite interfaces with
common, 93, 108, 166, 249 (n.
39); effect of, on city social order,
111–14, 127–28; class hostility of,
115, 127–28; memorialization of
common, 194–95, 196–97
Sons: enlistment of, as woman's sacrifice, 32, 38–39, 53, 63; loss of,

"View from nowhere," 4–9, 14, 216

Walton, Mrs. Anderson W., 57
War materiels: outfitting of troops, 44, 46, 47–48, 85, 238 (n. 18); factories for, 45–47; donations for, 56–57, 59–60; Augusta as supplier of, 206, 237 (n. 11). *See also* Uniforms
Washington, Booker T., 6
Wayside homes, for soldiers, 57–59, 91–94, 104–5, 190–92
Wheeler's troops, 103–4
Whitehead, Elizabeth McKinne, 52
Widows, 93–95, 245 (n. 52)
Widows' Home, 190–92, 261 (n. 55)
Willis, B., 113
Womanhood, racial relations and changing definition of, 130–31
Woman's Christian Temperance Union, 211, 212
Women: gender roles of, 4–5, 13, 32–34, 109–10; employment of, 22–24, 43–44, 46–47, 48–62, 81–86, 173, 236–37 (n. 5); in household hierarchies, 24–28; sexual exploitation of slave, 25–27, 231–32 (n. 28); and enlistment of sons, 32, 38–39; contradictory position of, 38; heading households, 43, 45, 50–51, 70; in New South, 211–12. *See also* Confederacy, women's support for; Gender roles; Soldiers, support for families of; Subordination
Women's voluntary organizations, 12–14, 51, 58–59, 76–77, 90–94, 239–40 (n. 23); postwar, 182, 211. *See also* Ladies' Aid Society; Ladies' Memorial Association; Ladies' Volunteer Association
Woodward, C. Vann, 217–18
Wounded soldiers: numbers of, 96, 245–46 (n. 57). *See also* Nursing